David and Bathsheba is the
kind of reading experience hard
to find these days—engrossing,
enriching—so that you do not
want the book to end.
—CATHERINE MARSHALL

Roberta Kells Dorr lived in the Middle East for
almost twenty years. During that time she
researched marriage and family customs of the
Davidic period as well as pagan religous practices,
especially those of the Hittites. The result is *David
and Bathsheba,* an epic love story with carefully
documented details woven into a suspenseful
historical novel.

DAVID & BATHSHEBA

The Love Story That Changed History

ROBERTA KELLS DORR

LIVING BOOKS
Tyndale House Publishers, Inc.
Wheaton, Illinois

David and Bathsheba,
originally entitled *Bathsheba,*
published by arrangement with
Chosen Books Publishing Co., Ltd.

First printing, Living Books edition, June 1982

Library of Congress Catalog Card Number 81-85681
ISBN 0-8423-0618-8, Living Books edition
Copyright © 1980 by Roberta K. Dorr
Printed in the United States of America

To my very own David

FOREWORD

ROBERTA KELLS DORR began to research the Old Testament story of David and Bathsheba back in 1959 when she, her husband, and five children took a medical missionary assignment on the Gaza Strip. She continued her research during the next seventeen years and a transfer to the hospital of Jibla in Yemen. During this time she was able to visit archeological digs and geographical sites, study the culture, learn the language and gain new insights into the lives of men and women in ancient Israel. Out of this study grew the audacious idea of telling the David and Bathsheba story in novel form and from the basic point of view of Bathsheba herself.

Twenty-one years later, the result is *David and Bathsheba,* a book that is faithful to the biblical account, although the portraits of David, Bathsheba, Uriah, and others that emerge may contain some surprises for the critical biblical scholar. I view this book not so much as a historical novel, however, as a biographical account of those times, based upon the biblical record and going beyond it inferentially.

The Old Testament story in its own right is one of the outstanding pieces of historical literature preserved from the ancient world. The economy of writing, the bold delineation of character, the continuing focus upon what is happening in the struggle over David's throne within his household and among his advisors carry the reader along and require little comment. Even so, Roberta Dorr has added background and contours to the story that have enabled readers to enter more fully into the turbulent times and without moralizing or making the stories "edifying" has lent to them additional human and moral weight.

The author has lived up to the challenge of the literature. She has let the story carry its quiet testimony to the God of Israel, who finds His way in the struggle of men and women for life and health, who guides the processes of history but largely through the agency of His creatures, and who throughout insists upon both justice and mercy.

Walter Harrelson
Professor of Old Testament
Former Dean of the Divinity School
Vanderbilt University

ACKNOWLEDGMENTS

To my grandmother, Emma Benham Sherman, goes a very special thanks, for without her faithful reading of *Hurlbut's Story of the Bible* to me, year after year, I would never have come to know the Bible characters as the vitally alive, real people they undoubtedly were.

To Annie Sue Clift, missionary nurse and friend, a thank you for getting *David and Bathsheba* out of the chaos of its cardboard box and translating it into neatly typed pages. Thanks also to those who have typed more recently, especially Marjorie Johnson and Alice Watkins.

To Dr. Bob Lindsey and his wife Margaret and all the other friends in Israel, Lebanon, and Yemen, thank you for helping me meet people, get to out-of-the-way places, and for providing suggestions and encouragement along the way.

For special help in my research: Dr. Lindsey in Jerusalem; Dr. Menahem Haran, biblical scholar in Jerusalem; Dr. Walter Harrelson, professor of Old Testament and former dean of religion at Vanderbilt

University, and Dr. Philip Herzbrun, professor at Georgetown University, who read the manuscript and gave very helpful advice.

To my husband, David, and my children: Philip and wife Cheryl, Debby and husband Alex Carrick, Paul, John, and Jimmy, who have advised, consulted, corrected, and often typed the manuscript without complaint.

Finally a special thanks to all of those at Chosen Books, with a special thanks to Catherine Marshall LeSourd who first read the manuscript and then gave invaluable advice and encouragement and to Len LeSourd who as my editor has never ceased to have faith in *Bathsheba* and who has refused to settle for less than the best.

PROLOGUE

I⊤ was evident to everyone in the crowded, darkened room that the king could not last through the night. There was a silence that seemed part of the very atmosphere. It was not a fearful, foreboding silence, but a waiting silence, as though something very important and awesome were about to happen.

Family and friends tiptoed in and out of the room; old warriors awkwardly brushed tears from their eyes as they filed past his bed for a last glimpse; small grandchildren were held up to look at him and the women of the harem gathered together soberly in a frightened knot at the foot of his bed. They all sensed how barren and empty life would be without him and wanted to cling to every precious moment left to them.

The king reached out his hand to Bathsheba, and she took it and held it in both of hers, bending over to hear the words he was struggling to speak. "You must not weep for me. This illness is unto death, but do not grieve. The Lord Himself has come to see me. His Shekinah glory has filled the room, and He has spoken to me of all that shall come to pass in the future. He has given me a message of hope for my people." His voice was so weak she could barely hear him. "Nathan the prophet," he continued with great effort, "has written it that all may hear and be comforted."

He motioned for Bathsheba to bring out a rolled parchment from under his mattress. He watched her unroll it and hand it to Nathan to read to the people.

The room grew quiet, the king's eyes closed, and a gust of wind made the lamp's flame bend and flutter as Nathan held the parchment to the light to see more clearly. When he finally spoke, his voice was strong and vibrant but mellowed with emotion. "These are the last words of David," he said, pointing to the scroll. "David, the son of Jesse, speaks. David, the man to whom God gave such wonderful success, David, the anointed one, David, the sweet psalmist of Israel."

At these words the people wept and tore their robes and covered their faces. Their grief was that of small children who have heard their father is dying and don't know where to turn for comfort. "These are the last words of your king." Nathan spoke in a loud voice that carried over the noise of their grief. "Listen and be comforted." Slowly the weeping quieted and the keening died down. A young scribe raised the lamp so that it shone on the scroll, and Nathan began to read the words that God had given to David.

The Spirit of the Lord spoke to me, and His word was on my tongue.

The Rock of Israel said to me,
"One shall come who rules righteously,
Who rules in the fear of God."

He shall be as the light of the morning;
A cloudless sunrise
When the tender grass springs forth upon the
    earth;
As sunshine after rain.

And, *it is my family He has chosen.*

Yes, God has made an everlasting covenant with
    me;
His agreement is eternal, final, sealed.

He will constantly look after
My safety and success.

The godless are as thorns to be
Thrown away, for they tear the hand that touches
    them.

One must be armed to chop them down;
They shall be burned.

When the reading stopped, the room was quiet;
no one moved. It had grown dark and the shutters
were drawn against the mounting gusts of wind.
The king's bed was outlined by two flickering lamps
at its head and by the lamp held by the young
scribe. With a great effort the old king opened his
eyes and looked out past Bathsheba and the
people who stood round his bed. He struggled to
speak. "A great one is coming—an anointed one,
Messiah, will sit on my throne, and He will rule righteously."

For a moment his eyes were bright with all that
they were seeing. Bathsheba felt his hand close on
hers ever so gently and then relax. His eyes closed,
and he was gone from them. Bathsheba bent over
the dead form and sobbed. The women of the
harem began the terrible wailing for the dead, and
David's mighty men and counselors, tribesmen, of-

ficers, and servants let their tears flow openly and unashamedly.

Then Nathan the prophet and Beniah the captain of the house guards picked up the royal robe that lay across the foot of David's bed and the crown that had once belonged to the king of Rabboth Ammon, whom David had vanquished, and they placed them on Solomon and led him out into the common room where all the leaders of the tribes and men of state were gathered.

All the people came to file before Solomon to pledge their allegiance and acknowledge him as their king. Then the young Solomon turned to Nathan and asked him to bring his mother to stand beside him, that all Israel might know that she was indeed a handmaiden of low degree whom the Lord had seen fit to exalt to be the mother of the king.

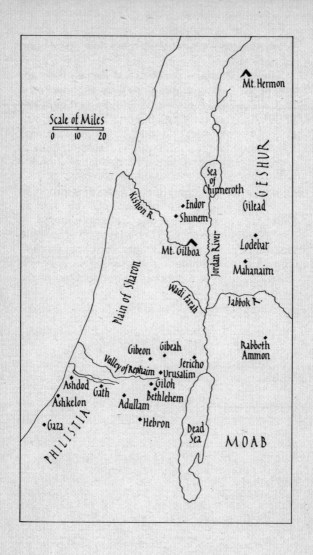

BOOK ONE

AHITHOPHEL

1

AHITHOPHEL, CHIEF ELDER of the village of Giloh, paced back and forth across the courtyard of his home, kicking the well-curb as he passed. He was not used to waiting. He reached over the stone well-curb and looked down into the depths of his lime-stone cistern to check the water level. The village could do without grain and fuel, but without water they would be at the mercy of the enemy.

He sat down on the worn stones of the well and stroked his gray beard reflectively. It was hot in his courtyard, and he jerked the long striped head cloth from around his neck and wiped the sweat from his face. "This silence is ominous," he mur-mured aloud. "If the battle had gone well we would have heard by now."

He stood up, flung the headcloth around his neck, and walked to the steps that led from the courtyard to the roof of his house. As he mounted the uneven steps, his thoughts churned: The Philis-tines could not have picked a better time to strike. If there had only been a little more time, a month or two, perhaps Saul would have seen his mistake and made friends again with David, his captain, and the men who had followed him into exile.

He paused to catch his breath at the top of the stairs and looked out over the cluster of houses and the city wall to the road which the young men of Giloh had traveled toward their meeting with the Philistines in the north. The road was now ominously empty; no donkeys with wares to trade, no women carrying jars to and from the well. He leaned over the parapet and looked south where the road led down to the desert around Beersheba and the caves of Adullam. "Thank God," he muttered, "my son is with David and not fighting the Philistines at Gilboa."

The roof was beginning to cool at this time of day, and Ahithophel usually left it to the women who spent their time there weaving at the loom which sat under the grapevine that climbed from the lower garden and fanned out over the western portion of the roof. Usually there was the steady sound of the worn, wooden shuttle, whispering through the cords, but today there was no sound from the loom. As his eyes became accustomed to the late afternoon sunlight, Ahithophel noticed that both Reba, his wife, and Noha, the wife of his son Emmiel, were at the loom as usual but were sitting motionless. This added to Ahithophel's impatience. He liked to feel things moving and throbbing around him.

"There's no reason to stop the loom," he said to them. "If there were bad news we would have heard it." Noha obviously had been crying, and now she covered her face with her mantle and wept louder. Impatiently he turned to his plump, efficient little wife. "Reba," he ordered, "see if you can stop this foolishness. There's no need for her to cry. Emmiel is with David and his men. Whether Saul wins or loses today, my son is safe."

Noha rose from the loom, sobbing uncontrollably. "Emmiel is not with David's men," she exclaimed as she hurried past him. "He went with the army of Saul to fight at Gilboa."

Ahithophel looked as though he had been slapped. He seized Noha by the arm. "It is not true. My son is with David and his men in the south."

"Emmiel has gone to fight the Philistines at Gilboa," she insisted through her tears.

Ahithophel dropped her arm and glared at her. "How do you know this?"

Noha checked her tears and met his gaze with red, swollen eyes. "Emmiel told me he was going," she sobbed as she fled down the steps to her room.

Ahithophel was astounded. His only son, Emmiel, the apple of his eye, the delight of his heart, had neglected his wife and left his own fields and flocks to share the life of an outlaw with David and his men. Ahithophel had counted on Emmiel's bitterness toward Saul to keep him from the battle.

He walked to the edge of the roof and looked down the slope to where his wine press and clusters of olive trees blended into the fragrant pines of the lower hillside.

"I don't believe it," he muttered.

In the turmoil of his own emotions he had completely ignored his wife, Reba. Now she came to him and placed a firm hand on his arm. "Emmiel is strong and brave. I'm sure he will be all right."

Ahithophel did not look at her. "You think he went, then? Why should he go? I don't understand."

"He would go," said Reba, "because he loves his country. His quarrel is with Saul. That a king could be so jealous of a young, successful captain like David that he would seek to kill him is repulsive to our son. He would never fight for King Saul. But Israel? That is different."

"But why? Why did he tell that sniveling wife of his and not his own father? I don't understand."

"My lord, our son is emotional and impulsive, and he knew that you would try to dissuade him with logic."

Ahithophel sighed. Reba was right. His family, friends, and neighbors all looked up to him as a man of wisdom and had chosen him as the ruling elder of Giloh. He was considered wealthy by village standards; his olive oil brought the highest prices, his granaries were bursting with wheat, his flocks overflowed the sheep cotes every spring.

Pragmatic to the core, Ahithophel wasted no time in religious discussion or reflection. He believed in observing the feasts and times of sacrifice, the circumcising of children, giving the first fruits, and being careful to touch no unclean thing. In return he expected and even took for granted that the God of Israel would reward him with good health, abundant crops, and deliverance from his enemies.

He was known as one who was loyal to his friends but a bitter opponent to his enemies. Above all, he cherished his family. Though his wife, Reba, kept close to the loom and the grindstone, when she chose to speak, it was noted by the amused villagers that Ahithophel usually listened. And though he himself was critical of Emmiel for choosing to live in exile with David ben Jesse in the desert caves of Adullam, he would listen to no complaint of him from others. He was proud of his two grandchildren: Machir, a boy of twelve, and Bathsheba, a spirited girl of six. However, it was his granddaughter with her big, brown, laughing eyes and thick, curling hair who really held the heart of Ahithophel.

Often when he was sitting at the town gate, discussing important matters with the elders, he would see Bathsheba's large brown eyes peeping at him from behind the carob tree that grew in the open square. He would always pause in his deliberations and hold out his hand to her, and Bathsheba would come running to him, her small brown feet leaving little curls of dust and her hair blowing out from under the embroidered kerchief. Standing on tiptoe she would whisper something in his ear, then scamper shyly away.

His eyes followed her with satisfaction as he commented to his friends. "She will be a beauty."

The daylight hours dragged into evening, and still there was no news of the battle. A meal was spread in the courtyard, but no one cared to eat. Gradually the old men of Giloh came by twos and threes to discuss with their chief elder the strange quiet and their fears for the army of Israel. As silently as shadows they appeared, wrapped in their warm, brown, loom-woven cloaks, to sit by the fire of fir twigs and dung patties in the corner of the courtyard.

"My boy went with only his shepherd's crook and sling," said one old man with terror in his eyes.

"Mine had a bow and arrows but no armor, only the clothes he was working in," another lamented.

"The Philistine chariots are swifter than eagles. Their iron weapons pierce the leather shields of our men as though they were made of air," voiced a third.

"My brothers," Ahithophel cut across the babble, "it is true. If the battle is lost at Gilboa the Philistines will claim the fords at the Jordan, roll on to take the trade route to Damascus, and sweep down the Jordan Valley to attack Bethlehem and our own village of Giloh. We must prepare ourselves." He rose to his feet and walked with them to the doorway.

"You, Philemon, and your family will serve as our watchmen. You, Asa, and your family will gather fuel and water. The rest of you must collect large boulders and stones to be thrown from the walls if we are attacked."

He closed the front gate behind the frightened villagers and turned back into his courtyard. The women had retired to their quarters, and Machir sat listlessly on the roof, cutting holes in some dried gourds which would be used for storing honey. Bathsheba stood with large, questioning eyes watching her grandfather. When he sat back down by the fire, she came and cuddled up close to him, laying her head against his arm.

Ahithophel looked down and saw that she was fighting back tears. *She's not one to weep like her mother,* he thought. Feeling a sudden flow of tenderness for the little girl, he picked her up and put her on his lap.

"Now, now, don't be afraid," he said, patting her on the back gently but rather awkwardly. "Everything is going to be all right." When Bathsheba buried her head on his shoulder, sobbing, Ahithophel felt undone. He stroked her dark hair and noticed how the tendrils curled around his fingers. Somehow this was more touching than her tears.

At Ahithophel's call, a serving girl hurried out to the dimly lit courtyard, took Bathsheba's hand, and led her to the sleeping quarters. Ahithophel waited until they were gone, then with a sigh he joined his young grandson on the roof.

"Grandfather," whispered Machir, "someone is

coming down the road to the city gate."

"Where?" Ahithophel anxiously peered out over the dark houses to the moon-bright space before the city gate.

There was the sound of running feet and excited voices, followed by a frantic pounding on the barred gate. Several men were working to unlatch the bolts when Ahithophel and Machir reached them.

The big gate swung back, and three young men entered, breathing hard. Their clothes were torn and their bodies so covered with blood and dust that only their voices were recognizable. "Quickly tell us what has happened," Ahithophel urged.

"All is lost . . . all is lost. . . ." One young man spoke the words through great wracking sobs.

"What is lost?" Ahithophel demanded. The people of the village had gathered behind him in the shadows.

"Israel has lost to the Philistines. It was a massacre. Wave upon wave of chariots and spears and arrows."

"Impossible!" gasped Ahithophel.

"Saul was killed," said a second man from the shadows.

"His sons, too, all but one," said the third.

"There are only three of you. Where are all the other men of Giloh?" asked Ahithophel.

"The men of Giloh," one young man said sadly, "may all be dead. If any are alive they have fled with Saul's son, Ishbosheth, to the city of refuge at Mahanaim."

Ahithophel's voice throbbed with emotion. "My son: did you see Emmiel—my son?"

The men struggled for words to answer the agonized plea, for Emmiel had also been their friend. "We don't know for sure. We were all scattered like leaves before a mighty wind," the older man said.

"I thought I saw him with one of Saul's sons," answered another.

"Then there is hope. They may have escaped to Mahanaim in Gilead," Ahithophel insisted.

Before the men could answer, a scream pierced the night, and then one by one the women of Giloh joined in the terrible lament for the dead. The men at first stood stunned and silent. Then they, too, began to weep unashamedly for the gallant men who they now feared would never come home to the pleasant hillside to till their fields again.

"Don't give up your hope!" Ahithophel shouted. "Some of our sons are alive and well in Mahanaim." But his voice was drowned by the wailing of the women.

Then a call came from a villager standing on the town wall. "Bethlehem is in flames!"

Before the people could climb the wall to see for themselves, there was another loud, insistent pounding on the town gate. The refugees from Bethlehem poured through the opening gate, screaming, "The Philistines have ridden up the valley from the Jordan! They are looting and burning Bethlehem!"

Some of the fleeing people carried goatskin packs of wine and cheeses, and others struggled with coarse, cloth-wrapped bundles of flour and seed wheat. All were terrified and eager to hurry on.

"You will be next," they cried. "The Philistines are going to march up and take the whole ridge." With that they hurried off, leaving the villagers of Giloh in a state of panic.

Ahithophel moved among the people. "You can go if you like, but I am not moving. I will not be driven off my land as long as I have a strong right arm and a good sword. We can lock the gate and shoot our arrows from the walls."

An old man pushed through the crowd and came to where Ahithophel was standing. "It's no use," he shouted over the din. "There are thousands of Philistines. They will climb our walls, rape our women, dash our young ones against the wall, and take our land. Pack up, Ahithophel, and lead your people to safety in Gilead."

"I'll not leave my good land for those fiends of Dagon. I'll not have them drinking my wine and using my good oil." Ahithophel suddenly noticed Reba was standing beside him.

"My lord, I have taken the liberty to pack our things. I have the oxcart ready with some wheat and the grinding stones. I have all we can carry of the wine and oil. Noha is riding with me on one of the donkeys, and Machir has the mule. Bathsheba can ride in the cart with the wheat."

Ahithophel was astonished. "What makes you think I am leaving?"

Reba looked at him firmly. "If our son is alive he will be in Mahanaim with the family of Saul, and we must get to him as soon as possible. Here we are helpless."

Ahithophel considered her logic, then looked around and saw that it was indeed true; there were no young men to defend the city. But the journey to Mahanaim, located in the Gilead mountains east of the Jordan, would also be perilous. Since the Philistines were pouring down from the north and would soon be coming along the ridge road, the people of Giloh would have to follow the wild goat trails used by the shepherds.

Ahithophel stepped back into his home for one last look around. He saw the gourds lying where

Machir had left them; the cook room still gave off the faint odor of warm bread; in the corner was his old, broken yoke. He went to the steps and mounted slowly to the roof.

The loom sat silent and motionless, the half-finished piece of work still in place. He looked to the south, toward the burning city of Bethlehem, and saw that it no longer darted with flames but glowed like a hot, red coal. *Reba is right,* he thought, *we have no choice but to leave.*

He hurried back down the steps across the courtyard, pausing by the well to run his hand over the smooth, chiseled stones. They were worn smooth with age and still gave off heat from the afternoon sun. They almost seemed to have warm blood running beneath their surface. His land and his home and all of Giloh were like a woman to him: his woman. How could he just walk out and leave her to strangers?

Faint and far away he could hear the people beginning to leave from the village gate. He looked frantically around for something he could save at this final moment. "Water," he told himself out loud. "We will need water." He grabbed the goatskin wine pouch from the wall and was filling it from one of the clay jars when he heard running feet on the cobblestone path outside. The door of the courtyard was pushed open, and Bathsheba stood there outlined by the moonlight.

"Grandfather, we must not leave the snowy doves. They would be so frightened." She ran to the corner where they sat perched on the old yoke and tenderly coaxed them into her arms.

The water jar slipped from Ahithophel's grasp and fell with such force that it broke on the stones at the base of the well. He ignored it. With a strong push he plugged the opening to the wine pouch with a twisted cloth. "We must go," he said, hurrying over to Bathsheba.

She stood holding the doves in the folds of her skirt and looked at her grandfather. "What will happen to my father if he comes and finds us gone?"

Ahithophel did not answer her. With one quick movement he flung the wine pouch over his shoulder, swept Bathsheba with the two doves into his other arm and rushed from his house.

A small group waited for them at the gate. Reba and Noha were on the gray donkey and Machir was on the dappled mule, holding the reins of a donkey for his grandfather. The others from his house were riding out, leaving only a big cart filled with wheat standing under the rounded portico of the gate. Quickly he placed Bathsheba in the cart, mounted his donkey and motioned for the little group to go before him.

When they had all passed, Ahithophel drew himself up, squaring his jaw and raising his eyebrow until his face assumed a stern fierceness. He flicked the donkey's hindquarters with his whip and rode behind them out the gate and down the road to the north without looking back.

2

BATHSHEBA SAT in the cart, holding tight to the sides as it bounced and bumped along in the darkness on the narrow goat trail that wound through tall fir trees past the rounded dome of Moriah. The route to Mahanaim led close by Saul's fortress at Gibeah, and Ahithophel twice called a halt to discuss with the village elders whether the Philistines might already have occupied the defeated king's strong-hold. Now, however, the only sound was the thud-ding of the mule's feet and the noise of the cart as it scraped through the bushes on either side.

They had traveled only a short distance when Ahithophel again signaled them to halt. "Giloh is burning," he cried, pointing to a faint glow on the horizon behind them.

Bathsheba saw the small fingers of light in the distance and felt tears sting her eyes. She clutched the doves to her cheek and looked up at the shadowy forms of neighbors and friends crowded around the cart. Some moaned as though in phys-ical pain. At last they started slowly on again, their eyes drawn back to the distant glow for as long as it could be seen.

As they approached the narrow path that forked just below the fortress of Gibeah, they heard sen-tries on the walls of Saul's palace calling back and forth among themselves. Immediately Ahithophel guided the entire group into an acacia brake. Then he assembled a band of men to creep forward and determine if the guards were Israelites or Philistines and whether it would be safe for the refugees to pass along the rocky path below the fortress.

Ahithophel insisted on leading the men. Bathsheba listened anxiously as they stole out of the brake. The moon had long since set, and there was not a gleam of light. She was uncomfortable in the cart; the grain scratched and her feet were numb, but she dared not move.

Suddenly the night outside the thicket came alive with the sound of shouting. There was a whir of arrows cutting the air, and Bathsheba instinctively ducked down.

"Philistines! Philistines!" Around her people shrieked as they urged their donkeys and mules forward out of the brake and down the steep mountain path. In the confusion Bathsheba was forgotten.

Quickly she jumped from the cart and tugged at the leather thong that bound the mule. It would not loosen. Already she could hear a guttural, strange language as the Philistines warily approached the thicket. They would discover the wagon any minute now.

Frantically she reached down into the grain and drew out the doves. The mule brayed suddenly in fright. Bathsheba turned and ran wildly down the hill, pushing through the tangle of vines and undergrowth. There was a shout behind her, and the child knew that the Philistines had found the cart full of grain. That would stop them for a moment. At last she came to a stop beneath a huge, overhanging rock.

From the opposite direction there came the sound of a mule being ridden at full speed. Bathsheba flattened herself against the rock. She heard her own name called and recognized the voice of her father's friend Judah.

"I'm here!" she cried.

"Thanks be to God you are safe," he whispered, as he lifted her onto the mule in front of him. There was a sound of snapping twigs and guttural voices from the thicket. Bathsheba felt Judah's strong arms tighten around her as he dug his heels into the mule's flanks. Soon they were moving down the path so swiftly that pebbles flew in showers from the mule's hooves.

Once out of danger, Judah steadied the mule to a slower pace. "Don't worry about your grandfather," he said gently. "I'm sure he got away. We'll no doubt meet him at the Vale of Farrah where we turn down to the Jordan." They continued down the steep rocky trail, the mule finding his way in the darkness.

They did not meet Ahithophel at the Vale of Farrah, but Judah reassured her: "Your grandfather will no doubt meet us at the Jabbok before daylight."

She leaned back against Judah's strong left arm and felt the steady beat of his heart through the woven material of his cloak. In this same way her father had once taken her to ride with him. She tried to remember Emmiel's face and voice. Although she loved her reckless, impulsive father, he had been gone from home so much she hardly knew him.

It was a long and tedious ride down to the Jordan and then across to the Jabbok where Ahithophel was indeed waiting. Her grandfather came to where Bathsheba sat sleepily cradled in Judah's arms and gently carried her back to ride before him on his donkey.

Bathsheba smiled drowsily as Judah followed with the doves and placed them in her arms. As the sun burst over the eastern hills she heard Ahithophel give the command, and the caravan began to move in single file up the path that led into the mountains of Gilead.

It was evening as they approached the ancient walled city of Mahanaim. The name meant "two camps" and was said to be the place where Jacob met his brother, Esau. It had been declared a city of refuge for Israel. Anyone seeking asylum within its walls was safe from his pursuers.

Now it was past the curfew hour and the large wooden gates covered with beaten brass were closed. There was a brief exchange, and the gates were unlocked for Ahithophel and his villagers. They moved silently up the narrow street between the houses. People were everywhere, in the shadowy doorways, looking down from the rooftops, leaning out the narrow windows. No one spoke or called a greeting. An air of gloom pervaded the ancient city.

A young man with a torch led them through a narrow doorway into an open court where groups of people were huddled around small fires. Babies were crying and animals wandered about. Bathsheba noticed that no servant came to wash their feet.

The boy with the torch stopped and began to curse a young woman with two children who had fallen asleep on some wineskins. "Move, move," he shouted. "There are many more still coming."

Finally the people of Giloh found an open area close to a wall. Bathsheba and Machir climbed up on some bales of straw, their eyes anxiously following Ahithophel as he left to find his son. They were given pieces of half-baked bread with curds, but Bathsheba could not eat. The choking smell of smoke; the stench of scorched olive oil, smoked cheese, peita bread; odors of thyme and cumin, all mixed with a terrible fear in the pit of her stomach.

Ahithophel forced his way through the crowded streets to the court where Abner, his one-time friend and general, was viewing the wounded and dying men stretched out in rows. "Don't touch these men," Abner warned as he pulled Ahithophel away from the stretchers. "Some are dead. You could become defiled."

"What is defilement to me if my son is here among these men?" Ahithophel countered.

When Abner did not answer, Ahithophel seized him by the shoulders: "Abner, in the name of God, where is my son?"

Abner put his arm around Ahithophel and spoke gently. "I can assure you he is not here among these wounded."

Ahithophel drew back. "If my son is not here, where is he?"

"Come with me to the king's court where we can talk."

Woodenly Ahithophel followed the general past the grimy, blood-stained men, some groaning with pain.

Inside the courtyard of the king, Ahithophel found himself surrounded by the men of Benjamin. They were waiting for Saul's only surviving son, Ishbosheth, to come out into the courtyard to be crowned with his father's crown. Seeing Abner, the king's general, they crowded around and plied him with questions.

"Why is Ishbosheth delaying?"

"It is important he be crowned at once."

"Patience," Abner admonished the men. "Please be patient with the young prince. He has just received word that the headless bodies of Saul and his sons have been hung from the walls of Bathshan for all to see."

A moan swept over the men. They began to cry out their frustrations to the God of Israel who had deserted them in their hour of need. "This is not the worst," Abner shouted, motioning for silence. "Word has also come to the young prince that the heads of his father and brothers are being sent around to all the Philistine cities so their people might mock the men of Israel."

With that, the men of Benjamin began to wail and weep, tearing their cloaks and beating their breasts. Some even dropped to the ground and wept with their foreheads touching the rough-packed dirt of the courtyard.

Ahithophel was caught up in the general grief, but he did not forget his purpose. He clutched the cloak of Abner and shouted over the din, "My son. What of my son?"

Abner turned to him with bloodshot eyes. "Ahithophel, your son died nobly on Gilboa with the king."

Ahithophel staggered and fell back as though wounded himself. "No, no, not my son. You are mistaken. It could not have been my son."

Abner put his arm around him, drawing him away from the rest of the men. "Ahithophel, I would not lie to you. As I live before God, your son died a hero."

Ahithophel began to tremble. His teeth chattered as with great cold so that he could say nothing. Although his whole body shook with sobs, tears would not come.

Now Ishbosheth was led into the courtyard by priests bearing incense and holy water. Though the young prince appeared overcome with grief, the ceremony of crowning him king proceeded as though it were taking place back in the palace of Saul, and soon Ishbosheth stood awkwardly in the center of the court with the great robes of state that had been rescued from Gibeah hanging large and loose on his slender frame.

At last Ahithophel found his voice. He looked wildly around at Ishbosheth and the others. "Why did they die?" he shrieked. "Why did they die? Where was the God of Israel when the roebucks of His people were being cut down by the chariots of the Philistines? Is our God not strong enough to deliver us from men who ride in chariots of iron?"

He moved around the courtyard, pain twisting his face as he demanded answers of the silent men. Suddenly a young priest named Gad stepped forward. "It is no mystery why Israel lost to the Philistines. It was not that our slings could not match the chariots of iron, nor that our arrows were not as sure as their iron lances, nor that their thousands outnumbered our hundreds; no, it was something deeper. We stood on Gilboa and watched them come as though we were already dead and doomed. The God of Israel was not with us, and we were as men without armor or a soldier without his shield."

The young man's voice took on the cadence of a prophet. "The terrible anger of Saul against his servant David divided our forces. We were all weak men who trembled like aspens at the sight of their chariots. If David had been there he would have raised up a standard in our midst and shouted us on, and we would have been fleet like mountain goats."

Hearing the criticism of his dead father, Ishbosheth threw off his royal robe in a rage. "By my father's good name, I shall not stand and hear you speak of him in these words and with the same mouth bless his enemy, David."

Gad stood his ground. "It was Saul who led us out to certain defeat. It was his obsession that led him to pass through the Philistine lines to seek out the witch of Endor in the far side of Mount Moreh. He made her call up Samuel from the dead; that is a known sin for our people. Then, faint with fear because of what Samuel had told him, he walked all night to rejoin us at Gilboa. Tired and fearful, he could not lead us out to victory against our enemies."

Ahithophel spoke in a voice strong with suppressed emotion. "It was King Saul who committed this great sin and not my son. Why then, Gad, did my son die?"

Gad closed his eyes and spoke as though reading from a scroll: "When kings go wrong they carry down to destruction whole nations, not just themselves."

With that he turned and walked from the court, leaving it shaken as though God Himself had spoken. Only Ahithophel was unmoved. He followed Gad to the street and shouted after him.

"My son did no wrong! It is not fair that he should die when he did nothing wrong."

Angrily Ahithophel returned to his family. He ignored the comfort of Reba and turned to Machir and Bathsheba. Placing his hands on their shoulders he looked into their eyes with a commanding challenge. "Never forget this night," he said. "You are all that is left of your father's line. Never forget his blood runs in your veins. Be proud. Be strong and see that you are a credit to his dead name."

Several days later, when he held his first court, Ishbosheth awarded Ahithophel and the refugees from Giloh the nearby Canaanite village of Lodebar: ". . . until the Philistines are defeated and you can return to Giloh." Though some of the Canaanites still lived in Lodebar, most of them had fled north to Syria months before, at the outbreak of the hostilities between Israel and the Philistines. "Until Giloh is retaken, Lodebar is yours," the young king said, glancing for confirmation to Abner, his general, who stood beside him directing all that he did.

Next morning before dawn, Ahithophel, his family, and the other villagers rose and packed, then rode through the still, dark streets of Mahanaim toward the gate that led out to the Lodebar road. Bathsheba sat behind her mother on a small, sleepy donkey.

Suddenly Noha pulled the animal to a stop and pointed to a lighted window in the wall just above their heads. "That's the house of Rizpah, King Saul's concubine. Now they say she's taken up with General Abner. Look! She's still up, entertaining him."

"You can't be sure," Reba whispered, reining her own donkey in beside them. "It's more likely she can't sleep, with her husband so recently dead."

At that moment a man's head appeared in the window. It was indeed Abner, drawn by the sound of the people passing below.

At the town gate Noha waited for Reba. "Did you see? I told you it was Abner. That should be proof enough of the evil that is going on within the king's house."

Bathsheba could tell by the way her grandmother answered that Reba was upset. "Trouble is not over for the house of Saul," she agreed, "but let it not be the house of Ahithophel that sets fire to the dry brands of gossip. I wish to God I had not seen it." With that Reba prodded her donkey forward into the morning mist.

The doves Bathsheba had tied in her scarf fluttered, and she grabbed hold of her mother's waist to keep from falling. She was tired of riding on donkeys. It would be good to have a home again. She hoped with all her heart that they would be happy in Lodebar.

3

AHITHOPHEL RODE through the crumbling gates of Lodebar, settled his family into one of the empty houses, and set his mind against accepting this as anything but a temporary situation. Lodebar was situated on a smooth mountain slope with a small stream in the valley and plenty of thick grass for his sheep and cattle. It was better than he had hoped, and yet it rankled him that gentile hands had plowed and worked this soil.

Reba likewise hoped to be back in Giloh before the next harvest, but this did not deter her from working to make as clean and comfortable as possible the large, sprawling house provided them. Finding it filled with cobwebs and overrun with field mice, she enlisted Noha and all of the servants to clean and repair the floors. A mixture of mud, dung, and straw was applied to the walls while fresh clay was brought for the courtyard. "It is a good house, and we are fortunate," she said when everything was finished.

Bathsheba loved Lodebar. She enjoyed watching the craftsmen work in the near court where the seed wheat was stored and the animals bedded down at night. An old man came and sat in the warm sunlight while he chiseled a set of grindstones from a solid block of limestone. In another corner a carpenter fashioned a plow and a loom from some seasoned beams Ahithophel had purchased.

In her own small court that she shared with her mother, Bathsheba had made mud nests for her doves and pigeons. Then she hung a birdcage on the lowest branch of her lemon tree. The sun shone brightly during the day, and at night the crescent moon was often caught in the branches of her tree. It seemed a good omen to her that both heavenly dignitaries visited her court so regularly.

The first years in Lodebar were difficult for the new settlers. Every moment of their time was used to eke out a living. Ahithophel had few occasions to sit with his friends and brood over the death of his son. He was too tired after the hard day's work to discuss anything but the sowing and reaping of his fields.

Eight years passed in this way, and gradually Ahithophel did less and less of the work himself as his possessions increased and his household prospered. Once again he had time to sit with his friends and wax critical over the rule of Ishbosheth. He was not alone in his impatience. Many were stating openly that Ishbosheth was too afraid of the Philistines to fight them, and Abner, his general, had grown weak.

Abner drew their criticism because of his unlawful attraction to Rizpah, the dead king's concubine. Ignoring Ishbosheth's protests, he had openly brought Rizpah to his house. The young men speculated that with Abner so distracted by Rizpah, it would be better to cast their lot with David ben Jesse. "He may be outlawed," they reasoned, "but he is no coward."

David's strength was growing. He was now considered a king by his own tribesmen who called him "the lion of the tribe of Judah." In recent months two of Abner's men had fled across the Jordan to join David's forces in Hebron. "We will never be able to do battle with the Philistines and win back our lost villages unless we are united under one leader," they said.

On several occasions Abner attempted to wrest the fortress of Gibeah from the Philistines. There were a few unsuccessful skirmishes but no victories, leaving the tribesmen more critical than ever. "When Abner does gather our men to fight," they complained, "it is more against our own kinsmen—the men of David—than the Philistines."

One encounter at the pools of Gibeon was especially unfortunate. There Abner's men ran into some soldiers from David's army led by Joab. Their fight was short and one-sided. When Abner and his men began fleeing in all directions, Asahel, Joab's younger brother, pursued Abner himself.

"Are you Asahel, the brother of Joab?" Abner panted as he looked back and saw that the young man was following him.

"I am he," Asahel replied. "And I would have as my first victim the enemy of my lord, King David."

Abner clawed his way up a steep cliff until he could look down on Asahel. "Turn back from following me," he warned. "How could I look your brother Joab in the face if I should kill you?"

Asahel spat on the ground in disgust. "It is not I who will be killed," he shouted, scaling the cliff with great agility.

Abner knew he was no match for the younger man in a foot race. Raising his spear above his head, he hurled the blunt end of it at the young man.

It felled him instantly. Abner turned and ran, stopping only to look back once more before he rounded a curve in the path. There, he saw Joab kneeling in the dust beside the motionless form of his brother. Abner muttered an oath but kept on running until at last he joined some of his men, struggling across the fords of the Jordan bound for the safety of the Gilead mountains.

Joab tried to remove the spear, but Asahel was dead. Joab was enraged. Clasping the dead body, he swore an oath never to rest until he had killed Abner and avenged his brother.

When Abner and his men came straggling home to Mahanaim, there was grief and anger over the fine young men lost in battle. But when they heard of Asahel's death they grew silent and fearful. Remembering Joab's fiery temper and vengeful ways, some of the older tribesmen predicted that there would be no way now to unite the two houses of Saul and Judah peacefully. Some talked openly of going over to David's side.

Ahithophel listened to the battle reports and carefully weighed the evidence. For the present he decided to wait quietly in Lodebar until he was sure which side would win. He did not want to drop his ties with the house of Ishbosheth only to find that David was destined to remain a minor figure, ruling only the crowded, mud-brick village of Hebron.

Then in the month of Iyyar and only a few days before the wheat harvest, two men from David's court arrived in Lodebar. They carried with them an invitation from David himself, asking Ahithophel to come to Hebron to assume the position of chief counselor to the king.

As the men spoke, Ahithophel smiled to think of David's cunning. It would be no small triumph for David to pluck the strongest and wealthiest man east of the Jordan right out from under the watchful eyes of Ishbosheth's men.

He excused himself from the visitors and dispatched Machir on a secret mission to Mahanaim with instructions to bring back any news from the court of Ishbosheth that could influence his decision. "I'll not give them my answer until you return tomorrow," he assured Machir as his grandson saddled his swiftest mule.

4

THAT EVENING Ahithophel hurried to join the guests from David's court beside a low table Reba had set with brass bowls and silver goblets. *It is well,* he thought as he greeted the two men and sat down, *that they realize I am a man of wealth and standing.*

He was, as always, a gracious host. He saw that his guests were served the choicest figs, the tenderest green almonds. By the time Reba brought the damp towels scented with rose water to wipe their hands, he knew the questions he must ask.

"Do you think Joab really intends to kill Abner?" he began.

Sulim, the short guest with the intense, dark eyes, turned and spat the wine he was drinking onto the clean, earthen floor.

"We never mention Abner without showing our disgust for him."

Beniah, the taller guest, spoke with more reserve. "David's men want to avenge Asahel's death and at the same time seize the kingdom from Ishbosheth."

"That is wise. I would counsel the same," said Ahithophel, getting involved in spite of his resolve to be quiet and listen.

"There is only one problem." Sulim interrupted. "David will not agree to such a plan. He even accuses Joab of looking for a fight so that he can avenge Asahel's death."

Ahithophel was astounded. "David does not see this as his chance to take the throne?"

"Yes, he sees that if Joab should kill Abner, everyone would call it a just revenge. He also knows that this would put a finish to the claims of

43

Ishbosheth who would be too weak to fight our army without his captain." Beniah spoke with quiet resignation.

Sulim leaned forward, eyes flashing with frustration. "We were all ready to fight. It was the moment we had all waited for, but David insisted he would not have the crown of Israel taken in such a fashion."

Ahithophel pondered this information. "But will not Joab seek to kill Abner and avenge his brother anyway?"

Sulim glanced at Beniah and spoke softly. "We all know that Joab will not rest until he avenges his brother and kills Abner."

Ahithophel rose and walked to the doorway, his mind full of unanswered questions. Could this lion of the tribe of Judah ever unite the land, defeat their enemies, and regain their villages? Was David a man of real strength or an idealistic dreamer? He looked from Beniah to the impulsive Sulim. "Tomorrow evening I have planned a celebration to announce my granddaughter's betrothal. I will have an answer for you then."

The two men exchanged disappointed glances. To ease the tension, Ahithophel called for more wine, then began to reminisce about the days when the nation had been united and victorious.

Everything had been so easy then. David had slain the giant from Gath. His armies had driven the Philistines back to the coast. The nights after battle were spent in feasting and revelry in Saul's great stone hall. David was always at the center, full of vitality, singing, playing his harp and telling stories the villagers still remembered.

"That was before the trouble," Beniah agreed.

Ahithophel's face clouded at the unpleasant memory. It wasn't the Philistines that had brought an end to the glory of those days, he reminded himself. It was something that crept up out of the darkness so subtly that no one saw it until it was too late. Old Saul was jealous of David. First he took Michal away from David and married her to rich old Phalti. Then he drove David out to live in the caves below Hebron. The battle of Gilboa was just the final tragedy at the end of all the other tragedies.

Although he had talked late into the night with his guests, Ahithophel rose at his accustomed time and walked out from the village to his wheat fields. He always loved this early hour of the morning. It was an ideal time for reflection. *David can win,* he thought, *if he makes the right moves.*

Some people said that God determined who would win or lose. Since his son's death on Gilboa Ahithophel had scoffed at such thinking. "No," he reasoned aloud, "those who are clever and bold win out. If David chooses wise counselors and develops a strong army, God will be on his side." He blew the husks from the wheat cupped in his hand and tossed the kernels into his mouth.

A bitter smile crossed his face. Since he was not one of those God favored, perhaps it would be wise to join the man considered to be God's own anointed choice. Above all he would be cautious; he would wait to see who was the stronger man. "I don't need help or favor from God or man," he told himself, squaring his shoulders. "I will succeed well enough by myself, using my own wits."

He passed the vineyard belonging to Judah. The grapes would not be ripe until the month of Tammuz, but he could see that Judah was skilled at vine tending and would have a large crop. Yes, he had done the right thing to promise Bathsheba to Judah.

Bathsheba was now fourteen and very beautiful. *Such young women can fall into scandalous situations,* he thought. *But Judah is wise and strong. A beautiful woman needs a man like Judah as her husband. If a man does not find the proper husband for his daughter, she could disgrace him even though she is married.*

Ahithophel had seen several of the women of Israel stoned for adultery. His eyes narrowed. There was no reason for a man to take a woman in this way when he could have both wives and concubines under the law with no criticism.

He thought of Bathsheba as she had looked just the night before. She was no longer a little child but a beautiful young woman, slim and graceful as the willows by the stream and with rich black hair that rippled down to her waist drawing everyone's attention, when it wasn't hidden under the mantle Noha insisted that she wear. Her eyes were dark and laughing with long lashes that edged them in a most becoming way.

"Yes," he muttered, "when young girls ask questions about grown men it is time they marry." She had been so interested in his guest from Hebron and so impressed when she discovered that her grandfather had known David quite well when both were in Saul's army. She had begged and begged him to describe David to her and had not been satisfied with simple answers.

"Is he tall?" she had asked quite casually.

"Taller than I am," he had answered without paying much attention.

"What color are his eyes?"

"I don't know." When he saw her disappointment, he had added, "They are unusual eyes; you might say they were hazel flecked with blue."

"Is he strong?"

46

"Very. Muscular but very gentle. It is difficult to describe him."

"Tell me, Grandfather," she said finally, "is he handsome?"

"Oh, yes, yes," he had assured her. "He is very handsome. All the women are in love with him."

It was time Bathsheba had a husband.

Somewhere beyond the mud brick wall of the courtyard, a cock crowed. Bathsheba stirred in her sleep and smiled. The shutters on her small window slowly opened, letting in a ray of sunshine as Jessica, her maid, pushed her head through the opening and made cooing noises imitating the pigeons in the courtyard. Bathsheba smiled again and turned over toward the wall letting her dark hair fall in great rivulets across the homespun mat and clay floor.

Jessica disappeared from the window and a few minutes later entered the room with a steaming bowl of groats. She set the bowl on a stool near the window and bent over the sleeping form of Bathsheba with a long feather from one of the pigeons.

"Time to wake up, my pretty one," she cooed softly as she tickled Bathsheba's nose with the feather.

Bathsheba brushed at the feather, pouted, stretched, then sat up and reached for the bowl. She held it for a moment enjoying its warmth and then sipped a bit of the warm broth.

"You don't seem to remember all the things you have to do today," Jessica said as she turned to shoo the pigeons out the door and latch it so they couldn't come back.

"You must hurry and dress. We have much work to do in preparation for tonight."

Bathsheba set the bowl of groats down quickly. "I hope Machir gets back from Mahanaim in time for the celebration. I know he thinks Judah is too old for me, but he does like him better than anyone else."

Jessica's face grew serious. "And you, my lamb, do you also like Judah better than anyone else?"

"Judah was my father's best friend. And he saved my life once. I'm sure I will be very happy with him."

Jessica shrugged. "Hurry and dress now. Your grandmother wants us to grind more flour. The jar of water is on the floor in your bath." She closed the door quietly, and Bathsheba stood up, shivering with the cold of early morning. She flung open the shutters, letting in the warm sunlight to heat her room, and reached for her shift as she hurried with bare feet into the courtyard.

The bath across the court was a cramped, dark room built of clay bricks daubed with mud and brushed with white lime. Jessica had put the stone basin on its clay shelf and the water in a crudely turned clay jar on the floor. Quickly Bathsheba poured water into the bowl and bent over to wash her face.

She was surprised at the clearness of the reflection and it held her attention for a moment. *I do have rather nice eyes,* she observed to herself with satisfaction, thinking of Judah and how he must see her. *But my nose is too long and my mouth is a bit pouty. Grandfather says I am the most beautiful girl in the Gilead, though he could be wrong.*

"Bathsheba, your mother is getting impatient." Jessica was standing in the center of the court holding her dress. Bathsheba held out her arms and Jessica slipped the robe on her and tied the embroidered band which was wound twice around her slim waist. "Jessica, do you think an older man would find me attractive?" she asked.

Jessica studied her young mistress. "You are pretty just as you are with a sort of freshness about you. Soon I will teach you to apply color to your cheeks and a bit of kohl around your eyes."

"Bathsheba, why must you take so long?" Noha stood in the arched doorway, wiping her hands on the hem of her dress.

"Mother, I am coming," Bathsheba replied as she tied another knot in her waist band. It seemed that her mother was always irritated about something. It made Bathsheba wonder if her mother's bitterness had been the result of a great love cut short or of no love at all. Noha had remained in the house of Ahithophel after her husband's death on Gilboa, in a somewhat higher position than the servants, but not quite a full member of the family.

Noha softened a bit. "We'll need more bread today, with the visitors here and the festivities tonight." She brought out a large jar of wheat and called for Phineas to bring the grindstones.

The servant came struggling in with several round stones and adjusted them so they would turn easily. Noha waited until Bathsheba and Jessica were seated, one on each side of the mill. Then she scooped up some plump brown wheat in her hand and, bending over the stones, let it run down into the hole in the center of the top stone. Jessica grasped the wooden handle and began to turn the large top stone. The grinding was monotonous and took a long time, but of all the work to be done, Bathsheba enjoyed it the most. She liked to handle the warm grain and then see the stones almost come to life as Jessica caught the rhythm of the whirling mill stone and made it spin faster and faster.

The women of Ahithophel's house were always busy. There was the daily bread to make, water to be carried, wool carded and woven, garments mended, and the gardens and animals tended. There were always plenty of servants to help, but everything had to be checked and rechecked by either Noha or Reba.

Ahithophel had come by his servants in different ways. The years of meager harvest or famine forced some of the villagers with large families to offer him a child or two. In time, these servants were returned to their families and new ones came to take their place. They were usually grateful to work free in a large house where there was plenty of food and the mistress was not stingy with cloth for their clothes.

Jessica was different. Ahithophel had taken her captive after a battle with the Amalekites. As a captain in Saul's army he had ordered his men to kill everyone in the village without mercy. Jessica's husband and other relatives had been slain, but she had been saved only by the kindness of Ahithophel.

He first saw her standing among the ruins of her home. She was wearing a fine linen dress and had a golden band woven through her long dark hair, which signified a noble birth. She looked like a frightened gazelle, and Ahithophel could not raise his sword against her. In the moment he hesitated, Jessica fell at his feet. "My lord, I can read and write as well as any scribe. Please, if you have children, let me go with you. I will teach them all I know."

Ahithophel had recognized this as an unusual bit of good fortune. He brought her home and instructed her to teach Machir his early lessons. Later he agreed to let Bathsheba study with Jessica in the same way.

No one thought of Jessica as one of the hated Amalekites; she was as a daughter to Ahithophel and Reba and an older sister to Bathsheba. Now, as the two girls worked together, they talked as equals and friends.

"I wish these men from Hebron had never come," Bathsheba said impatiently.

"If you are tired of the grinding," Jessica reassured her, "take heart; there's only a little wheat left."

"No, it isn't the grinding I mind. I just don't want grandfather to go with these men to Hebron."

Jessica was surprised at the unexpected outburst. "It is an honor for your grandfather that King David wants him as his counselor."

"I know, and I'm afraid Grandfather will be tempted to go. He wants David to fight the Philistines and win back his village."

"Don't you want to go back to Giloh too?"

"I was so young I hardly recall it. When I think of it I remember only the doves, the pigeons, and a large well-curb. I keep thinking, what if Grandfather does get Giloh back and it isn't the way he remembered it?"

The grain was finished. With a great effort Jessica lifted the top stone and swept the particles of flour into the pile beside the stones. Then catching up the corners of the tough, homespun cloth, she tied the ends securely and stood up. She dusted off her skirt and quickly put the flour in a basket which she placed on her head. Then she hurried out to the ovens in the far court.

Bathsheba sat for a moment thinking. *I don't really believe Grandfather will leave Lodebar— not when I am married to Judah and living just down the lane from him.*

She smiled, thinking ahead to the party that

evening. "It will be good," she told herself, "to live so close to home and grind grain for the house of Judah."

5

AHITHOPHEL WAS sitting with his visitors in the receiving room when the sound of hooves was heard on the dry-packed dirt in the narrow lane outside. Machir was returning from Mahanaim.

Phineas was nowhere in sight, so it was Ahithophel who lifted the bolts and swung wide the gate before his grandson had time to dismount or knock. Ahithophel was startled to note how much his grandson looked like Emmiel, his long-dead son. They were the same height and noble bearing with the same open friendliness and suggestion of strength. Machir, however, was not a man thirsting for battle as his father had been, nor did he hunger for prominence like Ahithophel. He was content to plow his fields and prune his vines, taking each day as it came.

Ahithophel quickly led his grandson to the roof where they could talk without being disturbed.

"Ishbosheth has ordered Abner to return Rizpah to the women's court of Saul's house," Machir began, "but Abner has refused to give her up. Ishbosheth sees this as an attempt to claim the throne and is threatening severe punishment for Abner."

"I knew it would come to this," Ahithophel sputtered indignantly.

"The whole court is in total confusion. Abner is threatening to leave and join David in Hebron."

"Fools, fools, all of them are fools!" Ahithophel stormed as he pounded his fist on the parapet. "How can Abner think of going to David when he has killed Joab's brother—David's own nephew? How can he be so foolish when Joab has sworn to kill him?"

"That is only part of it," continued Machir. "Abner has already contacted David, and David has asked that he bring Michal back to him as an assurance of his good faith."

Ahithophel stared at his grandson in amazement. "After all this time do you really believe Michal will go back to David? She's been married to Phalti for years now, and he worships her."

"Grandfather, Michal is going back. In fact, she will meet Abner here at our house, and they will travel on to Hebron together."

"Michal and Abner here!" Ahithophel stared out over the rooftops baking in the hot afternoon sun, remembering Michal as he had first seen her in her father's palace. Tall as all Saul's family were tall, aloof, proud, decked in gold bangles, she was a young woman of twenty who had a reputation for getting what she wanted.

"She must see this as a chance to rule the country from the court of the women," Ahithophel growled. "She has always gotten what she wanted, even David. When she first saw him with nothing but his sling and shepherd's harp, she begged old Saul to let her marry him."

"David must have wanted her too," Machir interjected. "I used to hear the old men talking about it, how David had to bring a hundred foreskins of the Philistines as a dowry for Michal."

"He didn't really like it," said Ahithophel remembering. "I was one of those who went with him. He didn't mind killing the Philistines, but he really did mind getting those foreskins. Somehow for the first time, the Philistines suddenly seemed real men to him. I found him standing over one young boy with such a look I will never forget. 'Ahithophel,' he said to me, 'do you think I am going to enjoy Michal with a hundred men looking over my shoulder?' Maybe that's why it didn't work out between them."

Ahithophel was silent, sorting out all that he had heard. If Abner was going over to David, and Michal as well, Ishbosheth was finished. How strangely things had worked out. David had resisted those in his own ranks who wanted to fight him for the throne; now everything was working out in his favor. *It is almost as though God really is for David,* he mused.

"Machir!" Ahithophel startled his grandson with his stern tone of voice. "I am going to Hebron with these men tomorrow. I don't want to wait and go with Abner, in case his luck takes a turn for the worse."

Machir smiled. "As usual, you are always thinking ahead."

Ahithophel did not seem to hear him but sat with his hands on his knees, his eyes gazing at the mud-packed floor of the roof. "There are many matters I must leave in your care," he said. "I will betroth your sister to Judah tonight at the celebration, but she need not be married for a year. In the meantime, we will not draw up any formal agreement with Judah's family until later."

Detecting reluctance on Machir's face, Ahithophel abruptly concluded the matter. "It is good to join two great families; don't mistake it. A man must use his head if he is going to get along."

For a moment there was silence. "Grandfather, I'll leave to you all the big family matters, but there is one matter in which I must insist on having my way. It concerns Mephibosheth, the only son of Jonathan."

"Saul's grandson? The lame one?" asked Ahithophel.

"Yes, the lame one. I have invited him to live in Lodebar with us so he will not be torn apart by the contentions in Saul's house."

Ahithophel was again taken by surprise. His grandson seemed to have none of the wisdom he had expected him to inherit. "Machir, it is bad enough to have Michal and Abner stopping here, almost as though we were members of the family. But for you to keep Mephibosheth is dangerous."

"I'm not taking him because it is convenient but because his father, Jonathan, was a friend to my father."

Ahithophel shrugged in resignation. "I warn you, wherever members of Saul's family bed down, there is trouble."

Darkness came early to the mud-walled courtyard where Ahithophel welcomed the villagers he had invited for the celebration. The whole village was alive with the news that Ahithophel was to leave in the morning to become David's chief counselor.

The men gathered around him while the women slipped quietly into the far court. The pleasant smell of date cakes and crushed coriander filled the night air with fragrance as the men sat around the courtyard and talked excitedly with Ahithophel and his visitors. Phineas came to announce that Judah and his father, Reuben, were at the gate. Ahithophel rose and ushered them in, leading Judah to the chief seat under the crudely raised canopy stretched across the courtyard for the occasion.

With Judah's arrival the Canaanite dancing girls came in from the far court, shaking their tam-

55

bourines and singing in high-pitched voices the love poems of the Gilead Mountains. In the flickering light of the oil lamps the gold and silver of their jewelry flashed. At a signal from Ahithophel the dancers left and wine was served as the men discussed the news from Mahanaim. Finally, Ahithophel sent a message to Reba that it was time for Bathsheba to be presented.

Bathsheba stood in the center of her courtyard with the bright light of the moon glistening on her bare arms, making the gold bracelets and ankle jewelry sparkle. The night air was chilly, and she was wearing only her jewelry and the clumsy pantaloons worn by women of Lodebar. Shivering with the cold, she raised her arms and let Reba slip a new, brightly woven gown over her head. Then Noha placed a new sash around her waist, speaking one of the age-old blessings. Last of all Jessica placed a crown of flowers on her head.

Space had been made for the women at the back of the main courtyard, and a raised couch decked with field flowers had been prepared for Bathsheba. Ahithophel met them at the door and led his granddaughter to the seat of honor. Then he motioned for Noha to sit beside her while the children and village women crowded in close on every side.

The Canaanite women returned singing and beating drums to one side of the court, while the men of Lodebar rose and danced the village tribal dances. Arms linked together and feet beating rhythmically on the hard-packed earth, they concluded with a special salute to Bathsheba.

One of the old women now called out for Bathsheba to perform the dance of Mahanaim. Bathsheba blushed and drew back at first, but as the call for her became more insistent, she let them lead her out to the center of the courtyard. There she stood for a moment, her head thrown back, listening to the singing of the Canaanite women and the steady beat of the drum. Then slowly she began the graceful movements of the dance. The tempo increased and her feet moved faster, her hair blowing about her in rippling waves.

With a strong, staccato drumbeat and clapping hands, the dance came to an end. Bathsheba impulsively stopped before Judah and pulled the crown of flowers from her head and placed it in his outstretched hands. Then she hurried back to her seat amidst laughter and cheers.

Clearing his throat and trying to look stern, Ahithophel rose to make the betrothal announcement. He noted with pleasure the worshipful look Judah gave Bathsheba. He also noted her answering flush and sparkling eyes. *How right it is,* he thought, *to marry Bathsheba to an older man like Judah.*

Back in her small courtyard Bathsheba was glad that Jessica had remembered to leave the lighted lamp in the niche beside the door to her small room. A donkey brayed and the soft notes of a shepherd's flute could be heard outside her wall. There were voices in the distance as Ahithophel continued to talk with the lingering guests.

It had been a wonderful evening. She stood still under the lemon tree and tried to remember every moment. She could still feel the excitement of the dance, and she blushed as she remembered giving her wreath to Judah. She looked down at her small, shapely hand and remembered Judah's warm handclasp and bold look of adoration as the betrothal announcement was made.

She lifted the clay lamp from the shelf and carried it to check the pigeons in their mud-daubed houses. She loved to see their eyes blink open and shine like glowing coals in the darkness. She smiled, remembering how carefully Judah once had held the pigeons in his hands when he had brought them to her. Judah loved small birds and animals just as she did.

Returning to her room, Bathsheba lay down on the sleeping mat and was soon sound asleep. She did not hear Jessica's knock on the door; only when Jessica called her name did she awake. "Judah has left a present for you," Jessica whispered as she knelt beside her.

"Oh, Jessica, please let me see it." Bathsheba was instantly awake, brushing back strands of black, curling hair from her face as she sat up.

"I'm afraid you will be disappointed. It's rather a strange gift."

"What is it? Now I am really curious." Bathsheba threw back the coverlet and jumped to her feet.

Jessica shrugged her shoulders, turned and went to the door of the courtyard which was now deep in shadows. "All right," she said, "stay there, and I will bring it to you. Whatever you'll do with it I can't imagine. Now shut your eyes."

There was a faint tinkling of bells and a tapping noise on the hard-packed earth. When Bathsheba opened her eyes, there in the doorway stood a fuzzy white lamb with a sparkling silver collar and silver bells engraved with wild flowers. With wide-eyed delight Bathsheba knelt beside the lamb and felt its soft wool. "He's so sweet and clean and white and what a beautiful silver collar!"

Jessica was amazed. "I'm glad you like it. Really, I thought you would want bracelets or clothes for yourself."

"Jessica, you should know me better than that.

Don't you see? Judah knows how much I love animals. I believe he made the collar himself."

A cloud passed over the moon and a breeze sprang up, making Bathsheba shiver. "I suppose Grandfather has decided to go with the men from Hebron?" she asked suddenly.

"Yes, he has ordered his mule to be ready before daybreak."

Bathsheba was silent as she tried to picture all it would mean to them if her grandfather went to live in the court of David at Hebron. "I suppose I should consider it a great honor that King David has chosen Grandfather," she said finally. "It is strange, though, I don't feel happy about it at all. Not that I don't think Machir can manage everything. That's not what worries me. It's something I feel."

The little lamb nuzzled Bathsheba's hand with his nose. She bent down, burying her face in the soft wool.

6

WHEN AHITHOPHEL and his two companions arrived at the gates of Hebron they were greeted with flattering respect by David's men. A young servant came to wash Ahithophel's feet and another brought him fresh robes from the king's own storerooms. "The king has prepared a special feast in your honor," Beniah informed him as a young man with a flaming torch appeared in the open doorway.

He was guided through a dusty courtyard into a long, narrow room filled with young men laughing and talking. Ahithophel was shown to a long table at the end of the room and given the seat of honor.

An air of expectancy filled the hall. As the torches flickered there was the smell of burning oil and spices mixed with the heady perfume of aloes and spikenard. Shadows moved in great shapes along the walls, and out across the floor, blending with the raucous laughter, was the stomping of bare feet on stone and the high-pitched music of a flute.

Somewhere in the distance a horn was blown. The men became quiet as they looked eagerly toward the door. Ahithophel last remembered David as a young man with warm, laughing eyes and a homemade harp under his arm. He did not know what to expect now but was surprised when David entered the room almost casually, with no more fanfare than another blast of the horn.

There was no doubt that this tanned, muscular man was their leader and tribal king. Vitality radiated from him and drew people's attention almost magically. As David mingled with his men without ceremony, some of the old captains tried to hurry him along. The king ignored them and reached out across the table to greet his men and welcome strangers.

A short, stocky man with large protruding eyes and red, disheveled hair pushed on ahead of David to claim the seat to the left of the throne. It was Joab. Ahithophel recognized him immediately though it had been nine years since he had last seen him. Joab was a nervous, restless man, obviously driven by deep and conflicting emotions. *I must win the friendship of Joab,* Ahithophel decided, *if I am to succeed in the court of David.*

Joab had been a good friend to his son, Emmiel, and Ahithophel knew he shared his own fierce determination to regain the villages lost to the Philistines. With this in common it should not be hard to win Joab's friendship unless he learned of

Ahithophel's tenuous connections with the house of Saul. Inwardly he groaned at the thought that Machir would be keeping Mephibosheth at Lodebar. *We would have done better to have broken with the house of Saul long ago.*

As David approached the head table, Ahithophel started to kneel but found his arm caught in the strong grasp of the king. David's voice was warm. "My men and my God have made me a king, but to you, Ahithophel, let me be as a son."

The meal that followed was simple but adequate. Watching men eat with gusto, Ahithophel noticed that their clothes were plain and that their weapons hanging on the walls behind them were of both Philistine and Amorite styles, obviously taken in battle. As king, David possessed little of the wealth and security that Saul once boasted. If Michal was coming back to David with the expectation of enjoying such niceties as the court at Gibeah had boasted, she would be very disappointed. And if Abner came trusting in David's friendship and not reckoning on the treachery of Joab, he might soon be dead.

That night in his small sleeping room, with a solitary clay lamp flickering beside the pallet on the floor, Ahithophel pondered the wisdom of his choice. David was little more than an outlaw king living off the land, depending on the bounty he won through small skirmishes with the Philistines and petty village chieftains. Yet on the other side, Ishbosheth was too weak ever to move against the Philistines; Abner was so obsessed with his passion for Rizpah he was ready to sacrifice everything for her. *No good ever came of a man loving a woman,* Ahithophel reasoned. It was much better to manage life with logic as he had done for Bathsheba.

The air coming in through the small window was

cool. Ahithophel wrapped his cloak around him, sat down on the hard pallet, removed his sandals, and blew out the lamp. He stretched out and pulled the cloak over his head, shutting out the droning of insects and the dampness seeping through the wall.

Abner and Michal would be arriving soon in Hebron. *Abner is a fool to trust Joab. David is a fool to take Michal back. The world is full of fools.* He finally went to sleep in spite of his discomforting thoughts.

Ahithophel had been gone from home a full month when word came to Lodebar that Michal was at last on her way to Hebron with her crippled nephew, Mephibosheth, and the six orphaned sons of her sister. Bathsheba was eager to meet Michal. The reports were that she was overbearing and arrogant.

It had been said that Michal's bed in Gibeah was high off the floor, and the dark, carved teak of its frame was inlaid with ivory flowers. She had chests carved from cedar for her clothes, and the jars and basins for her bath were of brass and alabaster. Compared with such elegance Bathsheba could see that her own court and sleeping room with its mud-brick bath seemed poor indeed.

Bathsheba pulled the mats, cushions, and coverings out into the sunshine to freshen them and found they looked dingy in the bright light. "Jessica, we must hurry to the stream and wash these linens. I would be ashamed to have someone from Saul's house think we did not keep our rooms clean."

Jessica hesitated. "There are fowl to be feathered and a sheep to be dressed, as well as herbs to be ground and the bread mixed and baked."

"You and I can do this by ourselves," Bathsheba said, ignoring Jessica's reluctance. She had the linens laid out in two piles on the mud-brick tiles of the court. As she talked she drew up the ends and tied them, first one bundle and then the other.

With a sigh of resignation Jessica picked up one of the bundles and put it on her head. Bathsheba did the same with the other and followed Jessica through the large courtyard, out to the narrow lane that led through the bazaar toward the main gate of the village.

Once past the gate and out of sight of the elders who always gathered there, they hurried down the hill to the stream in the valley. Tender blades of grass were growing along the bank, and there were buttercups with deep green leaves and bright yellow faces. After a seasonal rainfall the vegetation was thick and rich along the stream.

Quickly they untied the bundles. Jessica sorted out the heavier material for her pile and left the lighter things for Bathsheba. A practiced eye could spot the stones that were most often used by the village women for washing clothes. Bathsheba dipped the linen in the water carefully, holding it at arm's length so she would not get wet.

Jessica laughed. "You're too gentle. See, you must go at it as though you're after the devil." With determination she doused the heavy stuff in the cool water and proceeded to knead and rinse it, bunching it up in little mounds and pounding it with a small smooth rock. Then she tied her skirts high out of the way with her sash, pulled off her sandals, and waded into the water to pummel the linen with her bare feet.

Bathsheba tried but soon tired of pounding the

clothes with a stone. Finding her hands too delicate to squeeze the great bunches of cloth, she placed the clothes in a shallow part of the stream and began to knead them with her feet as Jessica was doing. Unfortunately, she had not bothered to fasten her dress around her waist and in a few moments she was as wet as the clothes.

Her hair had come loose from the comb and her dress was not only wet but muddy. "Well, I know what to do about that," Bathsheba said, laughing gaily as she quickly untied her sash and threw it to the astonished Jessica. With one quick movement she pulled her dress over her head, quickly washed it clean, threw it over a nearby bush, and plunged into the cold water of the stream.

"Bathsheba, come back here!" Jessica screamed. "Look at you! Out in the open in your underthings." Jessica glanced up and down the stream to see if anyone was watching.

"I'm not going home all muddy." Bathsheba splashed the cool water on her face and arms.

"Your dress will never dry," Jessica scolded.

"Don't worry," Bathsheba laughed. "I'm clean, my dress is clean, and we're both wet so there's no problem." She came to the edge of the stream, pulled her wet dress off the bush, and struggled into it. She turned to Jessica. "As soon as the sheets dry in the sun, we will walk home, and no one will know anything about it if you don't tell."

Jessica began wringing out the linens and spreading them on the bushes to dry, grumbling about the cold Bathsheba would catch and the stringy condition of her hair.

"Never mind, now you can fix it as you promised you would for my engagement," Bathsheba urged.

Jessica didn't answer. Her attention was suddenly captured by a small green plant growing close to the stream. Carefully she dug around the plant. "Look, Bathsheba, it's a rare herb. Come smell its leaves. It makes a delicious tea."

Bathsheba pushed back her wet hair and fastened on her sandals. "Grandfather loves tea. I wish he were here to taste it."

Jessica laughed. "This tea wouldn't be for your grandfather. Egyptians call this a magic love potion."

Bathsheba came and fingered the fragrant leaves. "Do you believe in love potions, Jessica? I don't think I would want someone to love me just because of a magic cup of tea."

Jessica took the plant and carefully tied it into the end of her mantel. "What romantic illusions you have. People always love for a reason. Beauty or gold or land or influence. Or even a magic charm."

Bathsheba looked at her with wide, troubled eyes. "Oh, no, Jessica. I can't believe that."

For a while Bathsheba sat in the sun while Jessica walked up and down the stream looking in vain for more herbs. "Come, the clothes are dry," Jessica said finally, gathering them quickly and arranging them into bundles. Putting the bundles on their heads, the two hurried back to the village.

It was late in the afternoon when Jessica finally had time to arrange Bathsheba's hair. Bathsheba sat on a cushion under the lemon tree while Jessica knelt behind her, skillfully combing the abundant tresses that fell in shimmering waves down her back. With swift and practiced skill she divided and parted the hair, holding it with bits of bone and ivory and working small blue flowers into the hair around Bathsheba's face.

There was a sound of feet in the outer hall, and

Noha stood in the small archway. "They're coming," she gasped.

"Do you like my hair, Mother?" Bathsheba asked, never taking her eyes from the mirror.

"Bathsheba, there's no time to think of such things now!"

The sound of knocking on the outer gate caused Noha to hurry back to the outer court while Jessica snatched the mirror from Bathsheba and gathered up the bone pins and ivory comb. Bathsheba rose slowly and shook out her dress. *I wonder if Michal is going to Hebron because she loves David?* she thought.

Bathsheba walked through the small archway, down the hall, and out to the front courtyard already filling with people. Michal rode through the gate mounted on a white mule saddled with purple tapestry. Though her face was shielded from the wind with a thin mantle, everyone knew who she was by the golden ankle bands, the flashes of golden bracelets and rings and the regal way she rode.

Michal let her maids help her dismount and immediately flung back her veil to scan the courtyard. She handed her cloak to one of the serving maids, then ordered Phineas to take her mule to be watered and fed.

Drawing herself up imperiously, she turned to Reba, ready to accept her welcome. Bathsheba followed her mother and was surprised when Michal turned to her. "You must be Bathsheba. What a young lady you have become. You were just a scrawny, big-eyed little colt when I saw you years ago."

Bathsheba reddened at the attention. For a moment the two looked at each other, then Bathsheba realized that Michal was not really beautiful at all. Her mouth had a look of smugness and her nose was too prominent, but her figure was flawless. She had managed well with artistry what nature had left undone. There was a proud lift to her royal head and a sureness in every movement.

"I am tired from the journey and terribly dusty." Michal was again businesslike and abrupt. Noha hurried off to guide the young maids to the far court, while Michal still lingered as though waiting for something.

"I will need my hair completely redone before dinner. Is there someone here trained in the art of hairdressing?" She looked at Bathsheba's hair carefully, reaching out to maneuver a stray flower back into place.

"Oh, yes," Bathsheba blushed with pleasure, "my serving maid, Jessica. She will be glad to do your hair in any style you should desire." Jessica looked less than pleased, but she came forward and gracefully led Michal back to the small courtyard prepared for her.

Bathsheba lingered to see Mephibosheth, who was being helped from his mule by two servants. Just at that moment Michal's nephews came running through the gate and pulled the mule's tail, sending him bolting into the far court. Another boy came chasing after him and bumped into old Phineas, who was bringing water to wash the feet of the guests. Phineas dropped the basin and water went spilling out over the hard-packed earth of the courtyard.

In exasperation Machir reached out and grabbed the boy. "Where are you going in such a hurry, young man?" he demanded.

The boy was breathing hard and was anxious to get back with the other boys. "I am going to Hebron with my aunt," he said angrily as he tried to free himself from Machir's grip. "I'll be living in the

67

palace of that swine of the house of Judah they call David."

Machir was shocked, and Bathsheba was glad that there was so much attention focused on getting Mephibosheth carried to his room that no one seemed to have heard the boy.

"In this house you don't speak that way of . . ." Machir began.

"Don't say the next king of Israel, or I shall report you to my Uncle Ishbosheth." The boy drew himself up until he looked like a replica of his grandfather, old Saul. "The house of Saul rules Israel, and so it will always be."

Machir let the youngster go and turned to Bathsheba. "That boy will soon get himself in trouble in David's court with ideas like that."

When their guests had all arrived, Reba called for old Phineas to carry the serving dishes to the reception room. Finding he was busily carrying ashes to the front courtyard, she turned on him impatiently. "Why must you carry out cold ashes just as we are ready to serve the meal?"

"It is the guest, my lady. The husband of the Princess Michal. He sits weeping by the front gate. It was he who ordered me to gather cold ashes and pour them on his head."

"That ragged beggar is the husband of Michal?" Reba was astounded.

"My lady, he is Phalti, the husband to whom old Saul gave his daughter when he quarreled with David. Now she is going back to David, and Phalti is grieving for her."

"Poor man," said Reba.

"How he must love Michal," said Bathsheba.

"What a fool he is," said Noha.

When the food was ready to be served to Michal

and her maids, Bathsheba was sent to find out if Jessica had finished arranging Michal's hair. Bathsheba hurried down the dark hall and knocked on Jessica's door. When there was no answer, she pushed the door open and saw Jessica huddled in the far corner, sobbing.

"Michal has ordered me to go with her to Hebron tomorrow," Jessica wept. "She has sent me here to pack my things."

"Michal has ordered you . . . ?" Bathsheba could not at first believe what she had heard.

"She liked the way I did her hair and. . . ."

"Grandfather will not allow it!"

"He is not here. Besides, you dare not cross her now that she is going back to David."

It was the custom to give a guest anything that was requested, as a show of hospitality, but it was a very bold guest who would ask for anything of value.

"Look, Jessica," said Bathsheba suddenly, picking up the herb they had discovered by the stream, "Michal is just the one to value a magic herb. I will put this in a small gold box and take it to her. I will explain that she cannot have you, but as a token of my friendship I will give her this gift of great value instead. There's no need to pack. I'm sure the plan will work."

Bathsheba went quickly to her own courtyard where Michal was staying. Costly rugs now covered the floor and the crude clay lamps had been replaced by transparent alabaster bowls that gave off a hypnotic fragrance with their soft light. Two young serving girls were remaking the small pallet bed with fine gray linen sheets.

The worn wooden door hung open, and Bathsheba could see Michal sitting on one of the mud-brick seats of the bath that ran around the wall. She was talking to a servant who was rubbing rich oils into her feet.

Michal greeted Bathsheba with a cold smile. "I hope you don't mind that I have stolen your little maid. Of course I will pay you well for her." Michal's eyes then grew hard. "Such skill as hers is lost in these hills. I have told her to pack her things. She will go with me tomorrow."

"And I have told her not to pack." Bathsheba spoke calmly but her eyes flashed their anger. "I'm sure you will find someone to better suit your tastes in Hebron."

Michal looked at Bathsheba with surprise. She had been used to intimidating everyone and was astonished that this young girl would question her decision. "My dear, you wouldn't want to deprive her of this chance, I'm sure."

"And I am sure you would not ask for something that is too precious to give."

"I am not asking for something," Michal's voice was harsh and mocking. "I am taking something, my pet."

"My princess," Bathsheba said, returning Michal's glare with a gaze that did not waver, "I have brought you a gift of far more value than my maid." She held out the little gold box and opened the lid to show the green plant inside. "See, this is a rare magic love potion."

Michal touched a leaf with her finger. "Surely you would not have been able to find such a treasure without the help of a very clever Amalekite maid. Thank you." She reached out and took the box, snapping the lid shut. "I will be grateful to you for the herb and for Jessica. You will see that I will reward you richly."

"But I have not. . . ."

"My dear, the matter is settled. Come, it is time that we should dine." With a wave of her hand Michal summoned her maids to accompany her up the stairs to the roof.

Bathsheba felt tears of anger and frustration sting her eyes as she hurried out to the main courtyard where she hoped to find Machir welcoming Abner and his men. It would be difficult for Machir to defy someone like Michal, but he was now her only hope.

Abner had just arrived with his caravan. As Bathsheba pushed through the servants unloading the baggage, she bumped into a woman who was dismounting from her mule. "I'm sorry," Bathsheba said reaching out to steady the woman.

"You must be Bathsheba," the voice was soft and pleasant. The woman threw back her hood that half covered her face.

"And you are Rizpah," Bathsheba said, her eyes growing large at seeing the woman who had become so notoriously sinful as to live openly with a man she could not marry.

"Yes, I am Rizpah," she said bending to kiss Bathsheba on both cheeks. "You have been crying."

Bathsheba led her to her grandmother's room where she was to sleep that night.

"What is wrong?" Rizpah asked gently as she sank down upon one of the mats and loosened her mantle.

"Do you know Michal? I mean, do you know her very well?"

"Yes, yes. I know Michal quite well." Rizpah sounded guarded and hesitant.

Impulsively Bathsheba knelt down beside her and spoke earnestly. "If she wants something very badly, does she have the power to take it?"

Rizpah looked around cautiously before she answered. "Whatever Michal really wants, she will have. I have never known anyone strong enough to stop her."

"Even if that something—or someone—belongs to someone else who prizes it very much?"

Rizpah leaned forward and whispered the words, "If she sees it is something you prize, she will be all the more determined to take it."

Sadly Bathsheba returned to Jessica's small room. Opening the door Bathsheba threw herself into the older girl's arms and wept. "I hate her. I really hate her," she cried.

At daylight the visitors were fed early. Then they gathered in the courtyard where Jessica mounted a donkey in the midst of Michal's servants. Bathsheba followed her friend and fastened her few belongings securely on each side of the saddle. "When you get to Hebron, find Grandfather! He'll think of a way to get you back!"

Machir spoke to Abner as he mounted his mule. "Be careful in Hebron. There are those who will pretend to be your friends. But remember, it takes only one puff to put out a light."

"I know that Joab has threatened to kill me," Abner replied. "But when he sees that I have brought Michal back to David with the allegiance of all the northern tribes, even Joab will be forced to accept me."

Slowly the caravan began to move. Bathsheba watched with tears running down her cheeks. All she could think of was Jessica and the anger she felt toward Michal for taking her. She turned and ran to her courtyard that now seemed lifeless and empty. It smelled sickeningly of Michal's perfume. She slammed her door in angry grief and threw herself down on the pallet, weeping bitterly.

7

WITHIN A MONTH Ahithophel had made himself indispensable to David and his household. Though David had been living simply, his daily schedule was becoming more and more that of a king. He was overburdened with people, pressed hourly with decisions, and hounded with the necessity of finding enough food for his men and their families. One by one, Ahithophel was able to find solutions for these problems.

One morning when Ahithophel was sitting with David in the main receiving room, a runner came with the news that Abner was approaching Hebron with twenty men of his immediate family and Michal, as David had requested. Michal had left her husband, Phalti, at the village of Benhurim. They would all be in Hebron within the hour.

Ahithophel was quick to notice the change in David's demeanor at the mention of Michal. David ordered the court cleared and his best robes prepared, the torches lit and incense burned in his rooms where he would receive Michal.

"It is obvious that Michal still has power to turn the heart of the king," said Ahithophel, smiling.

"Don't worry," David smiled knowingly, "I'll not be led by a woman, no matter how beautiful."

"Is Michal then to stay in the king's chambers while the other wives of the king are crowded together in the women's quarters?"

David pondered the question. "Perhaps Michal does not know that I have other wives and concubines. She will be jealous, but I suppose she must be given a room in the court of the women. Talk to old Mahat; see that she gives Michal a good room, Ahithophel, with whatever luxuries necessary to please her."

"A final question, my lord. When do you wish to see Abner?"

David studied the ring on the index finger of his right hand. "Joab will not like my decision to make peace, but he will not dare to move against me once it is done. See that a dinner is prepared in Abner's honor and mind you, spare nothing. He must see that while we once lived in caves, we have not become jackals." With a smile that matched the twinkle in his eye, David strode from the room.

Ahithophel was one of the few trusted men allowed to speak with David's wives. Now he went to the latticed door leading into their courtyard and struck the gong that would summon one of the servants. Almost at once the sound of children playing and the scolding voices of women stopped and there was silence. How these women of such different types and backgrounds could possibly get along together he could not imagine.

Ahinoam, David's first wife after Michal, was sweet but plain. David had married her on impulse when he heard that Saul had given Michal to Phalti. She had borne one son named Amnon, a willful boy who was allowed to do just as he pleased. Since David never called for Ahinoam anymore, she lived more and more for her son, spoiling him outrageously.

Maacah, the daughter of Talmai, king of Geshur, was the most beautiful woman in David's harem. She had her perfumes brought from Egypt, cloth for her robes from Sidon, and in the spring her maids lined her bed with rose petals. Michal would be a threat to Maacah as she was also the daughter of a king. As long as Michal had no children, however, Maacah would feel secure. Maacah boasted among the women that her son, Absalom, was David's favorite, and Tamar was his only daughter.

There were other wives such as Haggith and Eglah, and several concubines, but the wife Ahithophel sought as he stood outside the door of the women's quarters was Abigail. She was both attractive and practical. When David first met her, she was managing her husband's estates and organizing his workers. When her husband died very suddenly, David married her soon afterwards. If Ahithophel wanted something done efficiently and well, he called on Abigail to help him.

Now as he struck the gong a second time, he could hear the sound of soft-soled shoes on tile, a lattice opening, and then the round moon-face of one of the slaves peeped out at him. He asked for Abigail and was promptly ushered through the door and into the small receiving room where women of the harem received their visitors.

Abigail was always calm and efficient, but when Ahithophel informed her of Michal's imminent arrival, she shook her head in dismay. "We have no room. We're overcrowded as it is, and Michal will expect the best of everything."

Ahithophel stroked his beard and nodded. He remembered the large, sprawling fortress of Saul in Gibeah. Michal's furnishings had been elegant. Would she understand that David was not yet a king as her father had been? He doubted it. *Well,* he thought, *if she doesn't like it here, let her go back to Phalti.* It would be better for David and the new, united Israel. The house of Saul had brought them nothing but trouble.

He thanked Abigail, asked her to manage as best she could for Michal, and then returned to the main room where David would receive Abner as his guest for dinner that evening.

David was not in Hebron when the caravan of Abner arrived. An urgent message had come from Joab, asking for consultation on battle strategy against a Philistine advance, and David had ridden off in great haste. Above all he wanted to be sure his impulsive nephew did not return while Abner was there as his guest. It was left to Ahithophel to welcome Abner and Michal to Hebron.

Ahithophel led Abner to his rooms while old Mahat showed Michal with her servants to David's personal quarters. For a moment he thought he had seen Jessica in Michal's entourage. But there had been something else that made him feel uneasy. He had glimpsed Rizpah riding behind Abner into the large courtyard. He decided that she must have gone to the room with Abner. David would not look favorably on the way Abner had taken Rizpah.

Michal was angry that David had not come out to meet her and was apprehensive when she saw that he still seemed to be but one step above the young outlaw she remembered. Looking around his room, she grimaced at the big bed with its sheepskin covering, the tile floor spread with the animal skins, and small openings high in the wall through which the flies swarmed. She brushed past Mahat and ordered her maids to take the sheepskin covering from the bed and replace it with her fine linen sheets and mattress of softest down. She made them roll together the skins from the floor and put down soft carpets of woven black goat's hair. Last of all, she had the ugly torches taken away and small pottery lamps put in their place.

"There," she said, "it's barely liveable, but it will have to do until tomorrow."

Jessica was putting the last touches on an elaborate hair arrangement for Michal when they heard shouting and singing in the courtyard and realized that David had returned. Michal turned pale and reached for her polished brass mirror.

"Do I look my best, Jessica?" she asked nervously. "It has been years since we last saw each other." Quickly she slipped into the beautifully embroidered robes. *Who would have thought the "desert fox," as my father called David, would ever become king!* she thought.

"Come, Jessica," she called, handing her a thin golden circlet. "Place this in my hair. It will be a reminder to him of my royal blood." Jessica inserted the thin circlet in place as Michal fidgeted nervously. "Should I be standing at the window watching the sunset, or perhaps lying on the bed as if exhausted from my trip?"

Jessica had no time to answer, for at that moment a servant announced the coming of the king. Jessica grabbed the chain holding a bowl of glowing incense and swung it gently back and forth. Then when she heard the king's footstep on the stair, she gathered up her skirts and fled the room.

When David stood alone in the opened doorway, Michal was pleasantly surprised. The young boy she had loved so long ago had grown into a tall, broad-shouldered man who obviously commanded respect from everyone. For the first time since she had decided to come to Hebron Michal was unsure of herself. She sensed it would not be easy to manage this confident man.

David saw only Michal. As memories flashed through his mind, he thought she had never looked more lovely than she did at this moment standing in the soft glow of the lamps. He came to her and tenderly took the small hand she held out to him.

"Michal," he said, his voice husky with emotion as he reached to embrace her.

She pushed him back firmly. "Not now, not in

77

front of these." She motioned to the two boys playing on the floor and to her serving maids.

"Send them away," he said, still looking only at her. Michal was startled by the commanding tone of his voice. Again she felt uncertain. She pulled her hand away and turned her back to him while the servants hurried the boys from the room and closed the door.

"Michal," he said, reaching to put his arms around her. She pulled away from him again and laughed nervously. "See, I have transformed this horrible room so at least it will be bearable tonight," she said.

For the first time David looked around and saw how changed his room was. His puzzled expression somehow made Michal feel less afraid. She took a step toward him with a hurt, pouting look. "You do see that I, a daughter of Saul, could never have lived in this room as it was?"

"I did not intend for you to live here. This is my room. I have had a room prepared for you with my wives." David's eyes were now cold.

For a moment Michal was too shocked to move. "A daughter of Saul to live with the common women you call wives? Never."

"Michal, listen to me. . . ."

"Never, I will never. . . ." She spat the words at him defiantly.

With one swift movement he picked her up in his arms, carried her to the bed and tossed her onto it. For a moment she lay stunned and silent. "Michal," he said, towering over her, "once before you chose your father's house instead of the caves with me, your outlawed husband. Now things are different. I have wives with sons. All of them are of good families, and one is the daughter of a king greater than Saul."

She looked at him from the bed. He could barely hear her whisper between clenched teeth. "Do you mean to say that you intend to keep these women now that I am here?"

If only she had looked hurt or unhappy it might have melted his heart, but the cold, unreasoning anger he saw hardened his tone. "They are my wives; I love them. They have borne me sons."

"Love them, ha! I have heard that word when it was used better to speak of feelings for one's dog." She sat up and adjusted the combs in her hair.

"Michal, do you question my love?"

"Can you cut love like a sweet cake and serve a piece to everyone who catches your eye and still have any cake to give?"

"Michal, stop. We are fighting." David's voice softened. "I had imagined our meeting so differently."

"Ah, yes, you imagined the daughter of Saul coming to you, the shepherd boy of Bethlehem, begging a room in your harem."

David stared at her coldly. "All right, keep the room. I'll find another."

"Where will you go?"

"Any place but here."

"You must stay here with me. I demand it."

"You can demand nothing. You will come to see me as my other wives do and at my invitation."

"I will never come to you if that is how it is to be."

David did not even hear her last words. Already he was out the door, walking with long strides toward the hall where the dinner was to be held in Abner's honor.

Michal turned from the door and angrily began pacing back and forth across the room. "Well," she said finally, "I am not living with his other wives. I have not lost everything yet. If he is to be king, I shall be queen. And once I am queen, I shall do as I please."

The feast for Abner was a great success. When the food arrived in great abundance on platters of silver and gold, Abner and his men remarked that there had never been a feast in Saul's house to equal it. They drank date wine from delicately wrought goblets. When the piles of roast lamb, chicken, and beef were removed, young boys brought basins of rose water in which the guests washed their hands before being served from large trays of fruit and sweet cakes.

As they ate, David and Abner exchanged extravagant compliments, each reminding the other of the many battles they had fought together against the Philistines before Saul's jealousy had banished David. David did not promise Abner that he would be made commander of the army in Joab's place, but those listening could sense that this was what David intended to do. Uneasily they wondered what Joab's reaction would be.

Abner, in turn, promised David that he had contacted all the northern tribes, and they would be sending messengers soon to pledge allegiance to David as their king.

The food had been carried away and David was prepared to retire when two of his men came forward bringing his harp. David seemed about to refuse. Then he suddenly smiled, took his harp and strode down into the midst of his men. At first he began strumming, testing the strings and listening to their mellow tones. Impulsively he threw back his head and began to sing.

Ahithophel had heard him sing before in Saul's house in Gibeah but not like this. The torches gave everything a soft glow, and their light falling on the strong face of the king revealed lines of sadness. The songs he sang were melancholy melodies in a minor key.

Ahithophel observed this and wondered if all had gone well between David and Michal. He watched as David stood with bowed head and strummed chords, making the crude, homemade harp fairly weep. Then very quietly David began to sing the lament he had written for Jonathan after his death on Gilboa.

Saul and Jonathan were lovely and pleasant
    in their lives
And in their death they were not divided:
They were swifter than eagles,
They were stronger than lions,
How are the mighty fallen,
And the weapons of war perished.

No one moved as the last notes faded away.

David stood for a moment in silence, tears flowing into his beard. Then at a signal from him, the servants began to remove the torches, and he said good-night to his guests. The men rose from their seats and followed him quietly from the room. Only Abner and Ahithophel were left with their torchbearer.

"He is indeed the sweet singer of Israel," said Abner. "What does he have that others don't have, Ahithophel? I am convinced he will be king, but why?"

"I don't know," said Ahithophel. "I often wonder about it myself. There is no fear in him, and yet his main strength is not in his fearlessness. It lies somehow in what you saw tonight."

"Perhaps it is his ability to care, to really care. You know, he really did love Jonathan but not because he was the king's son. Others buried their love for Jonathan long ago, but he still remembers and weeps."

They were standing at the door of the courtyard, and the cool night air was refreshing. Ahithophel looked out into the evening sky, clear and brilliant with stars hanging just above their heads. "Maybe it was written in the stars, or maybe it is just his destiny, but if you were to ask him, he would say it was God. He grasps nothing. All things flow to him. How I envy him."

Abner ran his fingers through his thick hair. "Everything in my experience tells me his approach is wrong. As the commander of an army, if I wish to advance upon a town, I must move my men up and fight. Those who get in my way I must crush before they crush me. Saul learned this too. The world will fall in on a man who tries to live by his faith. David will change; you will see."

8

ASSURED OF DAVID'S warm friendship, Abner arose early the next morning to ride with Rizpah and his men back to the Gilead Mountains. Relieved of the pressure he had felt during Abner's stay, David turned from saying his farewells at the gate, and went in to the small back room where Ahithophel sat tending to matters of the king's household. He found his counselor with some merchants, bargaining over vegetables and jars of olives. Since David's men were kept busy fighting and had no time to raise crops or herd sheep, they were often forced to trade the spoils of war for the food they ate.

Amid the things Ahithophel was trying to barter off was a small ivory jar with the stopper carved in the shape of a flower. David picked it up. "Do you imagine this would charm Michal?" he asked Ahithophel.

"I can advise you in all matters of state, but not of the heart." Ahithophel followed David to the door. "I have finished moving your things to the north room."

"Ahithophel, why do I love her? I have never had anything but trouble from her, and yet I love her."

Ahithophel shook his head. "What is love? You 'love' your wives because they are convenient to have around. They flatter you and cause you little trouble; but you are bored with them. You think you love Michal because she challenges you, but if she should submit and love you, you would find that she bores you too."

"As usual you are right, Ahithophel. Here, take this trinket and trade if for something more tangible than love—perhaps lentils, fresh lentils. A good pot of lentils is never boring."

As David handed Ahithophel the small jar and turned to go, he heard the sound of marching feet coming from the region of the city gate. "That must be Joab. Bring him to me quickly," he ordered Ahithophel. "When he learns of Abner's visit he will be angry."

Ahithophel soon discovered that Joab had already heard the news and was indeed angry. Red-faced, he started to push past Ahithophel but was stopped by the counselor's firm grip on his arm. "Joab, your uncle, David, wants to see you in the north room."

Joab pulled from him rudely. "If I find that you have planned this bit of mischief, Ahithophel, it will go hard with you."

Ahithophel watched the angry man stride down the hall. *Joab will always be in the middle of stormy encounters between the king and his people. I must be very careful not to get involved with him.*

Ahithophel returned to his room to find all the merchants gone and his scribe waiting for him. "Sir, there is a man here to see you. By his dress and speech he seems to be a Hittite. He says he wants to see you secretly on a matter of great importance."

Ahithophel nodded. "Bring him in. But mind you, scribe, see that you sit close on the other side. This may be some trick."

A large man in his early thirties, richly dressed but ill at ease, was ushered into the room by the scribe. The man's features were coarse, and his eyes, set in slits beside a long commanding nose, were hard as flint. His head was bald, and there was an ugly scar on his neck. The one hand that rested on the table was large and blunt-fingered.

Ahithophel, who made a practice of determining the character of each new man he met, decided that this was a man of average intelligence but clever; a man of many battles. In the cold fire of his eyes ambition burned.

"My name," the Hittite said, leaning forward, hands outspread on each knee, "is Uri. Uri of Urusalim. I will be brief. I have heard that David ben Jesse has desired the city of Urusalim, and I have come to help him take it."

Ahithophel was almost stunned by the man's directness. "My friend," Ahithophel said, "how can you make such an offer? You know even better than I that the city is walled and so impregnable that no army has ever been able to conquer it."

"That is true," nodded the Hittite. "No one can

84

take the city unless the secret is discovered, and even then it cannot be done without help from inside."

Ahithophel was astounded. "You know a way to take the city?"

"Yes."

"I'm sure this information has a price."

"A price? No, I am not such a man," the Hittite said, leaning forward and speaking in a low voice. "I am a foreigner there. My loyalties lie not with the Jebusites who rule Urusalim."

"You come with such information and yet ask no price? Speak frankly. This is no simple thing you want to do for us."

"When I say I ask no price, it is true. I am rich and so would only ask a good position among your fighting men." The Hittite leaned back and studied Ahithophel's face.

"A position in the army? This is not mine to give, but let me counsel with the king."

"I will arrange to stay until you bring an answer." The Hittite stood ready to leave, and Ahithophel noticed that he towered over him like a large rock.

Ahithophel found David in his chambers, standing at the window looking down into the court of the women where his children were seated with their mothers. His oldest son, Amnon, was alone in a corner eating ripe figs, while his second son, Absalom, sat with his sister, Tamar, as she wove a garland of field flowers. Impulsively she tried the garland on Absalom to see if it would fit, while Amnon looked on with glowering disapproval. Even from a distance it was evident to both Ahithophel and David that Amnon was jealous of his brother.

"It is too bad that Amnon is the elder," David noted as his counselor came and stood beside him. "What a fine king Absalom would make. You know, I was the youngest of my brothers and still Samuel anointed me king."

David motioned for Ahithophel to sit near the brazier and offered him dates rolled in honey paste. "I imagine you are impatient to know how I managed with Joab. I can tell you he is as stubborn as his mother, even if she is my sister. He will have no solution but to march against Abner and claim his revenge. I tried to show him we had won the fight without a battle, but. . . ."

Ahithophel nodded. "A war among our own tribesmen is what he would have. In that sort of war no one wins. What would he have you do with Michal?"

"Send her back to Mahanaim and declare war at once; then fight until Benjamin is devastated and East Jordan is humbled."

"That would take years and the best of your brave men. He is a hot-headed fool. Perhaps he needs to be distracted—challenged by some difficult endeavor."

David's eyes flashed with interest. "What would you suggest? It must be strong enough to make him forget his love for his dead brother and his hatred for Abner."

"Perhaps such a challenge as the taking of Urusalim would appeal to him."

David had been poking the wood in the brazier with a stick. Now he looked up, every muscle alert, "Urusalim! The citadel! The village of the eagles, perched on a cliff so high no army has ever taken it? The only city that has been besieged by all the great armies and generals and yet has never been captured? There is a challenge indeed. I admit it is my dream. But we are mostly a band of shepherds and farmers. The Philistines hold most of our land from Bethlehem to Gibeah. If we are going to fight, should it not be first against the Philistines?"

For a moment Ahithophel was tempted to tell him of his Hittite visitor, then decided against it. This Hittite might be judged by David as a traitor, and if so he would have nothing to do with him. "The Philistines expect you to fight them. They are prepared and waiting for you. Suppose you have proof it is God's will for you to take Urusalim as your city; would you march out to take it then?"

"If I knew it was His will, I would be sure to take it."

"Supposing someone like Joab should come and offer to attack the city?"

"Joab is not one for caution, but even he knows the difficulty of taking Urusalim. Yes, if Joab and you, Ahithophel, my very cautious counselor, advised this, I would surely consider it a miracle."

"You are right; I am cautious. But Urusalim seems just the place to unite east and west, north and south. It is the perfect city from which to rule Israel."

A dreamy look came into David's eyes. "I first saw Urusalim one day as a small boy out herding my father's sheep. I wandered with them north toward Mount Moriah where Abraham was tested by God. Suddenly, coming around a steep cliff, I saw it. The setting sun had turned its walls and mud-brick houses to brilliant red. It looked like a huge ruby set in the tall, jagged rocks. Around it on every side were high mountains. The words came to me, 'As the mountains are 'round about Urusalim, so is the Lord 'round about them that serve Him.' I stood there and sang this phrase over and over until the sun went down. I built my fire out on that hillside and watched the moon come up and shine upon the city. The sheep soon went to sleep, but I stayed awake for hours. God was there. He was more real than my campfire or the moon or even the city. To me Urusalim is not a city; it is a dream."

Someone pounded with great force on the door to David's quarters. The king's shield bearer, who had been polishing his leather breastplate and greaves, jumped up from the corner by the window to open the door. A wildly angry Michal, surrounded by five of David's chief captains, stood outside in the hall. She swept into the room and up to David, who stood holding his hands out over the glowing coals of the brazier.

"Where is Joab going with his soldiers?" she demanded.

David was completely taken by surprise and stared at Michal in silence.

"Did you know that Joab sent a messenger in your name after Abner, requesting him to return to the city gate?" she stormed.

Eleazer, captain of the thousand, stepped forward to confirm all that she had said. "It is true," he nodded. "Joab sent for Abner, and he is at the gate now waiting for Abner's return."

David was instantly alert. "I did not send for Abner to return. Eleazer, take ten men and hurry to the gate while there is yet time. Tell my nephew Joab that he is to return to me at once." David pushed the brazier aside. Without another word he hurried from the room with the rest of the men following behind him.

Michal did not move. She stood silent, listening, until faint and far away upon the morning air there came the dread sound of women keening for the dead. Quickly, she grabbed up her fine linen skirts, ran out the door, down the hall and up the dark steps to the roof where the small town of Hebron spread out before her eyes like unbaked honey cakes. Shielding her eyes against the sun she looked toward the north gate. Then she saw them—the men of Benjamin, her relatives and the relatives of Abner coming from the city gate carrying the body of someone on their shoulders. She knew immediately that it was Abner.

Fierce hatred rose up and choked her. To think that Joab had so triumphed was more than she could bear. She clenched and unclenched her fists until her knuckles turned white. She pulled her mantle from her shoulders and tore it, gritting her teeth and deliberately calling to mind the words of her father on the day of her wedding to David: "I am giving Michal to David as a snare."

"Oh, God," she prayed bitterly, "if there really is a God, let my father's words come true. Let me be a snare unto David and to the whole house of Judah."

BOOK TWO

URIAH

1

AHITHOPHEL WAS THE first of David's men to meet the mourners who came bearing Abner's body. Their faces were distorted with rage and their voices harsh with lamentation for the shrouded form they carried high above their heads.

There is not a minute to spare, Ahithophel thought with growing panic. *David must be warned before it is too late.*

The mourners pushed through the door and marched into the receiving room toward David's throne with the body of Abner. Ahithophel watched numbly, trapped by the crowd of people pouring into the room. Fearful for David's life if he came before them while they were in the heat of such terrible anger, Ahithophel struggled vainly to free himself. But it was already too late to warn the king.

There was a distant sound of a trumpet, then suddenly David himself stood in the doorway quietly taking in the scene. He was still dressed in the royal robes of state which he had worn when he swore friendship to Abner, bidding him "God's peace" not more than an hour before.

David's eyes moved around the room until they rested on the shrouded form of Abner lying at the foot of the throne. The mourners drew back as he moved toward the body of Abner. The weeping and wailing subsided as all eyes focused on the king. "He is weeping," someone said. "He is weeping for Abner."

As David slowly raised his head, they saw a wrenching anguish in his face. Suddenly he grabbed his rich linen cloak at the neck and rent it with a great tearing sound. Then with a loud voice he shouted, "Let not this sin be charged to me and my people, but let it be on Joab and his house forever. In each generation of his line let there not fail to be found one that is a leper or cripple or poor or cut down by the sword."

Weeping, he rent his cloak again while the men of Benjamin stood in stunned silence. Nothing they had anticipated doing to avenge Abner was as fearful as this curse spoken by David upon Joab and his family. Slowly, one after another, they put up their knives and sheathed their swords.

David then commanded his mighty men, his counselors, and his whole house to rend their clothes and put on sackcloth. "A truly great friend and brave warrior has died, and we will not see his like again."

As Ahithophel watched, David insisted on sitting with the mourners while the body was prepared for burial. He followed all the way to the cave where Abner was to be buried, and at the cave David again wept and recalled the times he had marched into battle as a young man under Abner's leadership. "He was a great man," he said, "and he did not deserve this evil thing."

Later the same day, the king issued orders that

Joab was not to come before him or set foot inside the hall of meeting. He also refused to eat with his men saying, "May God strike me dead if I touch anything before the sun goes down."

As David strode into the courtyard toward his own chambers, he was stopped by a woman who broke loose from the crowd and fell at his feet. She flung her thin arms around his ankles and clung to him, weeping, begging for protection. Several of Abner's men tried to pull her away, insisting that the king release her to them.

"Who is this woman, and what is her crime?" David demanded.

"This is Rizpah, the concubine of our kinsman, King Saul. She has defied the law and openly lived with Abner without the consent of her father or her kinsman, Ishbosheth."

"To whom does this woman belong?" David asked.

"She belongs to the king. She was the concubine of Saul until he was killed and then she became the property of Ishbosheth, who was crowned our king after Saul's death."

"Her sin is great," David agreed. "What do you intend to do with her?"

One of the men stepped forward and brought several large stones out of his bosom. "We intend to rid Israel and the tribe of Benjamin of this iniquity. When Abner was living we dared not act, but now that he is gone we will justly punish this woman."

David looked from the men to the woman who still clung to his ankles. "Do you have anything to say for yourself?"

When she raised her head, David saw that she had once been beautiful but was now hollow-eyed and ravaged with grief. "All that they say is true. I am the mother of two of Saul's sons. May the king permit me to live until they are full grown that they may not lose their mother, having lost their father at Gilboa."

David's face softened and then grew stern again. "You have sinned grievously, and the law would have you die. How can I do otherwise than give you over to your kinsmen that they may do justice as they see fit?"

To David's astonishment she did not weep and grovel. "Let the king be merciful," she said simply. "Let me live as a servant in the court of the women. I will serve your wives, as I am one who knows much of birthing."

David looked at the men before him and sensed that their anger had abated, that there had been enough of death with the murder of Abner. "Go then to the court of the women, and if you are clever as you say, you will live."

To Ahithophel's surprise, the men of Saul's family accepted David's decree without protest. The tribesmen were pleased by all that David did to honor Abner and were coming over to his side. He marveled at the king. How had he instinctively done just the right thing—first with Joab, then with Rizpah?

Ahithophel wished he could look into David's soul in order to ferret out the secret, self-serving motives that must be there. Did the king really regret Abner's death or was he secretly glad to be rid of a formidable foe? Since Ahithophel felt himself in danger of coming to revere his young king, he needed to find some fault in David to restore his comfortable cynicism.

The events of the following day further perplexed David's counselor. Early in the morning two men named Rechab and Baanah rushed into the large hall and asked to see the king about a matter of great importance. When David arrived, the men proudly unrolled a sheet before him. There before him was the bloody head of a man lying in its folds. Ishbosheth!

As David stared in dismay at the horrible sight, the two men, sure of his approval, both started to talk at once. "We have run all night from Gilead to bring you the good news that we have slain your sworn enemy. He was asleep upon his bed when we fell upon him and killed him. We have brought you his head as proof."

The two men stood back smiling, waiting for the king's praise. Instead he lashed out at them. "How long are we to be plagued with fools who seek to administer justice as though they were God?"

He turned to his own men. "Listen and gain wisdom. God is the one who determines the day we are to be born and the day we will die; He decides who is to win and who will go down in defeat. Saul and his household are our brethren, and we should dwell together in peace. If we must fight and plot and kill, let it be against the Philistines, who are our enemies, but not against those of our own flesh and blood."

Then turning to his guards he ordered, "That this may be a warning to all who plot evil against their own flesh and blood, kill these men. Let their hands and feet be cut off and their bodies be hanged over the public pool."

Rechab and Baanah turned pale and began to sink down before the king. Before their knees touched the ground, two of David's young warriors had driven spears deep into their ribs. A solemn silence fell upon everyone as ropes were tied around the dead bodies, which were then dragged from the hall. Then David knelt over the head of Ishbosheth still lying in the sheet.

"Ah, my brother, I remember you as a boy with Jonathan. This same hair now dripping with blood was golden in the sun, and your lips now blue with death were always laughing. It is good that Jonathan did not live to see this evil that has come upon the house of Saul!" David reached down and gently covered the head with the cloth.

Ahithophel, who was standing close to him, heard him whisper, "Michal, Michal, how will you be able to bear it? First Abner and now your brother. All of the golden ones of Saul's house gone and each dying as a dog dies, without honor or pity."

Without a further word to anyone, David turned and went to his chamber, where he stayed without eating or sleeping all that day and night. The next morning David ordered the head of Ishbosheth to be buried with honor.

A strange thing began to happen throughout Israel. Men from every tribe and village began to journey to Hebron. They crowded into the large receiving room and spilled over into the great courtyard outside, wanting to pledge themselves to David. All wanted to band together to defeat the Philistines who still held a number of their towns and villages.

David was full of emotion as he stood before them. "We have waited seven years to take back the villages of our people. The Philistines hold my own village and family lands in Bethlehem, the village of Giloh, the fortress of Saul and tribal lands of Benjamin at Gibeah. The tombs of our ancestors all lie in their hands. It is time to unite Israel and take them back."

He could say no more, for the people shouted and stamped their feet, laughed and cried, embracing each other. Some prayed, rocking back and forth with tears running down their faces; still others linked themselves together arm in arm and danced for joy.

Two days later when all the tribes were represented, they chose Zadok, the priest, to bring the horn of holy oil from the tabernacle so that he might anoint David to be king of all Israel. Years before, the prophet Samuel had thus anointed David and now the people wanted to affirm this choice.

In the courtyard of the king's house David stepped forward and knelt on the warm, brown stones before Zadok. In thundering tones Zadok prayed a prayer of dedication. Then slowly he lifted high the sacred horn and let the golden oil flow in all its rich abundance on David's bent head until it ran down his face and dripped from his beard onto the stones of the court.

As the last drop fell from the horn, a trumpeter on the wall sounded a blast on the shophar that almost paralyzed the entire assembly with its insistent, piercing cry. The shophar was sounded only at times of special crisis and joy and always on the Day of Atonement. Now it seemed to summon them to a new hope, a new allegiance, and a new unity they had not known before. The women and children began to sing and beat drums and tambourines while the house and courtyard of David rocked with shouts and laughter of the men.

A white mule was brought for David. As he rode out from the crowded courtyard, women and children threw garlands of flowers in his path. In their enthusiasm some even climbed the nearby palm trees and broke off branches to wave.

To the music of trumpets and harps and drums, David's fighting men, tribesmen, and villagers followed their king out of the dusty little village of Hebron to the tents that had been set up on the hillside for the feasting and celebration to follow. Israel was united again under a king who would lead them out against their enemies to reclaim their lost lands.

During all the festivities and celebration that autumn Joab was forbidden to enter the village of Hebron. News of David's coronation celebration had also been kept from him lest he become bitter and vengeful that he had not been invited. Joab spent most of his time sitting moodily in a small room on the roof of his cousin's house in Beersheba, vowing vengeance on all the tribe of Benjamin.

Some months after the coronation Ahithophel arrived in Beersheba with a tall Hittite and asked Joab's cousin if he could talk with the disgraced army commander. The two men were led to an upstairs room where Joab sat cursing the cold, wet weather and the friends who had turned their backs on him since he had fallen from favor.

Ahithophel ignored Joab's hostility, introduced the Hittite, and proceeded to describe the plan to take Urusalim. Soon Joab could no longer conceal his interest. "A secret passage leading into the city of Urusalim, you say? How easy it would be to take it if we could just get inside with a few men."

"No, not easy," Uri cautioned. "I say it is possible; but easy? No. There are guards at the top of the wall, ready to attack anyone seen moving near the entrance to the cave. Then, if you get into the cave, you must still find the shaft that goes up into the city. And if you are able to climb up the vertical shaft to the top, you are in danger of having your head lopped off by one of the guards. No, it is not

100

easy, but with a few brave men and some help from inside the city, it is possible."

"There is nothing you could do that would please David more," urged Ahithophel. "Urusalim, with those Jebusites flaunting their power, has stood all these years in the middle of our land, dividing us. If Urusalim could be captured, it would unite the tribesmen of the north with the tribesmen of the south in a new and vital way."

Joab was interested but now cautious. "Why have you chosen me for this venture, Ahithophel?" he asked. "I had judged we were not enemies, but I have never thought of us as being great friends."

Ahithophel looked out from under his bushy eyebrows and slowly smiled at Joab. "No, we are not great friends, but we both have fastened our chariots to this shooting star of the tribe of Judah. There are times when we can both go farther by helping each other."

Joab nodded. "I understand. And this Hittite is the chariot we are to ride in. But what is there in this for him?"

Ahithophel leaned back and motioned to Uri, who spoke slowly and cautiously. "I do not need gold or silver. I am a rich man. Years ago when the Hittites ruled this whole area, my ancestors governed the Jebusites in Urusalim. After the Hittite empire fell, we were forced to live on among these people who are alien to us. I would that David ben Jesse were my king and I a fighting man among your men. I am ready to worship your God, to marry one of your women and, as proof of my good intentions, help you take Urusalim."

Joab was an astute judge of men. He noticed how tall and well built the Hittite was and perceived that he had a strong devotion to duty. Every army needed men who would obey orders and not think for themselves. A Hittite such as this one could be his armor bearer if he proved himself in taking the city of Urusalim.

"We must not tell David of the Hittite now," Ahithophel cautioned. "We will only tell him that you are sorry for all the trouble that you have caused and are ready to make proper sacrifice for your sins."

"No," said Joab. "I have committed no sin. It is within my right to kill the man who killed my brother. I will never agree to such an explanation."

Ahithophel made several other suggestions until an explanation was found that did not hurt Joab's pride. "I will leave the Hittite here with you, Joab, so that you can plan everything. Tonight I will broach the idea to David. You must be ready to come when I send for you."

That night Ahithophel found David in the cramped scriptorium, dictating a message to be delivered to Joab. It was obvious he was having difficulty finding proper words because several scrolls had been filled and discarded. "My lord," Ahithophel said smiling smugly, "there is no need to write to Joab now."

"No need? Why?"

"Joab is eager to get back into your good graces, and he is delighted at the prospect of taking Urusalim."

David was instantly alert. "A few contrite words won't undo all the mischief Joab has done. But you say he thinks he can take Urusalim?"

"Yes, my lord."

"And you, Ahithophel, what do you think our chances are to take the 'City of the Eagles'?"

Ahithophel's face was sober. "Politically it would be very wise. It would unite the northern tribes with the southern and give Israel a new capital, one not chosen from the tribes of Benjamin or Judah." He paused to study David's reaction. "But with its high walls, stone cliffs, and deep cisterns, Urusalim can hold out through a long siege."

Reflectively David looked down at the array of parchment and charcoal pieces before him. "Some of my men say that we should first take back our cities from the Philistines. What would you say to this, Ahithophel?"

"Our army is small and has few weapons that compare to the Philistines. We would do better to attack where they are not expecting us. The Philistines don't think we would dare march against Urusalim."

David nodded somberly. "The Philistines have never attacked Urusalim because the city is too strongly protected. How can we expect to take something that they won't attempt?"

Ahithophel shrugged. "You think we are not ready yet?"

"No, I wouldn't say that." David thought a moment. "Let me pray about it."

As David left the room, Ahithophel dismissed the scribe and idly sorted through the notes David had been composing to Joab. The king's mysterious method of coming to a decision bothered him. He suspected that David sat down and carefully considered all the facts for and against a certain action and made his decision logically. Then he told everyone that God had revealed it to him, so that no one would dare oppose him. But some of David's decisions baffled Ahithophel. These were the times when David acknowledged that God's will was not what he himself really wanted, and he then went ahead and did what he felt God wanted him to do.

103

Ahithophel had puzzled over this again and again for it went against man's nature not to gratify himself.

Now he wondered how long he would have to wait for David to find God's will in this new matter of taking Urusalim. Knowing all he knew about the Hittite and the secret passage into the city, he could hardly wait to see what David would do.

He had to wait only until the next morning. "We will march against Urusalim at the waning of the moon," David told him privately. "See that you get word to Joab and then tend to the preparations that will be necessary for such a campaign."

Ahithophel could not resist testing him a bit. "Has God also shown you how you are going to take the city?"

David smiled. "Not exactly. I am to go trusting in Him, and then at the right time He will reveal to me the way it can be taken."

Ahithophel was too astonished to answer. He watched David walk toward the main hall struck with the feeling that David lived life with some extra strength and knowledge that had been denied him. He resented this. It seemed that everything was made so easy for David while the hard work and planning were done by others.

2

DESPITE HIS IMPULSIVE nature, Joab was a man who planned his battle maneuvers carefully. As he and Uri sat together on the roof, Joab probed for additional details from the Hittite until he had a clear picture of the inner structure of Urusalim. Then he gave the Hittite his own understanding of the situation.

"The water for the city comes from this cave that lies outside the east wall," said Joab as he roughly sketched the outline of Urusalim on an old piece of parchment. "Here are the steps coming from inside the city and out the Eastern Gate down to the opening of this cave. In time of peace, this is how the women come to get their water."

Uri nodded silently as Joab continued sketching in the details as he thought of them. "You are saying that in time of siege, the women do not use these outside steps to get their water. Instead they use an underground tunnel that opens into the Gihon Cave below."

"Yes," said Uri. "The women enter the tunnel here, turn first to the left, then to the right and down a path to the vertical shaft which is right above the cave."

Joab's hand shook with excitement as he drew in the dimensions of the secret tunnel. "How do they lower their jars down to the water in the cave?" he asked without looking up.

"They use a hemp rope that hangs at the top of the shaft," Uri explained.

"Aha, there is a rope then." Joab's eyes flashed with excitement. "Is it possible for one man to go up the shaft from the cave below and lower the rope for other men to follow?"

Uri nodded. "But there are guards at the top of the shaft inside and guards on the wall above the opening to the cave outside. The guards outside will be watching the opening to the cave and can easily see anyone who tries to enter."

"Then suppose we come from Hebron at the dark of the moon and wait until the darkest hour of the night to approach the cave?" suggested Joab.

"Yes," Uri nodded, "that is the time to attack. It will be too dark for the guards to see your men and late enough so that the women will have drawn their water for the night."

"It will not be easy. We must first get inside the cave and then find the vertical shaft," Joab said thoughtfully.

"Once inside the cave you will veer to the left—here," said Uri, drawing a new diagram of the inside of the cave. "A dim oil lamp will be left on a ledge at the top of the shaft so you will see its reflection on the water. Without the light it would be impossible to find the shaft in the darkness."

Joab studied the map, stroked his beard and ran his fingers through his hair. "Just finding the shaft will be difficult, but then I must somehow wedge myself into it, edge my way to the top without being discovered, and hope there will be no guard waiting to lop off my head. Is that right?"

Uri nodded. "The shaft is part of a natural fissure in the rock, so you will have good footing; but it is narrow. I can only promise to have a light at the top of the shaft and to distract the guards until you are able to get out of the shaft."

"And how will you manage to distract the guards?" Joab studied the huge man beside him and wondered if he could be trusted to use good judgment in a crisis.

"You must understand. The guards are not directly at the top of the shaft. It was not thought appropriate that they should be where the women draw water. There is a path to the left that leads into a large underground cave. It is here the guards stay unless there is some disturbance."

"Timing," said Joab, "will be of the utmost importance. You must be there to distract the guards at the very moment I am leading my men up the shaft, or the whole plan will fail."

"We must arrange a signal that will tell me when you are ready to enter the cave. It must be a signal I can see from inside the city." Uri sat motionless, hands on his knees, as he pondered the problem.

Joab continued to stare at the parchment. "It must be something that will also mislead them as to our true intent, such as a movement of a part of our army toward the North Gate."

Uri slapped his knee. "That's it! When your army moves openly toward the North Gate, that will be the sign to me that you and your men are moving into the cave. The Jebusites will not be alarmed by a movement toward the North Gate, yet such a movement of your troops would give me reason to enter the water tunnel with pertinent information for the guards."

Joab nodded in agreement. "Once my men and I are safely in the cave, you must give me a signal that will let me know when it is safe to begin my climb up the shaft."

Uri thought only a moment. "I will remove the light from the ledge above the shaft and carry it back to the guard room. They will think I am changing the oil, but the darkness will be a cloak for your activities."

"Good." Joab's eyes shone with anticipation. "If we can get fifteen men inside the walls of the city, we will take it with little trouble." He stared at the Hittite approvingly.

Uri held out his hand. "You can depend on me. I will not fail you, and when it is finished, I trust you will not fail me."

Joab took his hand, affirming the bond of understanding between them. Then he went with Uri to the door and watched the massive man mount his mule and ride off toward Urusalim.

Ahithophel decided not to tell David anything about the plan he and Joab had worked out for capturing Urusalim. Instead Ahithophel encouraged David to summon the fighting men from every tribe to meet in Hebron at the waning of the moon to prepare for the battle.

The young men came eagerly from every tribe, carrying whatever pieces of armor or weapons they were able to acquire. Days before the appointed time the hills and valleys around Hebron were covered with crudely made goat's-hair tents with blowing standards before them carrying each tribe's insignia. Restless and raucous, the men laughed and sported, sharpening their weapons and organizing their equipment. At night they gathered around their campfires to sing songs and tell stories of the brave leaders of the past.

As enthusiasm grew, both Amnon and Absalom begged to ride into battle with their father. David hesitated, thinking they were too young. *It is good for a king's sons to have some knowledge of battle,* David thought, *though there is plenty of time. Amnon is only eight years old and Absalom is seven.*

Absalom was the most insistent. "I want to see Urusalim taken," he pleaded.

Delighted by the boy's spirit, David relented. "All right," he said, putting his arm around Absalom, "go find your Uncle Shimea. He is planning to take Jonadab, and he can take you and Amnon too. Mind you now, you have to promise to do just as he says."

Amnon was less enthusiastic than Absalom. He

knew he wouldn't enjoy the long marches, rough camp life, and scarce rations of army life. But by going he hoped to win some attention from his father.

"Father, can we be fitted with greaves and breastplates and carry real spears?" Absalom pleaded.

Amnon shook his head. "Are we better than our father, that we should go out to our first battle dressed in armor when he went with none to fight Goliath?"

David did not catch the slight Amnon meant for Absalom. "I was a good deal older than you are now," he said, turning to look at Amnon for the first time. "Very few men had armor in those days. I would have given anything for some real armor, and I shall see that you and Absalom are fitted with it tomorrow if our coppersmith must work all night."

As David left the receiving room he found Ahithophel waiting for him. "Is everything ready?" David asked his counselor.

"Joab is not here yet, but he will come," replied Ahithophel, watching David carefully.

"We need Joab, but he is hot-headed and makes too many enemies."

"Yes, Joab is hot-headed," Ahithophel agreed. "And you, my lord, are too cautious. You hunger too much after righteousness."

David looked at his counselor in surprise. "God wants us to do what is right."

"You are a king," replied Ahithophel. "What you want and what serves your cause is always right. If you have enemies, they must be destroyed; if a man disagrees with you, he is wrong. There should be no other standard but your wish."

"You forget one thing, my friend and counselor,"

David said, looking intently at the older man. "I am king because old Samuel came to my father's house in Bethlehem and by God's authority chose me, just as he chose Saul before me. Just as God withdrew His power from Saul, so He can withdraw His power and guidance from me if I do not walk according to His will."

Ahithophel shook his head in astonishment. "You take all this much too seriously. What can there be in a bit of oil anyway?"

"You speak just like Joab! When we were in the wilderness fleeing from Saul, Joab wanted me to kill Saul. He said it was the only way I would ever become king. But you see, I am king without that burden on my conscience."

Here again was that mysterious quality that David brought into everything. It annoyed Ahithophel. He wanted to reason things out, plan maneuvers, plot their course with logic. David always came back to this vague, mystical reliance on God and His guidance.

"Do you think God is really concerned about what we do?" he asked David. "Why would He reveal His will to you and not to the rest of us?"

David laughed. "You don't really want to know God's way or His will. You like to be able to control everything with your mind. There may come a day when you face a problem too difficult for your mind to solve."

Ahithophel thought a moment and nodded. "You are right. I don't want to know what God thinks I should do. If somebody is against me, I want to fight him by every means I have, and if someone is about to get the better of me, I want to be free to lie or cheat to get my way. This is the real freedom, my lord, the freedom to be oneself no matter how disagreeable that self may be to others. You are not

free to lie. I am. You are not free to be unjust. I am.
You are not free to take what you want just because
you want it. I am. You see, I have freedom, and you
have nothing but a bondage to your God and His
goodness."

David was silent for a moment. "I can't reason it
all out the way you do, my friend. But I know when I
stand before the gates of Urusalim on the morrow,
all of my strength and confidence will come from
the assurance that the God of Israel, Lord of Hosts,
Almighty God, is with us and will fight for us."

Before sunrise the next day the shrieking blast of
the shophar brought to life the men of Hebron and
the tribesmen camped in tents on the hillsides. The
tribesmen quickly fanned the fires that had burned
down during the night, ate hastily, assembled their
weapons and prepared for the long march to
Urusalim. The tribesmen had only a few spears and
bows among them. The rest would fight with the
sling or wooden mace and shepherd's crook. They
were rough-looking men in sheepskin and coarsely
woven cloaks. The older men were bearded, wearing headpieces and sandals, while the young men
wore cloaks cut to their knees and were often
barefoot with no headpiece covering their short-
cropped hair.

David's men gathered before the main gate in
the city. The captains of hundreds and David's special band of mighty men wore remnants of captured armor and carried swords and bows with
iron-tipped arrows. In their belts they carried slings
and battle axes. Some had pouches stuffed with
bread, cheese, and dried figs—food to eat on the
march if there was no time to stop. In the predawn
darkness, their armor caught the glint of the dying

fires as they assembled into orderly companies of tens and hundreds.

There was another blast of the shophar from a long figure who appeared on the wall. The city gates were opened wide and men carrying flares and torches ran out in front of the horses and chariots of the king and his company. As the king's chariot came clattering through the gate, drummers beat a steady staccato and the men standing in their companies shouted with a noise that was like the roar of the sea. "Victory! Victory! Victory to the Lord of Hosts and King David!" Over and over they shouted as the drums rolled, the torch-bearers waved their torches, the standard-bearers lifted high the floating banners with the crudely designed lion of Judah clawing the air on the bright woven cloth.

David motioned for silence, and the great multitude of men grew quiet. His voice was jubilant and strong. "The Philistines are expecting us at Bethlehem, but God is leading us to take Urusalim."

There was a gasp of surprise, as few of the men knew their destination. Then shouts and cheers followed until David again motioned for them to be silent. "The Philistines sleep in our villages of Bethlehem, Giloh, and Gibeah, but we will sleep tonight in Urusalim."

One of the men standing in the forefront of his battalion shouted, "How will we take the city? It has high walls and strong men to defend them."

The horses of David's chariot tossed their heads and pawed the ground. David pulled the reins taut as he answered. "Like Gideon of old, we will come against them with drums and trumpets, shouting and marching. Our God, the God of Israel, the Lord of Hosts, has promised to go before us, riding in splendor to take the city."

Again the men shouted with a great roar, "The sword of the Lord and King David! The sword of the Lord and King David!"

They were so eager to march it was with great difficulty that the captains were able to make them wait for further instructions.

"My brothers, my kinsmen, and friends," David shouted. "We will wait only for the priest to pronounce God's blessing upon us and sanctify us for the battle. Then I will go before you on foot to Urusalim." He dismounted from the chariot and called for Zadok.

When the priest pronounced the blessing, the men shouted with a loud voice that echoed and re-echoed over the dark mountains: "The sword of the Lord and King David! The sword of the Lord and King David!" The torches were then put out, the chariots driven back into the city, and David marched at the head of his army toward Urusalim.

They took the valley road and moved quietly with only the dull steady beat of the drum sounding in the darkness. They were tense and alert until they had passed Bethlehem and its fertile fields occupied by the Philistines.

The first streaks of dawn were spreading out across the sky when David's men climbed the last hill and stood looking out across the valley to the city of Urusalim. There it was, even more beautiful than they had imagined it. A dark crown of stone sitting on a great spur of rock, with the green, rich growth of the Kidron and Central Valleys meeting at its southern tip in a veritable jungle of fruit trees and flowers, bubbling springs and planned gardens. At a signal from David, his men crept into position on the mountains that circled the city. Then, just as the sun came up, the Levites blew their trumpets and the shophar shrieked its piercing wail to waken the city.

David's men expected to see the inhabitants rush up to the walls, worried and frightened. Instead, a few women climbed to the top of the broad walls with jars on their heads, several old men tottered along with canes; even small boys scrambled up the walls to see who had come to try and take the fortress of the eagles, the city of Urusalim. The people were soon taunting David's men who stood at the foot of the wall waiting for a command from David. "Send your best men," they sneered, "and our lame and blind will defeat them."

As the day wore on, David and his men examined every section of the wall and tested the gates. The king had not given his men a battle plan; he had simply said that God had promised them the city. Now the men and their captains began to question among themselves. "David could be wrong. Perhaps we are not ready to attack such a well-fortified city."

One of the captains spoke to the men who had gathered in David's tent. "It is obvious we cannot fight people who dwell behind such strong walls. We will have to starve them out."

Quickly David countered, "The early spring harvest of barley has just been gathered and the threshing floor is clean. They will not be hungry for a long time."

The men pondered the problem from every aspect. "These Jebusites cannot live long without water, and the source of their water is outside the walls in the cave where the Gihon spring has its source."

David shook his head. "Urusalim is well known

for its deep cisterns. There will be no scarcity of water for many weeks."

Another of the captains spoke up. "The Philistines know everything we do. Their spies will be reporting back in Ashkelon and Gath by nightfall all that has happened. Tomorrow the whole Philistine army could come up against us or block our road back to Hebron."

Beniah, captain of the mighty men, spoke reassuringly. "My lord, you did not bring us here without knowing all that we have said. What is your plan?"

David looked from one to the other calmly. "There seems to be no obvious way to take the city. But we must not forget God. God has promised me the city, and He is faithful. Go back to your men and hold yourselves in readiness for attack."

David dismissed his men. He sent his sons and his bodyguard out also and then knelt with his face to the floor and prayed.

"O Lord God, I am at the appointed place, and You are not here. My friends and enemies mock me saying, 'Where is your God?' I can see it in their eyes. They despise me for bringing them here with words of faith in what You will do for us. Oh, God! Why are You letting me be put to shame before my men, humiliated before the Jebusites? I have done all things as You commanded me."

The tears were flowing down his cheeks and into his beard, but he did not move to wipe them away. God seemed to have suddenly retreated into some far place where He could not be reached. David tried to reassure himself by remembering all the times God had helped him in the past, and yet, as he looked at each event—even the slaying of Goliath—all seemed simple compared to what he now faced. He tried to pray again, but it was no use. The words would not come.

He reached for his harp and idly plucked the strings, seeking comfort that always came when he sang.

I will love Thee, O Lord, my strength,
The Lord is my rock, and my fortress,
    and my deliverer;
My God, my strength, in whom I will trust.

There is my answer, he thought. *God has told me He will be with me and now I am supposed to trust.* He began to play with more assurance as he remembered the battles he had fought and the faithfulness of God in every situation.

By Thee, my God, I have run through a troop,
And by my God I have leapt over a wall.
As for God, His way is perfect,
He is a buckler and sword to all those
    that trust in Him.

Then he added a new verse as he thought of the high jagged rock face of the city of Urusalim.

He maketh my feet like hinds' feet,
And setteth me upon high places.

It was beginning to get dark and with the darkness came the cool night air. David lay aside his harp reluctantly, wrapped his cloak around him, and walked to the door of his tent. A short distance away he saw his armor bearer, his sons, and a few of the captains squatting near a fire. They were eating bread and white cheese before bedding down for the night. Out across the valley the fires of his men covered the hillsides that surrounded the city.

Urusalim itself rose dark and menacing as

though it had suddenly blended itself into the rock cliff on which it rested. He could see some lights flickering up the cliff within the city, and he wondered if his own candle would ever burn within those walls.

He moved toward the fire and warmed his hands. He could not see these men sitting around the fire without missing the familiar form of Joab. Joab was impulsive and vengeful, but he was a man who could be trusted completely. Where was he?

As if in answer, they all heard the clipped, tapping noise of an approaching donkey. Who, they wondered, would be so foolish as to travel across the mountains alone at night with the Philistines holding the entire ridge from Bethlehem to Gibeah? One of the captains called out the password. Back through the darkness came the answer in Joab's familiar voice.

The captains rushed out to greet him, and Joab emerged from the darkness with his arms around the shoulders of two of his friends. He was shorter than the others, but he always walked with such command that he seemed taller.

When Joab saw David standing silent and unmoving beside the fire, he stopped short. The two men stood there studying each other. Then Joab rushed to David and knelt, kissing his hand and raising it to his forehead in respect. "My king—our king—I have come only to serve you. Since I killed Abner in revenge, I no longer expect to march at the head of your men. I beg only to be allowed to fight for you."

When David quickly raised him to his feet, Joab moved closer and spoke in a low voice. "I must see you alone in your tent. I have news that will make it possible to take the city tonight, if you approve."

In his astonishment David completely forgot the

reprimand he was planning to give Joab. Instead he simply said, "Come then. If it is as you say, all will be forgiven between us."

Alone with David in his tent, Joab reached into his cloak and drew out the sketches of the city. He spread them out on the floor and explained carefully to David how the city of Urusalim could be taken by surprise with just a small band of men.

David carefully examined the crudely drawn diagrams and then looked at Joab. "It is almost certain death to any man who attempts it. How can a man climb up the shaft without making noises that will alert the guards at the top? They will throw stones down upon him or wait until he reaches the top and cut off his head with one stroke."

Joab's eyes glowed with excitement. "Then the real danger is to the first man up the shaft." There was a tense silence between them. "I will volunteer to be the first to climb the shaft and lead the men into the city."

David looked at him with disbelief that slowly changed to admiration and excitement. "You know the odds and still insist on going? What is there in this for you, my clever nephew?"

Joab smiled grimly. "Little enough, I assure you. Simply tell your captains that the first man up the shaft into the city will be the commander of the host."

"You would risk so much to be back in your old position? Fair enough. I'll call the captains, and we'll make our plans." David would not let Joab kneel but put a firm hand on his shoulder. "You did great wrong to smite Abner when he came to us in friendship. But if you succeed with this, I swear to you that all will be forgiven, and you will again go out as the commander of the armies of Israel."

3

WORD SPREAD QUICKLY among the discouraged troops that Joab's plan meant that action was near. The captains crowded into David's tent and listened eagerly as David and Joab outlined their daring plan to capture Urusalim.

"The Lord is with us," David said to his men as he stood at the door of his tent and watched them file out into the night where they would take up their assigned positions.

In minutes Joab and his men stood huddled together in the garden of the Kidron beneath the city's wall. The night was crisp and cool and with a stillness in the air that made every snapping twig and crunch of sandal vibrate loudly. As they listened they could hear the clank of armor and the guttural speech of the guards on the wall. Then came the sound of their own men moving about on the hillside behind them and forming into their companies. Finally there was the pounding of sandaled feet on the path circling around the outer limits of the valley and up the slope to the North Gate.

This was the signal. Within the city Uri should now be on his way down to the inner tunnel and the guarded room beside the upper section of the shaft. It was time for Joab and his men to cross the open roadway below the city wall and enter the cave.

"Now," Joab hissed to his men. Stealthily he led the way out of the sheltering foliage of the Kidron gardens and crossed the road, disappearing into the cave with two of his men, Benrud and Jethro, close behind him.

The rest of his men crept out of the shadows.

119

Suddenly one of them slid down a slight embankment, making just enough noise to alert the guards on the wall. With sharp exclamations the guards sprang into action, firing iron-tipped arrows that whizzed over their heads. Joab's men retreated into the trees of the valley, cursing their luck. Joab would have to go on without them.

Waiting just long enough to determine that the others would not be able to join them, Joab reached out in the darkness and grasped the arms of the two men. Without seeing each other or a word being spoken, they understood that they must move forward alone.

The cold spring water came up to their knees as they moved into the total blackness of the cave, feeling their way along the jagged stone wall that seemed to close in on them from both sides. The water was numbingly cold. The bottom was slippery and uneven, making it difficult to hurry. Joab squinted and tried to see a ray of light up ahead. There was nothing but blackness. He could not see his men nor even his hand before his face. The rocks were sharp under his feet, cutting through his worn sandals.

Surely by now I should be at the shaft, he thought, wondering again if the Hittite could be trusted. He felt a sudden, uncontrollable impulse to sneeze and was barely able to stifle it.

The three men stopped and stood motionless, listening as the darkness of the cave pressed down upon them. Faint and far away they could hear what sounded like voices. Encouraged, Joab pressed on. Within minutes he rounded a projection of rock and there on the water ahead he saw a wavering flicker of reflected light. Looking up he saw the shaft, angling upward, a long natural fissure in the rock that seemed to be wide in some places and narrow in others. With relief he saw that the light was still in place. Uri had not yet given the signal.

Minutes passed. More time to think and wonder about Uri while his feet were becoming numb from the cold water. Finally, the sound of voices above. This had to be Uri.

Joab dodged back into the darkness as the voices grew louder. Then the light dimmed and the voices faded. Joab and his two companions were plunged back into darkness. "Uri must have led the guards back to the guard room," he whispered to Benrud.

Joab moved quickly. He grasped a rocky projection, shook the water off his sandals and slipped his foot into a niche in the rock wall. Rising slowly out of the water, he pulled himself up into the base of the shaft. He felt a tingling sensation that was like the excitement he always experienced just before he launched an attack in battle or plunged into hand-to-hand combat. *Tomorrow,* he thought, as he pushed his back hard against the smoother side of the shaft and moved his feet up along the opposite, rougher side, *if all goes well and I am still alive, I will be captain of the host again.*

An intense awareness made him conscious of every small sound, each breath, the rubbing of his wet leather sandal on the rock, the faint, sliding noise his back made as it moved upward and even the pounding of his heart which seemed loud enough to bring the guards running.

His hands grew clammy with sweat as they pushed against the wall behind him, and his legs cramped as they doubled up in the narrower section of the shaft. Panic rose in him as he felt the distance below sucking him downward. He struggled desperately to gain just inches and freed one hand to reach out cautiously toward the top rim of the shaft. He could not reach it, and he could not go on. He was wedged tight in the narrow section of the crevice.

Momentarily he stopped struggling, leaned his head back against the hard rock and gulped the fetid air into his cramped lungs. Sweat was making his hands too slippery to grasp the smooth rock and his feet were slowly losing their hold. In minutes he would fall down the shaft into the darkness below. The cause would be lost.

Desperation drove him to action. With one tremendous effort he freed himself from his cramped postion and then, bit by bit, he moved upward until he could feel the smooth, worn stones at the top of the shaft. They were too smooth to grip. Once again he felt the sweat break out on his hands, and his breath came in gasps as he struggled and clawed at the unyielding smooth rock until he reached a position just below the opening.

Without concern for who might see him or what he would meet as he came out of the shaft, he grasped for the firmer, less smooth edge and pulled himself awkwardly out into the upper tunnel. There was no one in sight.

He quickly determined that the guards were just around the wall of rock in the cave-like room Uri had described to him. In the dim light he could see the rope the women used to lower their jars into the water below. There was no time to plan or think. Grabbing the rope in both hands, he kicked the large, rolled portion over the opening and heard it hit the water at the bottom of the shaft. Instantly he could feel the tugging on the far end as one of the men began coming hand over hand up the shaft.

He heard a shuffling noise behind, turned and saw one of the guards come out of the darkness. There was a muffled oath. The guard's face contorted with surprise, then anger, as he jerked out a sword from his belt.

Joab held the rope with one hand, drew out his dagger with the other. He could feel the steady pull of the man coming up the rope as he turned to defend himself. He strained with all of his strength to hold the rope and at the same time parry the full force of the blow from the sword.

Suddenly the menacing sword clattered to the ground as the guard fell beside the well opening, a knife in his back. At the same moment Benrud pulled himself out of the shaft, holding his knife tight in his teeth ready to fight.

Uri had seen the guard advancing on Joab and had stabbed him just in time. Realizing that Uri had betrayed them, all five Jebusite guards attacked him furiously. Joab muttered encouragement to Uri and Benrud who fought recklessly together in an effort to drive the guards back while Joab held the rope for Jethro. Just as he was nearing the top, one of the Jebusite guards broke through and slashed the rope sending Jethro hurtling down the shaft.

Joab was wild with anger. He swung around, knocking the Jebusite's sword from his hand with the loose end to the rope he still held. Then with one swift, catlike movement, he lunged at the Jebusite with his drawn dagger, driving it deep into his side.

There was no time to see if Jethro had survived his fall down the shaft. Joab grabbed the fallen Jebusite's sword and joined Uri and Benrud with such ferocity that two more of the guards were killed instantly and another mortally wounded.

The fifth broke loose and started to run up the sloping floor of the tunnel, knocking the clay lamps to the floor as he went and plunging the tunnel into darkness.

"After him," hissed Uri. "He will alert the guards at the mouth of the tunnel."

Moving as fast as they could in the blackness, the three men groped their way forward. Suddenly the tunnel bent sharply to the left and angled upward more steeply. Now there was some light from an oil lamp set in the wall, and they could see the escaping guard just ahead of them. With a burst of speed Joab sprang ahead and fell upon the guard. The wounded man gave a loud shout of pain and anger that alerted the guards at the mouth of the tunnel.

Frantically Joab flung the wounded man from him, and Uri kicked him to one side as they clambered up the last steep section of the tunnel. Here they encountered several bewildered guards, standing with their swords drawn, but stunned to see one of their own people leading two men dressed in the battle dress of the Israelite army.

"After them," shouted Joab as he lunged past Uri and sent the guards retreating before him in confusion. As they fled, one of the guards plunged the tunnel into total darkness by sending the only lamp crashing to the floor. For a few moments there was the sound of pounding feet, heavy breathing, and the clanking of metal. Then there was silence. Joab realized they must be in the guardroom at the end of the tunnel.

"Hold your swords," Uri panted. "The guards have gone."

In the darkness they felt for the door and found it barred and bolted on the outside. They huddled together in the darkness and listened. Quite distinctly they could hear heavy breathing outside the door.

"They've sent for reinforcements," Uri snapped. "We must act quickly." He aimed his huge shoulder at the door and lunged forward. There was a splintering, cracking sound, as the heavy door fell with a loud crash. Awaiting them were the shadowy figures of three guards who crouched with their swords sheathed. Then one of the guards hissed, "And you, my Hittite neighbor, have brought them to us. The Hittites are no better than dogs."

With a growl of anger Uri leaped at the guard and cut him down with his sword while Joab and Benrud attacked the other two. One fell. Then the remaining guard rushed at Uri with such fury that he drove the Hittite back against the wall and would have killed him but for Joab. The red-haired soldier of Israel sprang at the guard, driving his dagger into his broad back. When the guard fell, Joab stood there panting as he looked down at the silent forms lying at his feet, barely visible in the darkness. "Before this night is over," he exulted, "I will again be the commander of the king's army."

Uri clutched his arm. "You saved my life tonight, as I saved yours. You have my thanks. Now we must open the main gate. If we don't hurry, all may be lost. Let us walk down the street together as though we are men returning late from a friend's house. When we come to the open space before the gate, Benrud and I will attack the guards. Joab, you must lift the bolt and open the gate for David and his men. There is little time. I'm sure the alarm has already been given."

Joab and Benrud followed Uri out into the narrow street that led down to the bazaar and the South Gate, also called the Dung Gate. Since there was no moon, they could barely see each other and the few people they met in the street never bothered to look at them.

When they reached the lower end of the city and came to the open space before the gate, Joab was the first to rush out of the darkness and flatten one of the four guards with a single blow of his sword. Uri and Benrud followed up the attack with a swiftness that won Joab's admiration as he lunged past them and struggled with the great iron bars that held the gate shut. Normally it took two men to lift the bars, but Joab, strengthened by the excitement of battle, lifted and flung them to the ground. With a dull, grinding noise the gate swung slowly open.

As David and his men surged through the gate, the noise became deafening: loud commands of soldiers, the battering of barred doors, screams of women, cries of children mingled with the cursing of men and the clash of metal on metal, wood on wood, and the thudding of falling stone as whole walls were battered down in the heat of the struggle.

Joab no longer enjoyed breaking into houses; he had learned from long experience that most of them had no more to offer than a few sheep and goats and some earthen pots or hidden supplies of grain. The attacking soldier had to find a temple to get anything of value. Sometimes the temples had dancing girls, a better find than gold to Joab's way of thinking.

"Does your temple have any young dancers?" he questioned Uri as they stopped to catch their breath beneath the high wall of one of the houses.

"Yes, there are some young girls. But it's the young boys that most of us go to see."

Joab stared at Uri. He well knew the dark practices of both the Hittites and Canaanites. Most of their temples and high places were built for the goddess Ashtaroth or the Hittite god of thunder and lightning. The rituals always involved wine and sexual orgies.

Joab, in his moments of revolt against David and the strict Mosaic law, had often thought that he would enjoy living in one of these Canaanite cities where the temples were filled with dancing girls. But he could not understand such disgusting practices as the burning of children, castrating of young men, or the lashing of young girls. Just the temple with its beautiful girls should be enough for any man. But so often what started with dancing, music, and beautiful women seemed to always degenerate into cruelty and ugliness.

Looking back the way he had come, Joab could see huge fires burning out the lower part of the city; in the dim light men were still fighting, but the shouting and screaming were growing fainter. Ahead he saw that David and his men had opened the North Gate, and Israel's troops were pouring into the city. "Urusalim is ours," Joab said, as he stopped to listen to the shouts of triumph.

Uri grunted. There seemed to be no pangs of regret in his stoic expression, and Joab marveled at this man who had lived so long among these people and yet felt no pity for them. The taking of an enemy city was always a bloody business, but Joab was drawn to its excitement since it was not his city or his people.

"My part in this night's effort is finished," Uri said matter of factly. "I think I have served you well. When we come to the end of the street, I will be at my home, and that is where I must stop."

One more turn in the narrow alleyway and they stood before an impressive gate to a large house that opened directly off the street. "Welcome to my home," Uri said as he pounded on the great brass door. "Welcome," he said again as the door swung open. "I am to meet Ahithophel here. Will you join us?"

Joab had a glimpse of a pleasant courtyard lit by hanging oil lamps. "Another time," he promised. "Now I must go and make sure the business of this night is finished successfully. My uncle, David, must know it was Joab who gave him this victory and not some capricious God."

He reached for Uri's hand and clasped it firmly. "You, my good friend, have proven yourself tonight, and I'll not forget it." Without another word he turned and disappeared into the night.

4

AHITHOPHEL ENTERED Urusalim along with the troops that poured through the North Gate. Too old to take part in the fighting, he held back until he saw that the city was firmly in the hands of David's men. Then cautiously he made his way to the house of the Hittite where he found Uri impatiently waiting for him.

Ahithophel followed Uri from the gate of his home through a courtyard into a large stone house where he found such refinements and wealth as he had never seen before. Servants came with a golden bowl, fine linen towels, and rare perfume to wash his feet. He was ushered through dark corridors into a room of woven tapestries and silken pillows; a soft light flickered on the walls from alabaster lamps hanging by long silver chains from the ceiling. Even the oil in the lamps seemed to give off a sweet odor as though mixed with incense.

When the servants withdrew, Ahithophel sank down on the soft tiger-skin mat and leaned back against the linen pillows, ready to take a new look at Uri. This Hittite, who had seemed big and even ignorant back in Hebron, now in his own setting began to look impressive and commanding. His very silence gave him an air of authority. Granted, there was a strange, foreign atmosphere that was almost oppressive in this house despite all its richness, but Ahithophel shrugged this off as being of little importance. "I hope you do not regret helping us take the city," he said as he continued to study his host.

Uri settled down on a mat opposite Ahithophel. "The Jebusites are not my people. They are an inferior race of crafty tradesmen. My people ruled them when my forefathers were stationed here to keep peace and collect tribute."

Ahithophel knew well the story of the Hittites and how their once strong army had suffered defeat, leaving pockets of Hittite emissaries with their culture and wealth to fend for themselves in places like Urusalim. It was obvious Uri had no love for the Jebusites. "You wish to become one of us?" Ahithophel asked with growing curiosity.

"Yes, that is all I ask. I want to fight with your men, worship your God, and marry one of your women."

Ahithophel nodded and began to consider the situation from every angle. Uri had only his elderly mother living with him. He had been married twice, each time to Jebusite women who had borne him no children and, as he said, "caused me nothing but constant trouble."

The woman who marries Uri will be fortunate, Ahithophel reasoned. In all of Israel there was no one with such wealth and obvious refinement. He sighed and wished Bathsheba had not been promised to Judah. To live here in Urusalim and to be the mistress in such a house would make any woman the envy of all Israel. *Uri is not circumcised,* he thought. *I could not marry Bathsheba to a man who is not circumcised.*

"It is not easy to become one of us." Ahithophel

spoke, breaking the silence between them. "You realize that we worship a God who is rather strict with us. No temples with dancing girls or young men. Instead, there is the great mystery of the Holy of Holies, the shewbread, and the seven-branched candlestick. Then there is the sacrifice for sin and the Day of Atonement. It is really quite complicated."

Uri's eyes shone with excitement, and the scar on his neck reddened. "I am a man who loves discipline, and I find your God much to my liking."

Ahithophel was encouraged. "Look, my friend, there is one thing you must do to become one of us. You must be circumcised. It is a basic part of our religion, a covenant between each of us and our God. Once you have become circumcised, you will belong to our God, and then, of course, you will be one of us."

Ahithophel doubted that Uri would accept this ritual, but to his surprise the Hittite assured him he was eager to endure any hardship to accomplish his goal.

Ahithophel's mind raced over the possibilities this presented. *Would it not be better,* he thought, *to give Bathsheba to this Hittite than to give her to Judah ben Reuben, who could never dream of such affluence?*

He spoke slowly and watched the Hittite carefully. "You say you want to marry a maid of Israel of good family?"

"That is my wish and plan," Uri said simply.

Ahithophel became more enthusiastic. "I have a granddaughter," he said, leaning toward Uri and speaking confidingly. "She is without doubt the most beautiful maid in all of the Gilead. I could consider such a marriage for her, but mark you, there would be some difficulties. She is already promised—though not bindingly engaged—to someone else."

"I would be honored to have your granddaughter for my wife," Uri said, placing his hand on his chest and bowing very slightly toward Ahithophel. "I can assure you her life here in my house would be nothing but pleasure. She would have no work to do, and I would dress her richly, giving her as many necklaces and rings as she might wish. I would ask nothing of her but that she give me sons to build the house of Uri into the great house that it once was in the days of my grandfather. This should be little enough to request."

Ahithophel hardly listened as he was already planning the necessary arrangements. "First you must be circumcised," he said. Ahithophel struggled to put into words the mystery of the circumcision. He wanted Uri to understand that it was related to, but vastly different from, the pagan practices he was familiar with. Nor was it at all like one of the strange rituals the Canaanites might perform before their huge, round-topped monolith which rose from the floors of their temples like an enlarged phallus. The Canaanites worshiped the phallus and the gods of the phallus as the givers of life.

Ahithophel ran his hand through his hair and then cupped his chin in his hand as he thought. How could he explain that the Israelite, like the Canaanite, regarded the phallus as a symbol of man's great life force but not something to worship. Was not the first commandment given to man in the garden of Eden to be fruitful and multiply? Circumcision was God making His mark to remind man that even this part of his life was thought of first by God.

As Ahithophel looked at Uri, he realized that the Hittite would never be able to understand this deeper mystery. So he simply told him that he would arrange the time and place and obtain a priest to instruct him in the tenets of his new faith. He counted on his fingers the time it would take to make all of the arrangements. He would have to send word to Machir in Lodebar, telling him of his new plan to marry Bathsheba to Uri and ask him to break the agreement with Judah. Judah was a good man, and he would accept Ahithophel's decision without question.

So it was settled. They would leave for Lodebar within the month. In one swift moment Ahithophel had changed the course of Bathsheba's life and started a chain of events that would lead to consequences beyond anything he could have imagined.

The night was far spent when Ahithophel left Uri's house and headed for his tent outside the city walls. All fighting had stopped, and a strange silence had fallen over the city. As he walked into the street that led to the old temple area, Ahithophel paused by the steps leading up to the Jebusite temple. In the dim light he could make out a large pillar rising out of the ground, and as he looked closer he could see that there were dead bodies clinging to its base. These must have been the priests who took refuge with their god when the fighting reached them. A fresh breeze sprang up, and he noticed the torn curtains in the door of the temple billowing in its current.

Ahithophel shuddered. Though not a religious man it always unnerved him to see the destruction of a temple. These gods worshiped by the Canaanites were gods of the earth. It was said they could withhold the rain—that life-giving force that made everything fruitful. Worse than that, he feared they were powerful enough to find ways of getting even with men who disturbed their temples. It seemed only wise to give every god due respect and so offend none. He looked once more at the fluttering curtain and hurried down a narrow lane that led to the bazaar.

He had not gone far when he heard the sound of singing, at first faintly, then stronger and stronger. It was not sad music in a minor key but joyful, militant singing with the rhythmical stomp of feet beating in time to the music. What could it be? Ahithophel hurried toward the sound. As the singing grew louder and more insistent, Ahithophel realized the sound was like the movement of a great army, not marching but dancing. It was almost frightening, as though a flood of joy was pulsating up through the old city. Ahithophel saw some stairs leading to a roof and quickly mounted them so he could see what was happening.

Coming up the street were the captains and leaders of David's army, dancing the old tribal dance and singing the song of victory. Leading them was a man carrying a seven-branched candlestick and singing with more joy than all the rest. Ahithophel leaned over the parapet to get a closer look and saw to his astonishment that it was David himself, stomping out the rhythm of the dance and leading them all in the victory march.

At a crosswalk someone pushed forward a donkey and with a shout of joy the men swept David up and put him on the animal. David sat in their midst holding high the candlestick with one arm so that it could be seen by all the men. A shout went up as they saw it. "In the name of the Lord and King David! In the name of the Lord and King David!" Drunk with joy, they hugged each other and cried without shame.

Then Joab rushed out in front and grabbed the

bridle on the donkey and shouted, "Urusalim, behold your king! Your king is coming!" At this the men began to shout with Joab, "The king is coming! The king is coming!"

As the donkey began to move, the seven-branched candlestick preceded them into the night. They followed after it shouting, "The king is coming; the king is coming to God's holy hill!" As the words began to form into a chant the dance began again, and they wound their way up to the top of the hill right to the old temple area.

Ahithophel climbed down from the roof and pushed his way through the dancing, singing men toward the temple area. It frightened him to think of these men marching into that old temple courtyard with such raucous joy. What would happen he could not imagine. They seemed to have no fear of the dark mysteries of that pagan place.

In minutes he was in the courtyard of the old temple, surrounded by men who were shouting, singing, and breaking off into groups to stomp out the ancient rhythms of the dance—arms around each other, heads thrown back, feet stomping and leaping and crossing over, all the time chanting, "The king is coming to God's holy hill. The king is coming to Urusalim!"

The bodies of the priests were pushed aside and the tall pillar was toppled from its socket in the floor of the courtyard. Then the curtains of the temple were ripped from their rods. David leaped from his donkey and dashed inside the temple where with a great crash he pushed the pagan idol from its base and reverently put the candlestick in its place.

David appeared at the temple's doorway with his arms raised and his eyes closed. "He must be thanking God for the victory," Ahithophel marveled aloud.

David seemed not to notice the men. He was suddenly remote from them. Bit by bit the singing and dancing subsided, and the men began to gather around him. Still he did not notice them. Gradually he lowered his arms, opened his eyes, and saw that his men were overwhelmed by the mystery of what had happened to them.

Ahithophel had to clear his throat and wipe a tear from his eye. A nation had been born, and he was a part of it. The light of the candles made the old temple less fearful. Nothing had struck back at them when the pillar had fallen and the idol was broken and God's candlestick set in its place. Their God, the God of Abraham, Isaac, and Jacob, was stronger than the old earth gods.

"My harp, bring my harp, Beniah," David called, and in seconds the instrument was brought forward. David stood with one foot on the base of the pillar, strumming the strings while the men waited expectantly. This sweet singer of Israel was now their king in a way that Saul had never been. He threw back his head and looked up at the night sky full of stars while his strumming grew insistent and fierce, then tender and soft.

"Jehovah is King," he sang so softly at first that they could scarcely catch his words. He strummed a few more soft chords and then again, "Jehovah is King." Now he motioned them to sing and they sang with him, hesitantly at first and then louder and louder until the mountains echoed and rang with the words, "Jehovah is King!"

Let all the earth rejoice,
Tell the islands to be glad.

Now he sang, improvising as he went and always signaling the men to join in:

135

Righteousness and justice are His throne.
Jehovah is King, Jehovah is King.

Let those who worship idols be disgraced
For every god must bow to Him.
Jehovah is King, Jehovah is King.

Light is sown for the godly and joy for the good.
Jehovah is King, Jehovah is King.

May all who are righteous be happy
And crown Him our Holy God.
Jehovah is King, Jehovah is King.

Ahithophel could see that the men would not
sleep the rest of the night but would prolong this
moment as long as possible. For himself the joy of
the moment always seemed to be pushed aside by
the dark omens of the future. He must always be on
guard lest some unforeseen disaster creep upon
him. This was the price he had to pay for wisdom,
he assured himself, as he walked down through the
city streets toward the gate and his tent. What
would happen to David, for example, if the king
should slip and lose the favor of God and the approval of his men? No, Ahithophel thought, it was
better never to fly so high as to risk the arrow of
fate.

David's return to Hebron with a few of his trusted
friends was celebrated with music, singing, dancing, and general rejoicing. He rode through the
gates and up to his house, noticing for the first time
how small and ugly the city was compared to the
high, rock-bound city of Urusalim. His own house
seemed narrow and uninviting. How wonderful it
would be when he could move all of them to a new
palace in Urusalim. David hardly noticed the men

and women who lined the streets and crowded into the courtyard to welcome him. He wanted to see one face and one face only—Michal's.

He turned from his friends who urged him to sit with them and from the screaming, joyful company of his admirers to rush up the steps to Michal's room. He wanted to burst into her presence, hold her close in his arms, and recapture the love and happiness they once had. Remembering the unpleasantness of their last encounter, he paused and knocked.

He saw her the instant the door opened. Michal was holding her hands over the brazier, rubbing them together for warmth. She turned quickly, and he noticed her surprise. For a moment she looked as though she would rush to him and all would be as it had been years ago when she had begged her father to marry her to him in the old fortress at Gibeah.

He walked toward her hesitantly, watching the shadows play about her face, the slow hardening of her eyes and the way she brushed her hair back uncertainly. He sensed the struggle within her. She wanted desperately to come to him.

He reached for her hands and placed in them a small gift he had brought for her, hoping it would speak to her more surely than the words of love he was trying to express.

Michal looked down at the small box, then lifted the lid and looked inside. She bent over to smell the delicate odor of sandalwood. He could see that she was impressed. He was sure she had never seen anything quite like it. Once more he had the feeling she wanted to reach out to him, but once again something held her back.

On impulse he reached out and took her by the arms, forcing her to look at him. "Michal, I have taken Urusalim." Perhaps if he had stopped with these words she would have melted, but he went on to share with her his greatest joy. "God has been with me and has blessed me, and I know He will be with me and with the people of Israel. It is as though the heavens are His abode and Urusalim is His footstool."

Michal stiffened, and her eyes turned to steel-like gray. Before he finished she pulled away from him. "You think God has left my family and is with you? Well, it isn't true. God is still with us. The tribe of Benjamin was chosen first to rule the people, and my sister's sons will rule after you. You will live to see how your God will bless us."

"Michal, Michal, why can't you accept it? God is with me. See how He stretched out His arm and slew the enemy and helped me to take the city of Urusalim."

Michal laughed a harsh, bitter laugh. "It wasn't your God who helped you take Urusalim. It was that traitor, Uri, who helped Joab get into the city."

"Who told you this? You have heard only the gossip of some old women," David countered trying to restrain his anger.

"I have friends who tell me things. Joab was bragging of his cleverness after the battle. So you see, it was not your God who helped you; it was just a foolish Hittite who played traitor to his own people."

"Michal, listen, you must listen to me. I don't care how everything came about. God uses means that seem strange to us, but is was God who helped me, and He will continue to help me."

Michal began to laugh hysterically. "You think you are so great—you and your God. You think you are greater than my father. You will never be what my father was. Never."

David grasped her arm in a vise-like grip while a blind rage grew within him. She tossed her head in defiance and jerked from his grasp, tearing the delicate material of her robe. Her eyes blazed, and her lips curled in scorn. "I wish I had never left Phalti. He was a man in every way, and he worshiped me as though I were a goddess."

In one swift movement David lifted her and carried her to the great bed and tossed her down among the cushions. "I am your husband, Michal," he shouted, "and you will have me whether you want me or not."

When David had finished with her, he stood and looked at her lying limp on the bed, her defiance crushed, her proud manner gone. She began to cry, and he hated himself for what he had done, but he could not bring himself to ask for forgiveness. For a moment he stood looking down at her, and then he spoke with great feeling. "I have known women in tenderness, in lust, and in pride. But of them all, to take a woman in anger shrivels the heart as a fresh date shrivels the mouth." He turned and walked quickly from the room.

5

WHEN AHITHOPHEL'S messenger arrived by donkey in Lodebar, the villagers had already received news of the capture of Urusalim. As they pressed around him for details the man answered their questions as best he could and then asked for Machir.

When the two were alone, the messenger spoke eloquently of the role played by Uri, the Hittite, in the capture of Urusalim. "It is this same Hittite," he said, "whom Ahithophel intends to bring to Lodebar within the month to marry his grand-daughter. He wants you to make all the necessary preparations."

Machir was too astounded to ask all the questions that flooded his mind. The messenger in turn could give only partial answers to the questions he did manage to ask. He drank a cup of the warm, honeyed milk Machir offered and then excused himself, mounted his donkey and was off down the narrow street.

Machir stood numbly at the gate of the courtyard and watched him go until he disappeared at the end of the narrow lane where it turned down toward the market. *Ahithophel is noted for his wisdom and good sense,* he thought. *But in matters of the heart he is not to be trusted.*

He closed the gate and began to pace back and forth across the courtyard, ignoring the curious glances of the servants and brushing off the concern of Reba. *I must tell Bathsheba first, and then I will have to explain all of this to Judah.*

For the first time in his life Machir wanted to defy his grandfather. He could not endure the thought that his beautiful sister would be sacrificed to Ahithophel's ambition or that Judah should suffer this great disappointment. Judah had been as a father to Machir, giving him wise advice in planting his crops, loaning him tools, giving him choice seed, and always bringing the tenderest figs for Bathsheba.

It would be hard to tell Bathsheba that she was not to marry Judah as they had planned. Judah was someone she had known and trusted as her father's friend. His house stood just down the lane, and the daily routine was much the same as in the house of Ahithophel. A rich Hittite from Urusalim would be able to dress her in fine linen and costly jewelry, but their customs would be strange to her, the food different and the women of his house perhaps even hostile.

It was dark enough to light the small clay lamps when Machir finally came to Bathsheba's courtyard. She was sitting under her lemon tree feeding the pigeons grain from her open hand. Nearby Reba was trimming the wick of the clay lamps. Machir stood and looked at them, feeling such a wave of tenderness that he found it difficult to broach the unwelcome news. Reluctantly he sent for Noha, and when they were all together he told them of the message that had come from Ahithophel that afternoon.

They were stunned, unable to comprehend the enormity of all that this would mean to each of them. Reba was the first to speak and her voice sounded strained and tense. "He must have some reason for doing this. Ahithophel loves Bathsheba."

Noha began to cry. "There is never a reason. I have expected something like this to happen. Things have never turned out right for me, and why should they for my children?"

Bathsheba didn't cry but sat with the grain running through her fingers trying to understand all that Machir was saying. She had never heard of Hittites nor had she ever seen one. She had always pictured herself in the house of Judah bearing his children, grinding his grain, baking his bread, getting water at the well, and washing his clothes in the stream with the other women. Now everything was to be different. Uri was rich and lived in Urusalim. She would be leaving everything she knew and loved if she married this man.

"Oh, Machir," she said finally, "please tell Grandfather I can't go to Urusalim with someone I have

141

never seen before." Her eyes were round and pleading and Machir saw real fear lurking in them. Bathsheba had never been afraid of anything. Seeing her fear, Machir felt a wave of anger and resentment toward Ahithophel.

"We must do all within our power to dissuade Grandfather, but we know him well. Once he has made up his mind, no one can stop him." Machir rose slowly, hesitated a moment as he looked at all of them. "I will tell Judah tonight so he won't be taken by surprise."

Machir dreaded the mission entrusted to him. He walked quickly to the door and out into the darkness, intent upon finishing the unpleasant task as soon as possible.

It was late in the month of Tammuz—around midsummer—when Ahithophel finally made the trip to Lodebar with Uri. They arrived at the village gate, riding on mules with retainers and camels following behind loaded with wedding gifts for Bathsheba. They were met at the city gate first by the old men and elders and then by Machir who hurried out to embrace his grandfather and welcome the Hittite as was the custom. He led the two men up the dusty lane to their house where the servants were waiting to take charge of the animals and baggage. Reba and Noha greeted him warmly, and Ahithophel was pleased to see how genuinely he seemed to have been missed.

Ahithophel stood in his courtyard and breathed deeply, enjoying the fragrance of familiar spices and baking bread. He was surprised at how small his home was in comparison to the houses of Hebron and Urusalim. "Come," he said to Uri who stood waiting just inside the door. "We will have the servants wash our feet, and then we will sit down to the finest food this side of the Jordan."

Ahithophel motioned to Phineas and then turned to Uri. "When we have eaten I will call for my grand-daughter. You will see. She is more beautiful than the women of David's court and more desirable than the temple women of Bethshan."

Uri followed Phineas from the room and Ahithophel turned to Machir. "Did you get my message? Have you made preparations for the wedding?"

Machir nodded with quiet resignation.

"You will see what a fine man he is for Bathsheba. He is strong and brave, and he is rich." Ahithophel leaned forward and spoke the word "rich" with lingering enjoyment. "He has shown me boxes of gold and silver in his home." Ahithophel paused to note Machir's lack of enthusiasm.

"Grandfather, he is a Hittite. How can you marry Bathsheba to a Hittite?"

Ahithophel cleared his throat and adjusted his headpiece. "My dear grandson, he is circumcised and more devoted to our God than I am. He has been reading all our laws and goes daily to sit with Abiathar, the priest, for further study. He was even willing to change his name from Uri to Uriah—'the fire of God.' "

"He may be more devout than both of us, but I still don't like it. Bathsheba would prefer to marry Judah."

"Bosh!" growled Ahithophel. "Women know nothing of men. They don't understand a man's thinking and are totally incapable of making a proper choice."

Machir could see that his grandfather was un-movable. He led him out of the courtyard and into the small guest room where they could sit on mats and talk quietly without being heard by everyone in the house. As soon as they were seated Machir faced his grandfather soberly. "I can see that he is big and strong and even rich, but I also see that he is hard and without emotion, as all Hittites are. He will not make Bathsheba happy. She is like a tender plant, and he is like a great lump of clay. How can two such different people ever find happiness together?"

Ahithophel smiled. "You are much like your sister, so you too should marry someone practical. You can't eat dreams. No, Machir, I know what I am about. This Hittite is a good man. My granddaughter is like a priceless jewel that needs a proper setting. Urusalim is the place for her, and Uriah is the man who can give her everything she will ever need or want."

Machir sat for a moment in silence. "Grandfather," he said finally, "you have made up your mind, and there is nothing I can do about it. Let me ask but one favor. Have the engagement if you wish, but let Bathsheba remain with us for a year or two before she marries this man. She is only fourteen years old. There is time yet before she needs to be married."

Ahithophel laughed and shook his head. "I am not so foolish as you think. You wish more time, hoping that Uriah will marry someone else and Bathsheba can stay here in Lodebar. I can think of no greater tragedy than to lose a man like Uriah. He can give Bathsheba everything that really matters." He glanced at the door and then lowered his voice to a whisper. "Soon David will march out against the Philistines, and we will have our own village back. We will all go home to Giloh, and Bathsheba will be only a short ride away in Urusalim. I am thinking of everything."

Since Machir had grown to think of Lodebar as home, he was startled to learn that his grandfather would have them all move back to Giloh. "Grand-father, don't be disappointed if I choose to stay in Lodebar."

Ahithophel adjusted his headpiece and tightened his sash to hide his annoyance. "There is time enough to discuss our plans for Giloh when we get it back. I must go now. See that my granddaughter is dressed and ready to meet the Hittite when our meal is finished." He gave Machir a fatherly pat and went out to the courtyard where the feast was already being spread under the tall palm.

Bathsheba stayed in the seclusion of the women's quarters as it was not considered proper for her to be seen before she was presented to Uriah. She had heard the eager, excited voices when Ahithophel arrived with his guest, and without curiosity she had accepted the news that Uriah had brought her fine gifts. She clung to every shred of hope. Maybe her grandfather would listen to Machir or Judah would come and insist on his rights. Perhaps Uriah himself would find their customs too rigid and return home to Urusalim to marry one of his own people.

Her hopes faded as Reba came to lead her out to meet Uriah. Everything was going to happen as Ahithophel planned. There was no escape. She wanted to throw herself down on the warm brown tiles and sob, but she dared not. She must go down and try to look beautiful so this strange foreign man would be impressed with her.

From the door of the courtyard she could see her grandfather and the stranger drinking wine and laughing boisterously. The flames from the lamp lit the face and figure of the Hittite, revealing a thick-set body with huge, rippling muscles. His head and face were completely shaven. She could tell nothing about his eyes, but already she knew that this was not a man she could ever love.

When Ahithophel came to lead her inside, she kissed him as was the custom and welcomed him home, but she could find no words to express her apprehension. As they entered the courtyard she could see Uriah sitting among the cushions of the divan that had been spread under the palm tree. His back was to them, and she noticed only that his head was bald and on his neck was an ugly scar. He did not turn until Ahithophel touched him on the shoulder and said, "Here is my granddaughter— Bathsheba."

Uriah rose and turned to look at her while Bathsheba lowered her eyes and knelt before him. She kissed both his hands and raised them to her forehead in respect.

"She is fair," he said, and then added, "Is she in good health?"

Ahithophel answered quickly. "You are already thinking of a family. Don't fear. Bathsheba is well and strong."

Uriah took her hand and raised her to stand before him. Then he lifted her chin so he could see her face more clearly, and Bathsheba looked at him for the first time.

"Yes, yes, she is indeed fair."

Bathsheba saw that his eyes were small and calculating as they traveled over her face and down her neck and body and then back to her hair. *He is looking at me as though I were something he was about to buy, and he wants to see that he is getting a good bargain,* she thought, flushing with indignation.

With an authoritative air, Uriah turned toward the door, raised his hand and snapped his fingers. Almost immediately a slave appeared. "Go, bring the gifts and be quick about it," he ordered.

Ahithophel led Bathsheba to a seat among the cushions which had been prepared for her. She felt strange and out of place here in the familiar courtyard. Even Ahithophel looked foreign in his robes acquired in Hebron. Now a series of servants came carrying boxes and trunks all beautifully ornamented with rich carving.

Uriah opened the boxes one by one. He took several necklaces from one gold-covered box and placed them round her neck. From a small silver box he produced two rings, one with a large ruby and the other with a circle of emeralds, and put them on her fingers. "How beautiful my jewelry looks on her," Uriah said with satisfaction. Last of all, a young girl, Sara, was brought in and given as a personal maid to Bathsheba.

There were equally rich gifts for Ahithophel, including donkeys, camels, and rich spices. Ahithophel was ecstatic as he gloated over the treasures spread out around himself and Bathsheba.

It was evident to Bathsheba that Uriah thought of the whole transaction in terms of barter. Indeed, he had paid a handsome sum for her, and her grandfather seemed not only to think this quite proper but a high honor. Bathsheba did not intend to embarrass Ahithophel in front of Uriah, but it was obvious to her that she could not marry this large, bald-headed man with the small, hard eyes. Despite his circumcision he was a foreigner. She could never leave her family and home to go with this Hittite to Urusalim.

Bathsheba said "good-night" dutifully and then hurried to her courtyard to await her grandfather. Ahithophel came sooner than she had expected, jubilant with his newly acquired wealth. "You see how your old grandfather looks after your interests.

You will have everything your heart desires."

"Grandfather, it is impossible . . ."

"I know, I know. You are overwhelmed by his wealth, and you are feeling a bit shy and strange. But that will pass."

"Grandfather, you must listen to me. I don't care about the gifts. I don't want gifts."

A look of annoyance spread over Ahithophel's face. Then he relaxed and laughed. "There would be no marriages if fathers were moved by the whims of reluctant brides. You don't see now, but you will thank me in the future. I know what is best, my child. Just trust me." He patted her on the head fondly and then quickly left the room before she could answer.

Bathsheba sank onto her mat in the darkness of her small room. It was quite hopeless. Ahithophel would not listen to her. He would never give up the gifts Uriah had brought and, even more important, he would not be willing to give up his new relationship to a man of such wealth and position in David's army. Her wishes would seem childish and unimportant beside such gain. It was as Jessica had said; people did things for selfish reasons.

Her mind examined every alternative and realized there was no escape. She pulled her robe close around her and bunched up her mantle as a headrest. She lay down and tried to dismiss the more unpleasant aspects of her dilemma from her mind so that she could go to sleep. "Maybe," she murmured in the darkness, "something will happen, and Grandfather will change his mind."

6

As the news traveled through Lodebar that the granddaughter of Ahithophel was to marry a wealthy Hittite from Urusalim, the whole village was alive with the excitement. Every woman claimed to be a close friend of the young bride and all hoped to witness the ceremonial cleansing at the mikvah which Reba had engaged. Reba had also acquired the services of old Tiva, the village authority on marriage and death. Tiva was fat and ugly, with the added distinction of having been married five times. She could find husbands for plain and clumsy daughters and could manage a wedding excursion to the mikvah with seeming ease.

As a little girl Bathsheba had gone to the mikvah often with her mother and Reba. It had been great fun to run and play in the large courtyard while her mother sat and exchanged the gossip of the week with the other women. Now it was different. She would go as a maid to the mikvah with her mother, close relatives, and friends. But she would return with dancing and singing, riding upon a gray donkey, dressed and veiled for her wedding.

Since this was to be the wedding of the granddaughter of Ahithophel, Tiva had taken great pains to have the old stone wall around the area of the pool washed with white lime and the hard-packed earth swept clean of the carob leaves that dropped over the wall into the courtyard. She scattered brightly colored cushions around the tiled area under the awning, heaped baskets with fresh fruit, and heated a spiced drink for the guests.

The women led the way through the streets with singing and clapping, pausing now and then to exchange greetings with someone who leaned from a window or stood in a doorway. At the gate of the mikvah, Tiva stood sorting out the invited guests and their little girls from the uninvited followers who had hoped to slip by and partake of the festivities.

She led Bathsheba to the seat of honor under the awning and waved the others to brightly colored cushions. The women were already laughing and clapping, singing the sensuous songs reserved for such occasions. The words embarrassed Bathsheba. First one woman and then another would lead and the others would join in, improvising the words and music to describe the union of bride and groom on their wedding night.

Bathsheba pulled the large woolen robe more closely around her. She could not imagine why these women were so boisterously happy. She felt cold and dead inside, as though she were preparing for her funeral rather than her marriage. The women sensed none of her apprehension. It was customary for the bride to act shy and reserved. They offered her a cup of spiced drink, and when she refused they laughed and passed it on to another guest, joking and laughing about her loss of appetite.

At a signal from Tiva the clapping ended with a shout, and the women rushed forward to pull the woolen robe from around Bathsheba. She reached for it, but it was gone, and she stood before them naked. She felt the hot rush of blood to her face as she covered her young rounded breasts with her arms crossed in front of her. The women would have none of this. They poured water over her, rubbed her with salt and then poured water again. They washed her hair and rinsed it with lemon juice mixed with sweet herbs.

Now Tiva motioned for the women to be quiet as she came and took Bathsheba by the hand and led her to the pool. Bathsheba raised her hands and repeated the traditional blessing, then lowered her self into the pool. She shivered as the cold water closed over her thighs, then her breasts. Finally she stooped down and let the water flow over her. Once, twice, three times. The cleansing in the mikvah was a religious tradition. The bride was to go to her husband perfect—a virgin.

To Bathsheba the whole ritual had lost most of its meaning since Uriah was a Hittite. It would mean nothing to him that she was a virgin, purified by washing in the mikvah.

The women clapped and sang as she came from the water:

Thy breasts are as two turtle doves that meet to-
    gether.
Thy dark hair is like the water that rushes down
    from the top of Hermon
Thou art fair, O daughter of Israel,
Thou art fair.

Tiva led her back to the bride's bench, and once again the servants washed her hair and dried her with a large, coarsely woven towel. Fragrant oil was rubbed into her skin and intricate designs were painted on her hands and feet with black dye. All the time the women continued to sing and Bathsheba listened with a growing sadness.

Laughing and winking at the others, one of the maidens gave her clove to chew and honey to sip that her kisses might be sweet for her husband. The thought that Uriah would kiss her filled Bathsheba with panic. She wanted to jump up and shout to the women to stop. She could not endure the thought of even seeing Uriah again. How could she bear to be his wife?

Tiva motioned for the young maidens to bring the bridal clothes and dress for the bride for her wedding. The daughter of Reba's best friend placed bracelets on her wrists and gold bands around her ankles. "How fortunate is the granddaughter of Ahithophel that the groom's mother is not here to examine the bride for her son." The mikvah was not a pleasant occasion when the bride-to-be underwent a hostile examination by the groom's mother.

"With such beauty you have nothing to fear from your husband's mother," said another young friend, fastening earrings in Bathsheba's ears.

Tiva and one of the other young maidens helped Bathsheba pull on the harem trousers and fasten them with a cord at her waist and ankles while a third friend brought a fine linen robe and placed it over her head, letting it cascade around her as it gave off the subtle fragrance of jasmine. "How fortunate you are to be traveling to Urusalim," the envious friend whispered before she moved back into the circle with the other women.

Finally Tiva reddened Bathsheba's lips and brushed her cheeks with powder while Reba arranged the mantle over her hair so that it could be pulled down over her face when she was brought in to Uriah. The women clapped and sang and whispered excitedly as they led her to the door where both Ahithophel and Machir were waiting with a gray donkey to take her to Uriah.

The wedding took place in the courtyard of Ahithophel's house where a brightly colored canopy had been hastily erected to shield the bride and groom from the hot afternoon sun. Bathsheba sat next to Uriah, veiled and silent, while Ahithophel, as head of the house and chief elder of the village, signed the marriage contract that gave Bathsheba to Uriah. Bathsheba could see very little, but she

152

could sense the presence of Uriah sitting on the bench next to her and could see his hands resting on his knees. They were big and square. They may be hands that could kill a hundred Philistines, but they could never do delicate work in silver like Judah.

Now she felt her veil being lifted. Ahithophel was handing her Uriah's cup of wine as a symbol of their new union. She held the cup and stared down into the depths, appalled at the agreement it symbolized. She felt no sense of union with this strange man, but she raised the cup and drank the bitter wine.

The feast that followed was plentiful, with the usual laughter and drinking. At a lull in the merriment, the guests heard the clash of cymbals and the jangle of a tambourine in the street outside the wall. A servant opened the door to let in three gaily dressed Canaanite women with their drummers, who had come to provide the entertainment for the feast. An air of excitement swept through the guests. Custom was such in Lodebar that the dance became more and more sensual until the bride and groom were led to the bridal chamber where the marriage must be consummated and the bridal sheet examined for proof of the bride's virginity.

Bathsheba looked to see if Judah ben Reuben was one of the guests. He was not there. Then her eyes found Ahithophel standing near the wall looking relaxed and pleased. He had no idea how frightened she was. She glanced at Uriah. He was enjoying everything. One of the dancers winked at him and the guests laughed and clapped as Uriah reached out pretending to grab for her. Bathsheba observed the lustful way his eyes followed the dancer's movements.

The tambourines and drums jangled and beat more wildly while the dancers shook their shoulders and flung their heads back and forth, keeping time with their feet to music that beat more and more frantically. Suddenly, at a signal from one of the dancers, they moved toward Uriah and Bathsheba, grabbed them both by the hand, and led them to the small room that had been prepared for them.

The guests in the courtyard started to clap and shout advice to Uriah while he smiled and waved to all of them confidently. Bathsheba sent one fleeting, frantic glance across the room to Machir who was sitting on a mat beside Mephibosheth. His stricken eyes gave her the message: it was too late. The door to the bridal chamber was closed and Bathsheba was alone with Uriah.

She backed against the closed door and felt waves of panic rise within her as Uriah walked to the low bed and began to untie the girdle he wore around his waist. He did not even bother to glance at her but continued to undress, then pulled the sheet back on the bed and lay down. He waited for a moment while she stood frozen with fright.

"Bathsheba," he said gently, "I am ready for you." She did not move but stood tense and motionless.

"Bathsheba," he said more forcefully, "is this the way the women of Israel try to please their husbands? I command you to come."

Outside she heard shouts: "Why are you taking so long? Do you need our help?" Everyone then laughed.

The sound of drums and tambourines and shouting became more insistent when suddenly Uriah sprang from the bed, the scar on his neck growing livid. He grabbed Bathsheba with such force that she screamed in fright.

"No woman is going to make a fool out of me," he said as he carried her to the bed.

At the sound of the scream the guests became silent and a bit apprehensive. Someone laughed nervously, "It won't be long now."

The drums began to beat again in a slow, uncertain way, the tambourines jangled hesitantly. Everyone in the courtyard was listening so intently for the sound of voices that they did not at first realize that someone was pounding on the door.

"Is that you, Uriah?" shouted one man.

"Who else?" Uriah answered while everyone laughed with relief.

The door was unbolted and opened, revealing a smiling Uriah holding a sheet on which there was a bright, red stain. Everyone rushed forward to examine the bridal sheet while the women pushed into the room to see Bathsheba.

They found her sitting on the low bed wrapped in a sheet. Her knees were pulled up under her chin, and her eyes were dark with suppressed anger. "She must think she is the only one who has ever gone through this," said one of her aunts.

"Come, come," Noha said, "it is all over now." Noha turned to the other women. "Thanks be to God the sheet was red; you can all see she was a virgin."

"If she acts this way about such a little thing, what will she do when she has to birth a baby?" another quipped.

One after another they taunted and joked and laughed, hoping to cheer her up, but Bathsheba neither looked at them nor answered. Finally her grandmother impatiently pushed through the women and insisted that they all leave. Reluctantly they filed out, complaining as they went.

Reba sat down beside her granddaughter and began talking to her soothingly as though she were a small child. "Everything is going to be all right," she said.

"All right!" Bathsheba's eyes flashed as she looked at her grandmother reproachfully. "It was horrible. All those songs and jokes and everyone acting as though it was a happy time, and it was horrible." She hid her face in her hands and began to cry.

Reba held her in her arms patting her head. "I know, I know. Uriah doesn't understand; he is not one of us. I fear he is used to the temples of Baal and the groves of Ashtoreth."

"Grandmother, I can't, I won't go with him. I don't ever want to see him again."

"Oh, my dear," Reba said with very real concern, "you mustn't talk like that. A year from now you will laugh at all this."

"No, I will never laugh about this. And if Grandfather insists that I go with him, I am sure I will not live a week."

The grandmother soothed and talked to Bathsheba until she finally lay down on the bed and drifted into a fitful sleep. Then Reba hurried out to find Machir.

She found him in the courtyard and drew him aside, whispering, "I have seen other women upset on their wedding night but nothing like this. I can't reason with her, she just insists she can't go with Uriah tomorrow and of course she has to go."

"We can't let her go with him."

"There is nothing we can do. Bathsheba doesn't belong to us anymore. She doesn't even belong to herself anymore. She belongs to Uriah."

Machir was angry, "It is strange that I have more right to take Jonathan's son into my house to protect him from his enemies than I have to protect my own sister."

"We can do nothing but pray, Machir, and that is no small thing."

"There are only a few hours until dawn. I think Bathsheba is much too upset to travel with Grandfather and Uriah today."

"Don't underestimate your sister, Machir. I know she has led a sheltered life, but she has real courage. You will see. She will go with him because she knows it is her duty. Besides there is nothing else to do." Reba began to weep and Machir put his arm around her and led her to her room.

After leaving his grandmother, Machir walked up to the roof. The sky in the east was already light and soon the men would be saddling the donkeys to ride back to Urusalim. He clenched his fists as he imagined how helpless his sister must feel. If she so much as cried or fainted or refused to go, he was ready to fight Ahithophel and Uriah both to help her.

7

IT HAPPENED AS Reba had predicted. Bathsheba woke after a few hours of light sleep and bid a sad good-by to the wedding guests who still lingered from the evening's festivities. She would eat nothing. When the time came to go she mounted her donkey and rode out the door of the courtyard behind Uriah and her grandfather.

The narrow streets of Lodebar were empty at such an early hour, and the wedding party moved slowly down through the village with wisps of pre-dawn fog blowing in their faces. There was no sound but the steady tapping of the donkeys' hooves on the cobblestones and the rhythmic padding of the camel's cushioned feet mingled with the sobbing of Noha and the light chatter of Bathsheba's friends who would ride with her as far as the village well.

At the well Noha and the women of the bridal party wept openly and clung to Bathsheba until Reba sent them away so she could have some final words with her granddaughter. She reached up and cradled Bathsheba's hands between her own, looking at her with eyes made soft with love and concern. "You must be brave, my dove," she said, trying to control the emotion in her voice. "He is a good man but hard, as most fighting men are."

Bathsheba looked down at the bent frame and blowing white hair and was comforted by the warm, plump hands of her grandmother. "Don't grieve over me," she said with great effort. "I intend to make the best of it since this is what Grandfather has chosen for me."

When the sun rose over the mountains to the east, Ahithophel signaled that it was time to leave. Bathsheba felt her donkey press forward and her grandmother's hands loosen. She turned and waved to Machir and Noha. As the caravan climbed the path the cluster of women at the well faded from her view.

Soon the sun shone warm and bright, and the path wound endlessly through the pine and bracken along the way. Bathsheba thought with great sadness of all the familiar places and loved faces she was leaving behind. She thought of Reba and how she had seemed to age even in the last few days; of Noha and of Machir. And also Judah. She had heard he had left Lodebar a week before the wedding to join Gad's school of the prophets. Each memory was now painful, and she determined to fold them gently and put them away with that of her father. She tightened her hold on the reins. *I will do as I promised, Grandmother, and try to make the best of whatever I find in Urusalim.*

It was evening before they came to an inn on a dusty back street of the palm-shaded city of Jericho. The innkeeper pointed to the lamp-lit shelter for the animals and the platform where the men could bed down. Then he directed Bathsheba and her maid to a room above the stable. Bathsheba was relieved that the inn was crowded and that the women must sleep separately. Sara rolled out the sleeping mats for both of them and then spread out the bread and cheese for Bathsheba's supper.

"Your name is Sara, but Sara is an Israelite name and you are Canaanite. How is that?" Bathsheba questioned as she took the bread and began to eat.

The girl laughed and dropped down on the mat in front of Bathsheba. "All servants in the house of Uriah have had their names changed. When the master became a follower of Yahweh, he took a new name and gave all of us new names also. My real name is Iglat."

Bathsheba looked so interested that Sara continued. "Your husband's name was Uri and now he has changed it to Uri-Yah."

"I see," Bathsheba said nodding her head reflectively. "Uri means 'fiery' or 'light,' and when you put it together with the name of our God, it becomes Uri-Yah, or light of God." She repeated the name several times: "Uri-Yah, Uri-Yah." But when speaking the name, everyone pronounced it "Uriah."

Uriah must have taken his change in religions very seriously, she thought. In spite of her aversion to him she began to think of her husband more kindly.

"Has Uriah's mother become a follower of Yahweh also?" Bathsheba asked, feeling the first real curiosity about her new home.

"ImAshtah worships her son above all else and waits upon his every wish," replied Sara. "But she did not change her name, nor will she ever be a believer in the God of Israel. She has her idols, and I'm sure she would never give them up."

"Will she accept for her son a wife who is an Israelite if she is still so much a Hittite?"

"ImAshtah fears no one. She is strong and knows her son well. No woman can win him from her." Bathsheba's eyes widened so with astonishment that Sara continued. "She can give him everything. Even the temple women from Bethshan come at her bidding to entertain her son for an evening if he so desires."

Bathsheba could tell that Sara admired ImAshtah's strength. It would not be wise to confide in her for she would undoubtedly report all that she said to ImAshtah.

"There is something you can do that will make it much easier for you," said Sara as she prepared Bathsheba's mat for the night.

"What is that?"

"A son. If you give them a son you can have anything you want. Uriah's first two wives had no children, and ImAshtah got rid of them. Sent them back to their families. She would give anything for a grandchild."

Sara lay down upon her mat and was asleep within minutes, but Bathsheba lay awake thinking with new dread of the strange house she would soon enter—and of the mother of Uriah who was still a Hittite with her idols, a mother so strong she had already sent two wives back to their families. She turned over and listened to the night sounds of the inn and tried to forget Uriah and his mother. She heard a mouse scratching in the far corner, a mosquito droned above her head, and there was the sound of snoring from the floor below. Covering her head with her mantle to shut out the strange noises, she finally fell asleep.

The next morning as the sun came up over the mountains east of the Jordan, the small band of travelers was already on their donkeys slowly climbing the steep ascent of the west bank. It would take most of the day to reach the highest part of the ridge at Jebel Zeitun, known as Olivet. Then would come the descent into the Kidron Valley and to Urusalim. They stopped only once at the small town of Bahurim where there were many olive trees and where Ahithophel had to manage some business for the king. These people paid tribute to David in rich, fresh olive oil which was used for cooking, anointing the body, and filling the lamps that burned late into the night in David's quarters.

Bathsheba looked with interest at her grandfather, who knew so much about the ways of David's house. He seemed to be able to keep in his head all the supplies that were needed and also all the various amounts due from the vassals of the king. Even Uriah looked with new respect at Ahithophel.

The business transaction finished, Ahithophel mounted his donkey, and the small caravan moved on toward the crest of the hill. Shortly they would be riding into Urusalim and arriving at the house of Uriah. The thought filled Bathsheba with dread. She looked at her grandfather riding along so confidently and wished she could climb up in his lap and confide in him as she had done when she was a little girl. There had been no opportunity to talk to him and even if there had been, Bathsheba realized he would not understand. Ahithophel genuinely liked Uriah.

Ahithophel called for the caravan to stop under some olive trees at the top of the mountain and rode back to point out to Bathsheba the dark, rich growth of trees in the Kidron Valley and then the new city of David rising to the south along the ridge of the old Jebusite fortress. His enthusiasm rose as he pointed out the filled-in terraces of the Millo rising above the city walls and the steady flow of workmen carrying blocks of stone, crushed rock, and building materials up the long flight of steps into the city.

She tried once to voice her fears, but he did not hear her. Ahithophel was too engrossed in his own words. He rode back to where Uriah waited, and they began the descent into the Kidron Valley. Ordinarily Bathsheba would have been interested in all the new sights, but now her mind was clouded with anxiety. Ever since her wedding night, when Uriah had burst from the sleeping room to join the laughing guests, he had neither spoken to her nor acted as though she existed. Bathsheba had been puzzled at this but secretly relieved. Now that she was approaching Urusalim and the house of Uriah, she wondered if he would continue to ignore her.

The caravan entered the South Gate of the city and then wound up the narrow, cobbled streets to the northern section of the city, entering the courtyard of Uriah's house just at dusk. Servants seemed to be everywhere, adding to the general confusion as they led the animals away to the stables and unloaded the baggage. Bathsheba had time only to throw her arms around Ahithophel and beg him to come see her often before she was led wearily away to her room.

The house of Uriah was big and cut up into many narrow, dark rooms with small windows that opened at floor level. Bathsheba's room, like most of the others, she guessed, was dark and cold. But it was richly furnished and had a larger window than most. The mats were covered with a deep purple material that was soft to touch, and the rug was made of finely woven black goat's hair. The walls were gray with niches where lamps, incense, or ointments could be stored. In one corner of the room was a large carved chest which offered plenty of space for clothes or coverings. The brazier was made of the finest brass, and the drink Bathsheba poured herself was warm and tasty.

Though all of the furnishings were of the best quality, to Bathsheba the house was depressing. The only item of real interest to her in the room was the window. She could sit any place in the room and see out of it. As she rested on the padded cushion and stared out at the shadowy city, Bathsheba wondered about Jessica. Ahithophel had said that it would be impossible to take her from Michal, but perhaps when David's new palace was finished and the king's wives came from Hebron to live in Urusalim, then she would see Jessica. If only she could be with her now.

In a few minutes Sara was back. "ImAshtah would like you to come to her room as soon as you are freshened from the trip."

"Oh, Sara, I can't see her now. I am much too tired."

Sara was firm. "ImAshtah will not wait until tomorrow morning. I have brought water for you to wash."

Bathsheba sighed and went into the small adjoining room where she washed quickly in a beautiful alabaster bowl which had the Egyptian god, Horus, etched on one side and his mother, Isis, on the other. Then reluctantly she followed Sara down a long dark hall and into another room which was much larger and more elaborately furnished.

ImAshtah sat on a richly embroidered cushion, dressed more elegantly than any woman Bathsheba had ever seen. She was of fragile build, but there was a coiled, tensile quality to her body, and strength in the way she held her head and in the firm set of her jaw. Her eyes, small and bird-like, boldly probed Bathsheba until the new bride felt awkward and ill at ease.

Suddenly ImAshtah relaxed her gaze as though she had learned all she needed to know. "Come, sit by me and we will have our dinner," she said firmly. "I will send for Uriah, and we will eat together. We will introduce you to our way of life."

The servants brought the food and spread it out before them on a large silver tray. The full brass pot gave off a fragrant aroma of garlic, and the bread was brown and warm. ImAshtah snapped her fingers, and one of the man servants came and knelt before her. "Go bring your master," she commanded.

He rose and hurried to the door, almost bumping into Uriah, who paid no attention to him but came directly to his mother. ImAshtah held out one jeweled hand, and Uriah bowed, greeting her with great respect and deference. He seated himself beside her without even a nod to Bathsheba.

ImAshtah began to pick out the tenderest morsels and put them on his plate. "My son," she said as she looked carefully for the fullest cluster of grapes, "we must explain to your wife what we will expect of her. There will be some things she will find strange, and yet if she tries, I'm sure she can adapt herself to our ways."

Uriah nodded. "Ahithophel assures me she is a very even-tempered girl and will do whatever you suggest."

Bathsheba was shocked. She could not believe that Ahithophel had been so condescending.

ImAshtah noticed her reaction with smug satisfaction. "You must realize, Bathsheba, that you have married into an old, respected Hittite family. Our ancestors were building a great empire long before your people went down into Egypt. You will understand that we have certain standards and traditions. We will expect you to observe them as faithfully as we do ourselves.

"For instance, our women do not go about on the streets or sit on the roof talking to friends. That is for the servants and common people. We take great pride in dressing as nobility though we often find ourselves among people of low standards, lacking in taste." ImAshtah tore open a full red pomegranate and began to munch on one of the sections, spitting the seeds into a small silver cup. "We will have to make new clothes for you right away. That coarsely woven mantle and gown shout of the Gilead peasantry."

Uriah nodded in agreement but said nothing as he ate leisurely, wiping his big fingers from time to time on a large square of linen that had been saturated with rose water.

"Come, you must eat," ImAshtah chided Bathsheba. "You have nothing to do in this house but eat and sleep and perhaps work with my women in the weaving room. So you must learn to do that well." Laughing at her own humor, she continued to eat and talk. "You see, you have nothing but pleasant duties. We all have our duties and responsibilities. Mine is to make Uriah happy, and Uriah's duty is to make himself essential to the leaders of this new nation. They will be glad to have him when the Philistines come against Urusalim." ImAshtah reached over and patted Uriah's hand while their eyes met in mutual agreement. "Your grandfather says Uriah is more dedicated than most of David's own men. Not many men have changed their names to honor Israel's God."

Bathsheba began to understand how Ahithophel had grown to admire Uriah. His wealth was impressive. Ahithophel would have admired his house and costly possessions, but more than this it would have been Uriah's devotion to duty that would have attracted him. Bathsheba began to wonder if she had been too critical of Uriah.

ImAshtah was talking again. "There is one thing we do expect of you, my dear. It is normal and natural and . . ." Here ImAshtah looked at Uriah and then back to Bathsheba with a hard, calculating look. "We do expect you to give us a son."

Bathsheba lowered her eyes. "I hope I will be able to do as you wish."

There was silence again while ImAshtah studied Bathsheba's downcast countenance and then turned to Uriah. "Now, my son, what are your plans?"

Uriah frowned and ran his hand over his bald head. "The Philistines are massing for battle much as they did before they came against King Saul at Gilboa. There will be war, and soon. I hope to become one of them, to be listed with the thirty."

ImAshtah looked pained. "You are one of them."

Uriah shook his head. "Mother, you don't understand. I may never be one of them, but I am ready to spend every bit of my strength and wealth trying."

ImAshtah spat the seeds of the pomegranate into her hand with undue force. "My son, you must not try to be one of them. You are better than they are. You are a Hittite. Our nation at its weakest moment was greater than anything David can ever achieve."

Uriah seemed not to hear her. "They have some power, some mystery, these Israelites."

ImAshtah was immediately interested. "What do you mean, 'mystery'? I thought you studied with the priests and knew all their mysteries."

Uriah struggled to express himself. "They have an old wooden box covered with gold. No one has seen it in years. They call the box their ark. The Philistines once captured it in battle and took it home with them to Ashdod and put it in their temple. The next morning their great god, Dagon, had fallen on his face before this small wooden box."

"Perhaps one of the Israelites . . ." ImAshtah started to speak, her eyes pinched and speculative.

"No, Mother, no human force could wedge Dagon from his place. The men of Ashdod set Dagon back in place, and the next day they found the idol's head and hands lying outside the door of their temple, and the old box had not been harmed."

"What are you saying, Uriah? You think this box really has some magical power?"

"I am telling you this so you will see that the God of this box is stronger than the gods of the Philistines. All by Himself their God can do battle for them."

ImAshtah looked indignant. "It could have been done by David's men. They don't seem to be afraid of the sea gods or the old earth gods."

"It could not have been the men of Israel for they had been beaten badly. Those who were not lying dead on the field fled back over the mountains to their villages. There is some kind of strength in that box that is not in Dagon or Ashtoreth. This Yahweh is stronger than all of them."

ImAshtah cleared her throat and reached up to arrange a stray wisp of hair. Such talk made her nervous. "We dare not desert the old gods for the new. For things of the heart we need Ashtoreth and for the fields, Baal. You will see that David and his men will have some evil befall them yet for tearing down the gods of our temple and trampling them under foot. The old gods are watching, and they will strike when it is least expected."

Uriah looked down at the bunch of grapes he held in his large, blunt-fingered hands. "There is no harm in your making sacrifices to the old gods so that we will be at peace with them. But I am honor bound to put Yahweh, the God of Israel, first."

Bathsheba sat listening to them in stunned silence. Now she understood why Uriah had wanted to become "one of them." Why he had even changed his name. He admired the power and strength he had glimpsed in Yahweh, the God of Israel. ImAshtah, on the other hand, was willing to include Yahweh with her old idols as long as she could get what she wanted.

Glancing at ImAshtah, Bathsheba noted the strong set of her jaw and the precise way she seemed to snap the grapes from the stems. *If I don't produce a child for them within an accepted length of time,* Bathsheba thought, *it will not go well for me.*

ImAshtah pushed the bowl of fruit away from her and called Sara to come with the lamp. "Sara, my dear," she said looking at Bathsheba again with narrowed eyes, "take the young mistress to her room. It has been a long day for her."

Bathsheba rose and kissed the outstretched hand of ImAshtah and then paused and reached for Uriah's hand. He was picking his teeth with a bit of palm frond and ignored her completely. Bathsheba's face grew hot and flushed with embarrassment as she noted the smug, half-smile of triumph on ImAshtah's lips and caught the slight flicker of pity in Sara's eyes.

She turned and hurried down the dark hall to her room and closed the door behind her before Sara could enter and pry into her feelings. With tongs from the brazier she lit the wick of her lamp and watched the small flame elongate, flutter, and then go out, leaving her in darkness. She leaned against the wall and bit her lip to keep from crying.

She could still sense the hostility of ImAshtah, and she now felt almost like a prisoner in her small room. The ceiling seemed to be pressing down upon her and the walls moving in around her until she felt that she would be crushed. Quickly Bathsheba brushed the damp hair back from her face and rushed to the shutters, flinging them open with a bang, letting in great tides of moonlight. She sank down on the mat and breathed in the fresh, night air. She dreaded the moment when Uriah would come to her, but to have him reject her so obviously before others was the ultimate disgrace.

She began to cry, and through her tears she saw the courtyard below her window blurred and indistinct. The dark bulk of stone and cedar wood that was to be the king's new palace rose beside Uriah's house, blocking her view of the North Gate but leaving the open court and the old temple standing fully within her view. Out beyond the open court and city wall stood the mount of Abraham's sacrifice, Mount Moriah, now glowing like polished alabaster in the moon's soft light. "O God of Abraham, Isaac, and Jacob," she prayed as her grandmother had taught her, "give me strength to survive in this house of the Hittite."

8

EARLY THE NEXT morning Bathsheba awoke with sunlight streaming through the cracks and around the loose shutters of her window. She watched Sara lean over the brazier and patiently blow the dark coals to life so that the water could be heated. Her face flushed and reddened again as she remembered the embarrassment of the night before. She wondered if Sara had seen everything. It was a scandal and disgrace in Lodebar if the bridegroom turned from his new bride so openly.

Sara left the room and Bathsheba pushed back her coverlet. She shivered. It was cold, and her room was damp with the late spring dampness that always clung to houses in Urusalim. She knelt beside the wooden chest and drew out a warm gown of her own, home-loomed bridal finery. She hesitated, remembering ImAshtahs scornful words. With a shrug she let it fall to the floor and rummaged in the chest of clothes for one of the dresses from Urusalim. Testily she tried on a jeweled neckpiece and draped some unfamiliar, gauze-like material around her shoulders. She must remember that to place it over her head like the mountain women of Lodebar was ridiculed here in the city. Quickly she added ankle bands with tinkling bells and gold bracelets from the jewelry given her by Uriah.

She ran her fingers over the fine-tooled

neckpiece and enjoyed the jangle of her bracelets. *Am I doing this to please Uriah?* she wondered, and then was forced to admit to herself that she was loath to bear the scorn of being called an uncouth mountain woman by ImAshtah. Fingering the gauze of her mantle, she felt guilty as though she was being disloyal to her family and her friends in Lodebar.

Tenderly she picked up the crumpled clothes from the floor and buried her face in their rough folds. There was the lingering smell of pungent smoke and dried herbs about them that made her desperately homesick. She carefully folded each piece, then knelt by the chest and dug down to the bottom of the clothes to deposit her bundle.

"Your grandfather will be coming to see you tonight," said ImAshtah casually several days later. She was giving a dinner in honor of Uriah's appointment to David's group of mighty men. Uriah had been chosen out of the king's gratitude for his help in taking Urusalim.

"Grandfather is coming?" Bathsheba repeated the news as tears of relief sprang to her eyes. Over and over again she rehearsed what she would say to him. Surely he would understand and rescue her from ImAshtah and her son. He would feel it was an insult to their family that Uriah had brushed her aside like a servant and had not yet come to her in the manner of a husband.

As the day passed her hopes dimmed. She remembered Ahithophel's stubbornness, his joy in the rich dowry, and the disgrace it would bring to the little family in Lodebar if she would return home. Everyone in the village would blame her silently if not openly.

She began to see how impossible it was.

Ahithophel loved her, but stronger than his love was his pride. He would never admit he had not made the best choice for her.

Late in the day when Sara came to announce Ahithophel's arrival, Bathsheba had determined to say nothing of her problems with ImAshtah or Uriah. When she heard him mounting the steep stairs, she rushed to the door to greet him and threw her arms around his neck. He laughed. "I have not had such a welcome in years," he said, remembering how she used to run to him in Giloh. "My little girl must be very happy." He held her at arms' length so he could look at her. She managed a smile, and he nodded his approval.

Ahithophel stepped into her room and stopped to notice the rich carpet and cushions, the brass brazier with its shining pot and the fine silver cups sitting on the golden tray. His hand felt the smoothness of the alabaster lamp that hung by a chain from the ceiling, and he bent over to smell the choice incense that was being burned for the occasion. His practiced eye took in every detail, added and multiplied quickly the cost of everything. "I have done well to marry Bathsheba to such a rich man," he murmured.

He settled himself near the window and let his granddaughter pour him a warm drink in one of the silver cups. "You will not see me from your window these days," he said, pausing to look down into the courtyard. It was filled with workmen who were continuing their building late into the night by torchlight. "I am busy with preparations for the army and must leave these Phoenician builders to work out their own problems."

"Is there trouble again with the Philistines?" Bathsheba asked anxiously.

"Ah, so you are worried that your new husband

172

will have to go to war." Ahithophel looked pleased. "Joab has taken 300 men down to the caves of Adullam where they can better observe the Philistine villages on the plain. He has already sent back word that they are equipped and ready to attack us here. It could come at any moment. They are bloated with anger to think that David would dare to snatch Urusalim from under their noses while they still consider him a vassal paying tribute." He paused to take a long, noisy sip from the cup he held lightly between the fingertips of his two hands. "They expected David to fight them for his family lands in Bethlehem. Now they feel that they have been tricked and made to look foolish."

"If there is fighting will Uriah go with the army?" Bathsheba asked as casually as possible.

Ahithophel took another long sip of tea before answering. "As a new bridegroom he does not have to go, but I hear that Uriah is insisting on marching with his men. He will not hide behind the law as some men do."

"Then you expect the attack soon?" She could see that her grandfather assumed that her interest arose out of concern for Uriah, and that this pleased him.

"We have no idea when they will attack, but I'm sure it will be soon." Ahithophel quickly drank the last of the tea and set the cup back on the tray, wiping his mouth on his sleeve. "David assures us that the God of Israel has promised victory. I am hoping our men will quickly rout the Philistines and then march on to take back our lost villages. Can you imagine what that will mean? To see my own house again in Giloh, draw water from my cistern and eat once more the grapes from the eastern slope . . ." Ahithophel's eyes glistened with nostalgia. "We will go back to Giloh and be happy as we were before we were driven out."

As Bathsheba took a coal from the brazier and lit the oil lamp, Ahithophel was lost in his dreams of the past. "Giloh is not far, you know. It lies slightly to the west and then south of here."

When it grew dark in the room, Ahithophel rose and took the lamp Bathsheba had prepared for him. She watched him stoop to leave the room; at the stairs he turned and waved. Bathsheba watched as the light from his lamp flickered on the wall and ceiling above the stairs. Then the sound of his footsteps died away.

Back in her room alone, she was filled with indescribable sadness. The room was dimly lit, and dark, menacing shadows fell across the floor and mounted the far wall. Somewhere in the darkness below her window a solitary voice was singing a melancholy song; faint and indistinct were the sounds of feasting and revelry coming up from the guest room below.

"On this evening of his triumph, surely Uriah will come," she murmured as she sat tense and motionless on a velvet cushion. Hours passed before she heard the sound of the visitors leaving. She waited and listened. Once or twice she thought she heard someone climbing the stairs, but she was mistaken. More time passed until she realized that Uriah must have gone to his own room and to bed. He seemed no more eager to see her than she was to see him. Relieved but apprehensive, she pulled off her dress and crawled in under the warm skin coverlet and tried to sleep.

Long before daybreak Bathsheba was awakened by the piercing, insistent blast of the ram's horn from the North Gate tower. She flung open her shutters and leaned out to see what was happening in the court below. *The Philistines must have been sighted coming up the valley,* she thought, as her heart raced with fear and dread.

Down in the large court below, between the old temple and David's unfinished palace, fires were burning, and men moved like shadows to don battle gear and form into companies ready to march. Behind her in the house of Uriah, there was first a stir and then the pounding of bare feet running along the hall. When a woman's shrill voice rose from the lower courtyard, Bathsheba knew that Uriah was leaving to join the men of David's army. He was going eagerly without claiming the well-known exemption given by the law: "When a man hath taken a new wife, he shall not go out to war."

The men raised their banners and shouted their tribal chants lustily back and forth to each other until suddenly one voice, high and musical, could be heard above all the others.

The Lord hear thee in the day of trouble,
The name of the God of Jacob defend thee.

The priest stood in a cleared area, his head thrown back, intoning the words of petition while his hands rested on the head of a young lamb that was to be sacrificed.

With one swift movement the lamb was killed, and its blood was sprinkled on the altar built of rough, unhewn stones erected in the center of the court.

The lamb was placed on the altar and the priest could be heard again, his voice ringing loud and clear on the night air.

Some trust in chariots
Some in horses:
But we will remember the name
   of the Lord our God.

With shouting and drumming and blasts from the ram's horn, the men marched by companies out the gate, leaving the court empty and dark save for the glowing embers and a few darting flames that burned on the altar.

Bathsheba was deeply moved. *The altar is alive and warm,* she thought, *like a great heart beating in the darkness.*

The Philistines in their red cloaks, plumed helmets, and bristling green and purple banners had ridden up the Vale of Sorek in their chariots to camp at Rephaim, a scarce hour's march from Urusalim. At the same time Joab with his men marched up from Adullam and joined with the forces from Urusalim for a surprise attack against the enemy. Joab's men struck at dawn with the slingers of Benjamin moving in first to stampede the Philistine horses; the archers followed close behind with a rain of arrows to strike terror into the slowly waking camp.

Some of the Philistines struggled briefly in hand-to-hand combat, but most fled in panic back down the Valley of Sorek, riding in their chariots, crowding into supply vans, and mounting horses that pawed the ground and whinnied in fright.

The men of Israel followed, running along on the ridges above them and pelting them with stones and arrows, lances, and big clods of earth picked up at random on the steep hillside. David and his charioteers pounded after the Philistines, slaughtering masses of them before they could reach the plain.

So terror-stricken were the Philistines that their priests fled, leaving behind the cart carrying Dagon, their golden, fish-bodied god. The men of Israel laughed and shouted for joy at the victory that had given even the god of the Philistines into their hands.

Rushing down to the abandoned cart, the soldiers crowded about for a look at the ugly image so feared by their enemies. It was heavy with gold and the carving was intricately done. "We will bring it to Urusalim as evidence of our victory," they shouted. "It will prove that Yahweh is stronger than the dark gods of our enemies."

David alone stood firm, insisting that the god be burned and destroyed. "Already you are looking with wonder at the god of our enemies. You are marveling at its artistry and pondering the rituals of their worship instead of giving thanks to the God of Israel who fought for us this day. No, we must burn Dagon here at the place of his defeat, lest we first marvel, then grow curious, and finally serve him tomorrow."

Wood was gathered and a fire built under the idol, but Joab, with Uriah and some of the other men, whispered together that they must save the gold given off by the fire. When David heard of this, he ordered Beniah to bring the gold to him and before their eyes he had it beaten into powder and cast into the stream.

"This day we have won a great victory over the Philistines and their god," he cried. "Let there be nothing left of them to corrupt Israel—not even their gold."

For a moment there was silence, and then a great victory shout rang out from the men of Israel. Finally David mounted his chariot and led his men—dirty, blood-caked, and tired—back to Urusalim.

In Urusalim, three days had passed with very little news of the battle. On the third day, toward evening,

177

a distant sound of shouting and singing was heard. The door of the weaving room flew open, and Sara burst in to whisper the news to ImAshtah, who rose and hurried toward the hall. Then she stopped and turned to her daughter-in-law. "Bathsheba, we will do no more work. Our army has routed the Philistines, and our men are returning victorious."

"Have they taken back Giloh?" Bathsheba asked eagerly.

"No, no, not Giloh. But they have driven the Philistines clear to the Sharon Plain."

Bathsheba put up the thread and ran down the stairs and out to the open front gate where she could look down the street and see the approaching army. First came the runners in front of David's chariot, holding high banners with his sign, the lion of Judah. Then she caught a glimpse of David's chariot, and her heart began to pound with excitement.

The chariot came closer. The crowds of people surged around it, laughing, shouting, dancing, and singing. Then quite suddenly Bathsheba saw David himself. He was standing in the chariot, driving his own horses with his head thrown back and his light hair blowing in the wind. His wrist guards and greaves were made of pure gold; he wore a short battle garment, torn on one side, leaving his chest and arm bare. His muscles rippled easily under his skin as he balanced himself in the moving chariot. But it was not his appearance that attracted Bathsheba the most. It was that his manner was so vitally and recklessly alive. He gave the impression that he was enjoying life to the fullest and that he was completely free of fear.

The chariot passed. There had been just the briefest moment when he had looked in her direction. Could he have noticed her? With her heart pounding wildly she turned and ran back through the gate and up the stairs to her room where she quickly opened the shutters to catch another glimpse of David.

There he was, riding around the old temple, making the cobblestones rattle with the noise of his horses' hooves and the clanging wheels of his chariot. He was laughing and shouting to his men, and they were shouting back. He pulled the chariot to an abrupt stop in front of the roofless, pillared building that was to be his new palace and jumped to the ground, tossing his shield to his armor bearer and his spear to another man who rushed out of the crowd.

Bathsheba wished he would stay there, where she could see him within view of her window. She knew now why it was said that every woman in Israel was in love with the king. There was a magnetism about him that brought life and vitality to everything he did. Now he was reaching out to grasp the hands of his men as if commending them for their bravery. What could be more wonderful than to be singled out in such a way? Even though she was alone, Bathsheba blushed at the thought that he might have noticed her at the gate. If he were ever to reach out to her as he did to his men, she knew she would lose her heart to him.

9

URIAH DID NOT return with his men until the next day. He had penetrated far down to the plain, driving the Philistines back to the very gates of their cities. He came home amid shouting and rejoicing to find that ImAshtah had ordered a great feast in his honor.

"Tonight ImAshtah will take you to Uriah," Sara said as she stood in the doorway of Bathsheba's room.

"ImAshtah will take me to Uriah?" The mirror Bathsheba held almost dropped from her hands.

"Tonight is the full moon and all followers of Ashtoreth know this is the time when everything becomes fertile and grows." Sara seemed to enjoy the astonishment she had seen for a moment in Bathsheba's eyes. Quickly she gathered up the uneaten food and hurried from the room.

Bathsheba closed the shutters and sat down with her chin buried in her hands. She was beginning to understand why Uriah had not come to her. He wanted nothing from her but an heir, and so he had left even this for his mother to arrange.

The sound of hurrying feet in the hall aroused Bathsheba from her despondency. Two of ImAshtah's maids arrived with towels, jars of ointments, perfume, sticks of incense, and palettes of rouge to take Bathsheba to the bath. The bath was stifling. Young serving girls dressed only in their white undertrousers poured water on the heated stones until steam filled the room, and Bathsheba, sitting on the bath stool, could hardly breathe.

The maids scrubbed her mercilessly with the dry, pulpy interior of a gourd which they used as a sponge. Two older women wrapped a large coarsely woven towel around her and led her out to the dressing room where she had her feet and hands dyed with red henna. The beautician spent an hour drawing intricate designs with black dye on her hands and nails while another woman dressed her hair. Then they delicately applied thin, dark lines around her eyes and colored her mouth with a soft paste that would later be removed, leaving her lips moist and pink.

In a corner of the room a toothless, old woman dressed in rags fanned a bowl of coals and carefully placed sticks of costly incense into the center where they smoldered and burned, sending out perfumed clouds of smoke. She held Bathsheba's mantle and robe over the incense until the fibers were coated with a scent that would last for days.

Bathsheba listened to the gossip around her but said very little. She wondered why such care was being taken over her appearance. Waiting until she was alone with the old woman, she called to her. "Can you tell me why I must be bathed and dressed as though it were my wedding day?"

When the old woman sat as though she had not heard her, Bathsheba repeated her question.

With a sigh the woman gathered up the clothes and came to where she could speak quietly to Bathsheba. "It is hoped you will find favor in the eyes of your husband and of the goddess so that you will conceive and put an end to the tragedy of the house of Uriah."

When the woman started to shuffle away, Bathsheba reached out and held her by her skirt. "You have been a long time in the house of Uriah. You have seen his other wives. Where are they? What happened to them?"

The woman looked startled. "Who told you there were other wives?"

"It is no secret. It would be strange for a man the age of Uriah and with the wealth of Uriah to have had no wives before me."

The woman looked around cautiously, then whispered, "They were barren, all of them. Im-Ashtah sent them back to their families. It has given the master a distaste for women. He likes well

181

enough the temple girls and servants, but they are not the ones to give him an heir. It is hoped you will change all of this."

There was the sound of footsteps in the hall. Then ImAshtah stood in the doorway, dressed in a fine, purple robe and wearing a gold necklace and headpiece that glistened in the dim light. "Hurry," she commanded the maids. "The guests have arrived, and my daughter-in-law must come and greet her husband before he goes in to the feast."

There was a flurry of activity as the maids helped Bathsheba into a new robe, adjusted a jeweled headpiece on her head, fastened a heavy, jewel-encrusted necklace about her neck, and slipped soft sandals on her feet. Then she swept out the door behind ImAshtah and down the worn stairs to the lower floor.

Bathsheba saw her grandfather by the far door and noticed how his eyes brightened as he saw her. *Grandfather is happy to see me,* she thought, *but he is even happier to see my rich robes and costly jewels. No doubt he has already estimated the price of all that I am wearing.* She came and took his hand, bowing over it.

Ahithophel beamed at her. "Yesterday I saw the army of the Philistines flee before the men of David. God willing I will have Giloh back soon."

There was no opportunity to say more. ImAshtah grasped her arm and whispered in a loud, insistent tone, "Here is your husband waiting to greet you."

Bathsheba turned and saw that Uriah had been looking at her. She could not tell what he was thinking. His eyes were calculating, and yet there was approval in them. Quickly she bowed before him as she heard ImAshtah whisper, "She will be waiting for you in your room, my son, when you return from the feast. May the goddess bless this night."

ImAshtah led Bathsheba down some stone steps and to a section of the house totally unknown to her. They stopped before an impressive oak door. ImAshtah opened it, firmly guided Bathsheba inside, and then withdrew, shutting the door behind her and locking it.

The room was lit only by the bright light of the full moon which shone through a narrow window, revealing a huge bed surrounded by a gauze-like hanging. Bathsheba could not bring herself to sit on the bed but went over to the window and sat on a cushion, waiting with growing dread for the arrival of her husband.

When he did come, it was with a handsome young man carrying a lamp and the old woman Bathsheba had seen in the bath. The young man set the lamp on a stand and left, while the old woman busied herself blowing on some coals that were dark and cold in a brass pan. As she blew, the scent of jasmine floated across the room.

Uriah had been drinking wine, and his tongue was loose. He stared at Bathsheba for a long moment then laughed boisterously while the scar on his neck darkened. "Don't be frightened. I am in the mood for dancing, and I have brought this old one to provide the rhythm. Can you dance?"

"I know the dance of the women of Mahanaim and Lodebar," she said hesitantly.

He thought a moment. "I have never seen the dance of Lodebar, but if you can dance as the women danced at the wedding, that will be sufficient."

Bathsheba was shocked. "My lord, those women were Canaanites and whores."

Uriah shrugged, flung off his buckler, and the old woman removed his sandals. He lay back among the cushions on his bed. "This old one is clever with the drum. Let me see you dance."

The woman picked up a drum from one of the dark corners of the room and began to beat a steady rhythm. Bathsheba stood tense and apprehensive until she saw the old woman nodding encouragement, her eyes kind. Slowly, with all the dignity of the Mahanaim dance, she began to move her feet, trying to forget the man who was sitting on the bed cushions in the deep shadows. Her feet were mindless, and without effort they kept moving to the beat of the drum. As the old woman beat faster, Bathsheba's feet moved surely in the rhythm.

Suddenly the drum beats stopped and Bathsheba realized that Uriah had spoken. The woman put down the drum and came to her. "You have done well," she hissed. "He wants you to dance with nothing but your veil."

Bathsheba clutched the veil while the old woman tugged and pulled at her robes until they fell in a heap at her feet. "Now see that you dance as well as before, and you have nothing to fear." The old woman began to beat slowly, giving Bathsheba time to recover her composure.

Again the woman's reassuring eyes calmed Bathsheba so that she was able to dance the familiar dance of her people holding the veil to cover herself, letting her mind think only of the rhythm.

Suddenly Uriah snuffed out the flame in the oil lamp, plunging the room into darkness. The old woman hissed in Bathsheba's ear, "Now go to him." She pushed Bathsheba toward the bed and then disappeared through the door, closing it quietly as she went.

"Bathsheba, lie here beside me," Uriah said in a voice Bathsheba could hardly recognize. This time she did not cringe but lay down on the bed as close to the edge as possible. She could hear Uriah breathing, but she could not see him. He said nothing more. The silence between them was oppressive. Finally she heard him heave a great sigh and move toward her.

When it was over, Uriah turned from her and was almost immediately asleep and snoring. Bathsheba lay there rigid and cold. Now she understood everything. Uriah did not need a wife as other men. His mother cared for him and managed his house; for companionship he had the men with whom he fought and drilled. Her only function was to provide an heir.

The door of the room opened quietly and she saw dimly in the moonlight a figure approach the bed. It was the old woman. "Come," she hissed, "you may go back to your room now, and may it be that you are with child."

10

WHEN BATHSHEBA did not conceive a child as Im-Ashtah and Uriah had hoped, the house of the Hittite settled back into its usual routine to wait for the next propitious day. And Bathsheba's life in Urusalim became more and more difficult. In Lodebar she had been free to walk in the fields, help with the weaving, grinding, and baking, and visit with the other women of the village. In Urusalim most of these activities were not considered proper for the wife of a notable Hittite.

Her offer of help in the large kitchens was greeted with ridicule, as was her occasional visit to the scriptorium where she had tried to learn the

Hittite letters and read a few simple scripts. Bathsheba was allowed to work occasionally in the weaving room under the strict supervision of Im-Ashtah, go to the roof in the late afternoon, and once a month visit the local mikvah accompanied by one of the servants. As a result Bathsheba spent most of her time in her room, looking down from her window at the men working on David's new palace.

As the summer months passed quietly and the Philistines did not return, the tension in Urusalim began to subside. David and his men took advantage of the peaceful interlude to settle into their newly captured city. Men worked from daylight to dark filling in terraces, building walls, and helping Hiram's men finish the king's common room and raise the walls of the upper stories of his palace. It was now evident that the palace was going to be larger than they had expected and would not be finished until the next spring.

Fall came with the harvest and the Feast of Tabernacles. With it came the rumor of a new Philistine offense being planned down on the plain of Ashkelon, behind the high walls of Gath. "They will march before the early rains make it impossible for them to drive their chariots up the pass," said one old warrior as he readied his battle gear and rubbed oil into his leather helmet.

When the report came to David that the Philistines were assembling on the wide plain at the base of the Judean foothills and would be soon marching again up the Vale of Sorek to Urusalim, he called his men together in the courtyard. "I have been on my face before the Lord, seeking His guidance and asking if we should ride out against the Philistines. Now His word has come to me that we are to let them ride all the way up the valley and

186

camp for the night without interruption." There was murmuring among the men, and David motioned them to be silent as he continued.

"I propose to ride with most of the army down to the caves at Adullam. We will wait there 'til our scouts tell us the Philistines are moving up the valley. Just before dawn we will attack their forces in Giloh and Bethlehem and at the same time come against their army in a surprise attack from the forest of Bechaim. They will be expecting us to move out from Urusalim to the east but we will be attacking from the south. Instead of advancing on Urusalim as they had planned, they will have to divide their forces to defend their cities."

The men were pleased with his plan. They knew they could never win against the might of the Philistines in a direct battle, that they must always depend for success on a better strategy, advantages of the terrain, and the individual bravery and resourcefulness of their men. Saul, in his ill-fated stand on Gilboa, had taught them the necessity of using both their wits and the power of God if they were to defeat such strong enemies. "If it is still dark and we are so far apart from each other, how will we know when to attack?" asked one of the captains.

David smiled. "There is one signal that will not fail—the morning breeze! Just before sunrise, this breeze blows off the land and out to sea. It will stir the leaves of the olive trees around Giloh and Bethlehem and at the same time the mulberry trees in the Bechaim Woods. When we hear the rustling of the wind in the tops of the trees, we will know that the hosts of God are marching out before us. Then we will attack with the assurance that we cannot lose."

All that day the Philistines rode up the narrow valley of Sorek and camped at nightfall on the plain of Rephaim. They came in greater numbers than before and were more watchful and tense. Having stood in their chariots since before daybreak, riding over the rough terrain of the valley, they were exhausted. Since their scouts reported no movement of Israelite troops ahead, they camped for the night, feeling that the Philistine-held cities of Giloh and Bethlehem nearby afforded them protection. The night was moonless and quiet. In complete confidence they stationed guards around their camp and went to sleep.

At the darkest hour of the night David led his men up the ridge from Adullam and left Joab with several divisions of men spread out in the groves around the cities of Giloh and Bethlehem. Then he marched the rest of his men into the forest behind the Philistine camp. Just before dawn, the wind sprang up, stirring the olive leaves in the groves where Joab and his men were hiding. At the same time this morning breeze rustled the leaves of the mulberry trees in the forest of Bechaim where David and his men were poised ready for attack.

When the terrible blast of the ram's horn pierced the predawn darkness, the Philistines rose up startled and confused. Thinking that a large army was about to attack from the forest behind them, they rushed from their tents and mounted their chariots. Suddenly they realized that their chariots would be useless in the thick underbrush of the forest. Turning, they saw fires leaping up and around the town of Giloh. They headed south, crowding onto the narrow road that led to Giloh.

The fires set by Joab's men fanned out in the dry wheat and grass around Giloh and Bethlehem, catching the trees and the grapevines in great towers of flame. Some of the Philistines living in these towns flung open the gates and rushed out, only to be felled by swift sword strokes. Others who followed were terrified at seeing their townspeople lying dead in the roadway.

Joab and his men pushed into Giloh, going from house to house, kicking in the doors and battering down the walls, searching for anyone who still might be in hiding.

As the sun rose, the whole Philistine army was in full retreat. Some still rode in their chariots, most were on foot, but all were headed down the deep valleys that led back to their cities on the southeast coast. The men of Israel, led by David and now joined by Joab and his captains, followed the paths along the ridges above them, again picking them off as they fled. The terrified Philistines whipped their horses into a lather, trying to gain the safety of the flat plain along the coast where they thought the Israelites would not follow on foot.

Again they were mistaken. David's forces pursued them all the way to Ashdod and Gath. Never had the Philistines suffered such a disastrous defeat.

Before sunset David marched back up the valley with his fighting men, who were tired but triumphant and singing so boisterously they could be heard long before they came into view.

On the plain where the Valley of Elah joins the Sorek, David ordered his men to halt and make camp for the night. He called together the priests and ordered that a sacrifice of thanksgiving be made unto the Lord. The priests began to collect stones for an altar and gathered up the lambs they had brought with them for this purpose. The fat and special parts would be offered on the altar, and the rest would be fed to the men.

As the preparation began, Joab came to David. "My lord, the men are exhausted. Shouldn't we forget the sacrifice and simply feed these hungry men?"

David's face was dark with dust and streaked with sweat as he turned accusing eyes on Joab. "My nephew, surely you would not suggest we eat and neglect to thank the God who fought for us this day. Without the help of Yahweh we would be lifeless bodies hanging from the walls of Gath."

Joab shifted uneasily. "But, my lord, you speak as if it were not our strong arms that won the battle. I would like to see any of the gods fighting as Uriah and I fought today. I contend we owe God no thanks, and we owe ourselves a rest."

"Joab, Joab," David remonstrated, "you are too tired. It is God who made possible the victory. Together we won. If I have any talent or genius it is in this one thing: I see that we must put the wisdom of God together with the strength of men, and then we cannot lose."

Joab looked down at his dusty, blood-spattered legs and torn tunic. He ran his fingers through his hair stiff with dirt and blood. "David, my uncle, I follow you and I trust you, but you must remember that you are anointed with God's holy oil. You are the chosen, not me. God speaks to you, but to most of us He is silent. Do you think God would have cared if I had been killed in battle today? No, He would not have cared one jot. But you, you are the apple of His eye. You would not have fallen though they had driven a javelin clear through you."

David put his hand on Joab's bleeding shoulder. "You are chosen too, Joab. Not with holy oil but through the will of the people. Saul was anointed with the holy oil, and he fell on Mount Gilboa just like anyone else."

"Yes, he fell," Joab retorted, "but not just like

anyone else. He drew his own sword and killed himself."

"You have spoken a great truth, Joab," David said. "Perhaps to those anointed with the holy oil, the enemy lies within. It's worth some thinking about anyway."

Ahithophel had been awakened at dawn with the news that the Philistines had at last been driven from Giloh. He pulled on his clothes, mounted his donkey, and rode out the Valley Gate, turning southwest until he came to the top of the ridge. Up ahead was Giloh, his village. The first rays of the sun were hitting its walls and brightening the roofs of its houses.

All around him was a great devastation of charred fields, broken chariots, dead horses, pieces of armor, and men dead or dying. But he saw only the beauty of his village, Giloh, crowning the ridge of the steep hill.

Ahithophel covered his face with a headcloth to keep out the terrible odor of death and to prevent the smoke and blowing ashes of the burned grain from choking him. Inside the gate he pulled the donkey to a stop, lowered the headcloth, and looked around him at the open square. Everything was strange and different. The carob tree had been cut down and the dusty surface of the open space before the gate had been neatly tiled with small stones. To the right of the gate stood a small rectangular building with painted pillars that must have been a place of worship. Thrown out onto the pavement before it were the broken parts and pieces of a clay goddess.

As Ahithophel looked around the square, he noticed some of the houses had been torn down and replaced with shops and stalls filled with stacks of pottery, dried herbs heaped on woven mats, and piles of fruit in grapevine baskets. Near the gate was an apothecary's shop that probably sold incense and medicinal herbs. In all of his dreams of coming back to Giloh, he had never once thought of it as being changed. Digging his heels into the sides of his donkey he plunged up the narrow street.

With great relief he saw that the wall around his house was still standing. Cautiously he pushed open the gate and stepped inside. There was nothing that he recognized. The courtyard had been paved with small pebbles and there were pillars where solid walls had previously stood. Everything was open and painted with bright designs. The corner where he had stored his yokes and pruning hooks was bare and neat. The wall was stark and whitewashed. The mud-daubed nests of the doves were gone.

He walked in a daze to the stairs and noticed that the cook room had been cleaned of its familiar black char and no longer smelled of baking bread. He pushed the door open and was overwhelmed with a stiflingly sweet odor. Inside was the ugly god, Dagon, half fish and half man, his stony eyes glistening in the darkness. Ahithophel ducked back and pulled the door closed with a bang. There would be time to deal with that later.

He tried to open the door to the women's court and found it jammed shut. He pushed hard against it with his shoulders. It splintered and cracked, falling open suddenly and exposing a sight more frightful to Ahithophel than the pagan god. There in the small courtyard where Bathsheba had played so happily was a mother pig and her small piglets. To the people of Israel they were ugly, unclean creatures. Ahithophel threw his hands up in despair at the thought of ever restoring his house from such a defilement.

The pigs rushed past him and out into the main courtyard. At first too horrified to move, he watched them nose about the well-curb and the cook-room door. When he ran shouting after them, they all fled out the main gate with their mother.

He sank down onto the well-curb for a moment to catch his breath, mop his brow, and try to recover from the terrible shock. With resignation he rose and mounted the steps to the roof. Even the broken step had been mended, and the roof was no longer open to the sky but divided into separate rooms. The great loom was gone. "Perhaps it has been burned for firewood," he muttered ruefully.

He leaned over the roof and saw that the grapevine had been pruned back, and he realized that it was no longer needed for shade. He wandered like a stranger into the various rooms, opening chests of colored cloth and clothes, noticing ornaments and mirrors of brass, small tools and tables inlaid with ivory. His home had not been as grand as he remembered it, and certainly now that it had been made into a proper Philistine home, he no longer felt comfortable in it.

He walked slowly back down the steps, noticing the cistern with its stone well-curb. It was the same. Cisterns could not be disguised or replaced. He felt a great surge of relief. He ran his hands over the smooth stones and wondered if Machir would be willing to leave Lodebar. Would Reba feel at home here now? For the first time he realized that he could not reclaim the past. Nothing would bring it back as it had been. All of them had grown and changed, and even the house itself would never again be as it was before they left.

He had supposed he would come here as

though it were his home, but his life and interests were now in Urusalim. He slowly opened the door and stepped out into the lane. A cock was crowing, and the sun was shining brightly. Israel had driven the Philistines to the sea as they had dreamed of doing for years, and yet the taste of victory was not as sweet as he had imagined it. He closed the door and barred it. In so doing he claimed it again as his home, and yet as he mounted his donkey and rode down the familiar twisting lane, he felt a numbing sense of loss. If he had never regained his home he could not have lost it so completely. Now that he had it back again, so changed, even the memory was gone. He was unutterably sad, realizing he had lost Giloh—his Giloh—forever.

BOOK THREE

DAVID

1

WHEN SPRING CAME David was able to move into his new palace. There was still carving to be done and tapestries to be hung, but the basic building was finished. The swords and spears of his men now hung in the pillared common room, and there were benches around the walls for his friends. His new throne of olive wood, carved with the lions of Judah across its back, sat against the far wall facing the door.

For matters of business the common room suited his needs very well, but his favorite place in all of his new palace was a tent-like pavilion on the roof. Here with his mighty men he would sit for hours discussing matters of state and making plans for the battles that were likely to come with the first budding of the almond tree.

On this particular spring morning, David's men had been sitting in the pavilion busily mending their armor and discussing battle maneuvers. David usually enjoyed these times together, but on this day he grew restless. He was tired of sitting and tired of planning. He wanted to be out in the fresh air, walking across his own land. He rose from his dais, stretched, excused himself from his men, and went outside onto the parapet.

His city had never looked more beautiful. The Phoenician artisans had worked through the long, dark days of winter and were now packed and ready to return to their own country in time for the spring festivals. His wives had ridden up from Hebron on the first warm day and were noisily adjusting to their new rooms and courts. He smiled, remembering Michal's displeasure at finding that her rooms opened on the same courtyard as his other wives and then her final agreement to stay when she saw how they were lined with beautifully carved cedar wood.

He leaned out over the parapet to see the roofs on the houses below him and the narrow, winding lanes that crisscrossed the area, all coming together at the southern Dung Gate. He noticed that the workmen were still busy filling in the Millo that would level the area inside the walls, making more room for the houses of his men.

A rooster crowed, and he was reminded of his home in Bethlehem. He moved to see the road that led out of the city from the western or Valley Gate and over the ridge to Bethlehem. His father, Jesse, and his mother were back from their long exile in Moab. He hoped the Philistine lords would lie quietly this spring and not ride up to retrouble the villages they had lost. "Oh, God," he prayed, "let Jesse walk about his land in peace."

He was about to turn back inside and rejoin his men. Suddenly his attention was caught by a movement at a window in the old house of Uriah the Hittite which rose on the opposite side of the narrow lane from the palace.

There, sitting at the low window, looking down at the activity of the courtyard below, was the most beautiful woman he had ever seen. She was not dressed as a woman of Israel but had a golden ornament in her rich, black hair and thin gossamer material thrown over her shoulders, revealing a glowing golden necklace that went from her neck out to her shoulders in small jeweled platelets. Where the material fell away he could see that her rounded breasts were also covered with the same golden plating, molded miraculously to follow every curve. She seemed to be dressed as an Egyptian, and yet she had the bearing and features of a maid of Israel.

He forgot his men and the threat of war and even the beauty of his city. Nothing he had ever seen had quite captured his imagination as did this vision of loveliness. She reached for a cup that had small wisps of steam rising from it, and the way she held it in both hands, pursing her lips to blow on it, suggested that it must be hot broth or tea.

There was shouting down in the lower court, and she leaned forward and looked down, holding the cup suspended for a moment. Then someone seemed to call to her from inside the room. He saw her listen intently, pick up a brass mirror, straighten the gold coins that framed her forehead and then move from the window out of sight. "Could it be she is often at the window?" David whispered.

In just the few minutes he had seen her, she had captured his thoughts completely. He imagined the fragrance of her hair and the soft touch of her hand, the tilt of her head and the light in her eyes. He returned to his men but did not enter into the conversation. At mealtime he ate little but sat holding a brass cup in his hand and looking out over the heads of his men, lost in his thoughts.

"He is counting the wealth of his new city and estimating the men it will take to defend it," one captain whispered to another.

"No, it's not that. Even Moab and Edom fear his strength and will not come against him this year."

The next time David found occasion to walk upon the roof of his palace, he looked eagerly toward the window in the house of Uriah. The wooden lattice was open, and he could see into the small room. There were bright cushions, mats, carpets, and a hanging alabaster lamp, but the woman who had so inspired his imagination and taken over his dreams was not there. He was disappointed.

When it became evident that the Philistines were not going to ride up the valley as they had done in the past, David became restless and moody. For the first time there was peace and prosperity in the land. The men of Israel no longer had to go down to foreign cities to have their plows made or their spears sharpened; they had craftsmen of their own. The king and his officers now rode in chariots, and the soldiers had more spears, shields, bows, and arrows of metal than ever before. Their helmets and breastplates, greaves and arm guards were made of both tooled leather and silver. They were a formidable force, and none of their enemies was eager to come against them.

Even the Edomites and Moabites were lying quietly on the far side of the Jordan, allowing Israel access to both the king's highway and the harbor of Ezion Geber. David had thought it would be years before Israel would be at peace and yet now, so soon, everything seemed to be accomplished.

David knew he and his men would quickly grow restless without challenge. It must be something as fresh and difficult as fighting the giants of Gath, driving out the Philistines, or taking the city of

Urusalim had been to them in the past.

He sat down on his dais and leaned back against the skins, idly plucking the strings of his harp as it lay beside him. Yes, he thought, God had given him great victories over his enemies. He had established his kingdom so that he was both rich and powerful. He had given David the city of his dreams.

He had given him sons. They sprang up around his throne like the fresh young shoots around an old olive tree. They could all be kings. Amnon was first but Absalom was more talented. He thought briefly of how Ahithophel favored Absalom and how Amnon's mother complained of this. His wives were always complaining about something.

"Yes, God has blessed me," David mused. "If He were a neighboring king, I would pick out my richest treasures and with my men go to Him and pledge Him my allegiance. But He is not a king like myself. He is the Creator and Owner of everything. Urusalim is only His footstool, Moab His washpot, and over Edom He casts out His shoe. What could we bring Him that He does not already own?"

He picked up his harp and began to play, adding new words to an old tune:

"In Thy strength the king rejoices, O Lord . . ."

He could think of no further words, and so he hummed and plucked out the notes until he came to the last two lines and then he ended joyfully:

Thou hast given him the desire of his heart!
And the petitions of his lips
Thou hast not withheld.

The sound of the harp died, and David sat quietly meditating as an idea began to take form in his mind. *I now have a house of cedar. Men exclaim with wonder at my greatness when they enter*

*my house and see the tall, well-formed pillars
that support the roof and notice the carvings of
flowers and plants and smell the fragrance of the
pine. I have a house that brings honor to my
name, but my God is still living like a shepherd in
a humble tent. We must build Him a house; a
house more beautiful than the palace and more
costly than the temples of Egypt.*

Impulsively he went to the door of the pavilion
and called to his armor bearer. "Go summon my
captains, my mighty men, Ahithophel, and the
priest. Tell them we must meet together immediately." His voice was so vibrant with excitement
that the young man bounded joyfully down the
steps to carry out the order.

They came in twos and threes; big, handsome,
browned, and muscular, walking with half-
swaggering, confident gait of men who know they
can out-run, out-jump, and out-wrestle any assailant. They crowded together on the mats and
goatskin rugs, laughing and eager, happy to be together again for whatever purpose. Inside the pavilion they felt at ease, for it was a tent such as the
humblest shepherd might use, despite the fact that
it was constructed of the finest material.

When they were all seated and quiet, David stood
up before them. "With God's help" he began seriously, "we have destroyed most of the enemies of
Israel. We have overthrown the idols of Baal and
destroyed their high places. Through God's help we
are at rest this spring from our enemies; we are
living in new houses of stone and eating the milk
and honey our fathers dreamed of in the wilderness. With all of this, the house of our God—the
Tabernacle—is still a humble thing of poles and
skins and woven cloth: hardly a fit dwelling for even
the least of our soldiers!"

The men were immediately alert and expectant. "Perhaps," David continued, "the time has come for us to build a glorious temple to our God who is continually saving us from all our enemies. We will bring together our gold and silver and precious stones to make it as fine a temple as anything in Phoenicia or Egypt. It will be a work of love to our God carved with our own hands."

The men broke out with shouts of approval until David signaled for them to be silent and recognized Ahithophel. "My lord," Ahithophel said, "I am not a man who knows much of the ways of our God, but I do know that He will never gain the respect of the foreigner and the stranger as long as He is housed in a flimsy tent of cloth and skins like a desert dweller."

Seeing confusion in the eyes of the men, Zadok, the priest, rose and spoke forcefully. "The Tabernacle is meaningful to us because it was made after the pattern given to Moses by God Himself. But now that none of us is living in a tent, it does seem fitting to build a house for our God that we need not be ashamed of before the heathen."

"You have spoken well, but there is one problem," Abiathar said hesitantly. "Ever since the Ark of the Covenant was taken in battle by the Philistines and our Tabernacle at Shiloh was destroyed, no one is offering sacrifices for their sins or keeping the feasts of Moses. In the Tabernacle at Nob the Holy of Holies sits empty, and there is no one to light the candlesticks or burn incense. The table for the shewbread is empty and covered with dust."

"It is true," Zadok agreed sadly. "When the Ark was taken by the Philistines, everyone seemed to feel that God was no longer with us. They feared the Ark was just a common, gold-covered box and not the holy object we had thought it to be."

Zadok explained further. "Our people became disillusioned because the sons of Eli took bribes, slept with strange women, and claimed for themselves meat that was to have been sacrificed on the altar. Finally, when the Ark was taken, many lost faith in the God of Israel and went over to the worship of idols."

"I understand how they felt," David said. "I was disillusioned for a time myself, but when I heard how the Philistine god, Dagon, toppled to the floor when the Ark was placed next to it, my faith became stronger than ever."

Zadok nodded. "This was not true of most of the people. They saw that the Ark was gone, and they lost all faith."

"Whatever the reason, it is not right that we have forgotten the Ark for such a long time," David said. "Surely God is displeased with us."

David began to pace back and forth getting more and more excited as an idea began to form. "Before we talk of building a great temple," he said, "we must first go and find the Ark and bring it back to Urusalim."

Everyone quickly caught the spirit of adventure. Even the practical-minded Ahithophel joined in the excitement. "May I ask," Ahithophel's voice rang out over the hubbub, "where we are to find the Ark? Does anyone know where it has been all these years?"

Silence and shame fell upon the men as they realized that since the Ark had been returned by the Philistines no one had given any thought of it. "We never concerned ourselves with the Ark during the days of Saul," an old man said.

"I have heard the Ark was placed in the home of Abinadab at Kir-jathjearim," one captain ventured.

"We will send to the house of Abinadab and inquire after it," David said finally. "If it is indeed at his house, I myself will go on foot to bring it home." David immediately dispatched a messenger to the house of Abinadab.

It was evening when the messenger returned with his report. The golden Ark rested in a special chapel at the side of Abinadab's house. Abinadab claimed that during the twenty years it had been with his family, they had grown rich and prosperous.

There was great rejoicing at the news. Preparations were immediately started to bring the Ark to Urusalim and place it in a tent-like Tabernacle in the Kidron Valley.

A special cart was made and decorated with boughs and flowers. Two perfectly matched, white oxen were brought to haul the cart. A Levitical choir made up of the young men of Urusalim and led by David walked on foot to the home of Abinadab. It was a beautiful spring day. The sun was shining and the birds were singing. No one had any foreboding of the disaster about to take place.

The Ark was lifted onto the cart by priests, and Uzzah, the son of Abinadab, was chosen to walk beside it while David and the priests led the way, followed by the choir.

All went well until they came to the threshing floor of Nachon. The cart lurched to one side and Uzzah put out his hand to steady the Ark. To the surprise of everyone near him, he instantly fell on his face beside the cart.

The whole procession came to an abrupt stop. The priests drew back, making way for David who looked with horror on what had happened. "Uzzah is dead!" he cried.

His face grew dark with anger as he looked around at the people. Seeing doubt and fear on their faces, he was afraid they would never want to worship at the Tabernacle again. *Why?* he wondered. *Why did God let this happen just as all the people were ready to worship again as Moses had taught them?*

"There is some evil thing possessing this Ark," he said aloud to the people. "Is there anyone who will take the Ark to his house?" It was quickly obvious that no one wanted anything to do with it.

Finally one of the men suggested they take the Ark to the house of Obed-Edom, the Gittite, and pay him handsomely for storing it. This they did and were glad to be rid of the holy object that had caused them such trouble.

Back in his palace, David was puzzled by all that had happened. He spent hours alone in his pavilion, praying and thinking. Since the priests had no answer or explanation for what had happened, he became more and more baffled. Finally in desperation he prayed that God would send someone to help him understand why this evil had befallen Israel.

Late one night several months later, as David sat meditating on the roof of the palace, one of his guards announced that a stranger had come requesting to see the king with an urgent message. Behind the guard, in the shadows, David could see a tall man wearing the simple white tunic and long, uncut hair of the prophets. "Who are you?" David asked.

"I am Nathan, a Nazarite and a prophet of God." The man spoke in a firm manner as though it was perfectly natural that he should be announcing himself to the king. "I have a message for you from God concerning the Ark of the Covenant."

David's eyes flashed with interest. "Many have

lost their faith because of this terrible incident. I am eager to have an explanation."

"There are moments of darkness that come to all of us." Nathan spoke softly.

"Moments of darkness! There have been three months of darkness, and I have asked why, why, why? Always there is no answer. I have prayed, and I have fasted, always with the weeping women and the dead body of Uzzah before my eyes. He did nothing but try to keep the Ark from falling to the ground."

"My king, listen, and gain understanding. Our God is not made of stone and wood. He is God of the thunder and lightning, the wind and the rain, seed time and harvest, and He is the God of the inner mystery of the Holy of Holies. Sometimes we forget whom we worship, and we act as though He belonged to us and should do things as we want Him to. Moses had to learn while making the Tabernacle in the wilderness that each thing had to be made strictly according to the pattern. Each curtain was to be an exact size, each object followed careful measurements, and even the rituals of worship were to be carried out exactly. This is where you made your mistake. The Ark is to be carried on the shoulders of the priests and never placed on a cart."

"You mean that Uzzah paid with his life for a little thing like that?" David was astonished beyond belief.

"To you it was a small thing, but to God it was important. It was a matter of either doing this God's way or your way."

"But why did Uzzah have to die to teach me something like this?"

"We must not see it through our eyes but through God's eyes. Death looks like a terrible punishment to us, but perhaps from God's side death is as easy as going from one side of the Jordan to the other. Look at it this way, if Uzzah hadn't died, you would never have tried to discover what had gone wrong." Nathan spoke with an intensity and conviction which won David's admiration.

"Are you sure this is the answer? I have feared that some evil thing had taken hold of the Ark since it was with the Philistines."

"If you will investigate, I think you will find that in the past months Obed-Edom, the Gittite, has had many wonderful things happen to him. His neighbors feel that it is because he has the Ark in his house."

"If this is true, we will go again to take the Ark, and this time we will do it right." David's eyes were warm with gratitude as he bade Nathan good-by.

Several days later a large procession wound its way up and over the mountains north of Urusalim to the house of Obed-Edom. Upon arrival the priests entered the small room where the Ark rested, carefully fitted the poles they had brought through the rings on the side of the Ark and lifted it to their shoulders. When the people outside saw that no harm came to any of them they shouted for joy.

As the procession made its way back to Urusalim, it stopped at intervals so that an ox and fatling could be sacrificed. The priests blew trumpets while the young men sang and played cymbals, psalteries, and harps. As they neared the city the singing and rejoicing became more and more enthusiastic until people were dancing and clapping with joy before the Ark.

David had walked all the way carrying his harp and leading the young men in singing. As they neared the city, some of the young men joined arms and began to dance the tribal dance of celebration and joy. They sang with all their strength, keeping steady rhythm with stomping and bending and clapping their hands.

Jubilant that the Ark of God was coming to Urusalim after all the years it had been lost, David could stand the stiff embroidered robes of state no longer. He handed his crown to Abiathar and his royal robes to his armor bearer and pushed through the dancing men dressed only in the simple loin cloth and ephod such as the priests wore over their long robes. David picked up the rhythm of the dance and locked his arms in those of his men and danced with more joy than any of them.

The jubilant men marched past the old temple and David's new house of cedar, past the tall, dark house of Uriah the Hittite, and down through the tangled streets to the Kidron Valley below the South Gate.

Bathsheba, hearing the shouting and singing, rushed to her window, pushed back the shutter, and leaned out over the cushions to see down into the street below.

First she saw the shouting and laughing children, then the men with drums and instruments led by the standard bearer with the waving banner of the tribe of Judah. Then she saw David. He was singing a battle song of victory in the very center of his captains. Their arms were linked around each other and their feet were beating and pounding and clicking on the cobblestones.

Right beneath her window the song came to a finish with a great shout, and the men lifted David above their shoulders while they all shouted with one voice, "The Ark of the Lord and of David!"

As David was lowered to the street he looked up,

saw Bathsheba and smiled. Then the procession moved on.

Bathsheba sank back onto the cushions wanting to savor every minute. David had really noticed her and smiled. He was so full of vitality and enthusiasm. His men danced with grace and strength, but David had that extra zest and joy which made all eyes focus on him.

The procession passed from sight, and Bathsheba slowly pulled the blinds shut. Then she picked up the small brass mirror and looked into its blurred and wavering surface. *I wonder,* she thought to herself, *if David would find me attractive if we should ever meet?*

2

MICHAL ALSO HEARD the shouting and singing as the Ark was brought into the city. She too looked out of her window to see David dancing in his ephod with the young girls and women running before him shouting his praises. Her face grew scornful as she observed the king dancing like a common peasant at harvest time. She closed her shutters with a bang.

Late that night David returned to his palace still singing and laughing with his men to find the common room ablaze with torches and Michal in her most regal attire waiting for him. He almost laughed at the contrast. Michal was dressed for a formal reception, while he stood before her, his hair rumpled and his body dripping with sweat and dirt from the long walk. The linen ephod he wore was stained with the blood of sacrifices, and the men with him looked no better.

Michal smiled a strained, deliberate smile. "How glorious was the king of Israel today when he uncovered himself before the eyes of the handmaidens as might some of the vain fellows who shamelessly uncover themselves." She glared fearlessly at the king even though he towered over her.

"It was before the Lord God that I danced," David replied calmly. "He chose me in place of your father and your house, and He exalted me and made me ruler over all Israel. If I choose to play and to dance before the Lord, what have you to say? If it is pleasing to the Lord, I will yet debase myself even more, and the handmaidens you mentioned will honor me for it."

Michal turned in disgust and walked toward the door at the far end of the room.

"Michal!" David's voice had a note of command in it that she did not dare ignore. "Here in the presence of this company of my friends, I could divorce you, but I will not for Jonathan's sake. However, I swear as God gives me breath, you will see my face no more. And you will go down to your grave childless."

Michal froze with shock, then turned again to face the king. "You are still a crude, unlettered shepherd. You smell of the sheep cotes." In shrill anger she spat the words at him as she turned and left the room.

David's men were embarrassed. They had all heard of the trouble between David and Michal, but none of them had imagined that any woman could be so vain and arrogant or that David would curse her with childlessness. They had all hoped a child would unite their two houses and secure the kingdom.

Without a word to his men David left the common room and climbed to the roof where he paced restlessly back and forth. He tried to remember the days when he had been happy together with Michal and Jonathan. He wanted desperately to reclaim some part of that golden past. He had tried to love Michal and had failed miserably. *She hates me as her father hated me and without cause.*

Yet he felt strangely released from some oppressive bondage, though he was more lonely than ever before. The friends of his youth had all been killed or lost to him; his wives had become dull and uninteresting. They flattered him, said things to please him, or tried to win his favor with no real interest in him as a man, only as a king.

That was why Michal had been so important to him. He almost welcomed her tart hostility to the blandness of the others. But seeing old Saul's angry expression mirrored in her face had closed off something inside him, and he knew he was through with her forever.

Though it was late at night, he wanted to talk with someone. He thought of Joab, then Ahithophel, and finally his captains, but none of them would quite do. He wanted someone who would feel the deep joy that he had felt upon bringing the Ark back to its place in the Tabernacle. He longed for someone who understood this burning fire of holy emotion and who accepted it as a proper part of a man's life.

He sat among his cushions and began to idly sketch various plans for the new temple on the back of a sheepskin rug from his floor. He had seen temples in both Egypt and Phoenicia, and his temple must be richer than any of these. It was difficult for one who had spent so many years as a shepherd and a soldier to think big enough. The temple should be of stone like the temples of Egypt, yet fashioned like the Tabernacle of Moses and Aaron.

"So you are already making plans for the new temple." Ahithophel stood in the doorway from where he could see the sketches. "The old Tabernacle is a disgrace to Israel. We can never hold our heads up as long as our God is housed in a tent."

David looked up from his drawing. "You make it sound as though we want a great impressive temple for our own sense of pride. I would like to think that we will build the temple out of love for God."

"You always have such noble thoughts," said Ahithophel. He sat down beside David on the divan. "Your mind is so completely taken up with this new project you haven't given a thought to the trouble you're in."

David looked at him quickly. "Trouble?"

Ahithophel laughed a dry, mirthless laugh. "You have the whole tribe of Benjamin stirred up like a drove of hornets."

"The men of Benjamin?"

Then he remembered and laughed. "Ah, you have heard of my confrontation with Michal. I hadn't thought the news would travel so fast."

"David, this is serious. Michal is your only real claim to the throne."

David shrugged. "Michal has nothing to do with my claim to the throne. I was chosen by God and anointed with oil by Samuel, just as Saul was."

"There may be more Samuels going around anointing other young boys with oil if the tribe of Benjamin finds there is to be no joint heir to the throne through Michal."

"If there is someone else whom God would anoint in my place, then I am ready to step down and give him the crown."

"My son, you are not crafty enough. Think, just think what it would mean if the tribe of Benjamin should begin to search for the son of Jonathan." Ahithophel rolled his eyes to the ceiling.

David stared at his counselor in amazement. "Ahithophel, is it possible that Jonathan had a son and that he is still alive?"

"It is not only possible but it is a fact. Jonathan had a son. His name is Mephibosheth, and he is crippled. I have him safely hidden away where he should not be a threat to you. However, if the men of Benjamin get angry enough, they could seek him out and try to have him crowned."

To Ahithophel's great discomfort, David threw back his head and laughed. "So you know where the son of Jonathan is right now and could bring him here?"

Ahithophel nodded, his eyes wide with alarm. "Yes, I know where he is, but you must not do this thing. There would be instant trouble."

"If Jonathan had lived, he should have been king, and I would gladly have been his vassal. His son shall be brought to my house and be welcomed at my table for as long as he shall live."

Ahithophel groaned. "Why you want counselors I cannot understand, since you seldom take our advice. Mephibosheth is living with my grandson in the Gilead. I could have him brought to the house of Uriah, but this is not wise, my lord."

"You are right in your way and I am right in mine," David consoled Ahithophel. "I make my decisions trusting in God's goodness, and you advise me to act out of fear. It is as foreign for me to act out of fear as it would be for you to act on faith."

David started to question Ahithophel about the women in the house of Uriah, but he could not find the words to form his questions. The two men parted, and David walked out onto his roof alone.

Once again he looked down at the window across the courtyard from the palace. The shutters were closed. As he wondered about this mysterious woman, his pulse quickened. Had she really been watching him as he entered Urusalim with the Ark? When he had glanced up at her, she had looked right back at him with an openness and, yes, a sense of excitement that stirred him. What was she really like?

The next day Ahithophel sent a runner to Lodebar with the request that Machir bring Mephibosheth secretly to the house of Uriah the Hittite in Urusalim. Ahithophel was convinced that David was being foolhardy. He was always acting with such generosity and so little common sense. "Or perhaps it will work in just the opposite way," he told himself suddenly. "If Mephibosheth were here in David's house, it would be easy to keep track of him and know exactly what he is doing." It was also possible that the tribesmen of Benjamin would be so impressed with David's show of love for Saul's family that they would forget about Michal's unhappiness.

Ahithophel shook his head. There it was again. David had perhaps done the wisest thing even though he had not done it for that reason. *Just the same,* he thought, *someday he will act on this faith of his and will end up in real trouble.*

While Ahithophel was musing in his small office, David was again welcoming Nathan, the prophet, into the pavilion. He was pleased that Nathan had come and assumed that he was interested in plans for the new temple. David pulled out the sheepskin rug with the rough drawing.

Nathan remained standing and spoke quietly in that straight-forward manner that had so won David before. "When you first mentioned building the temple, I felt surely this would be God's will. It seemed so right. But in the night the word of the Lord came to me saying, 'Have I asked that a house be built for Me? When, since I commanded Moses in the wilderness to build Me a Tabernacle, have I asked for a house of cedar to be built? David will not build Me a house, but I will build his house.' "

When David started to reply, Nathan closed his eyes and continued to speak in the manner of the prophets. "And it shall come to pass, when his days be expired and he goes to be with his fathers, I will raise up his seed after him, which shall be of his sons, and I will establish his kingdom. This son shall be a man of rest, and I will give him rest from his enemies round about; for his name shall be Solomon, and I will give peace and quietness unto Israel in his days. He shall build a house for My name and he shall be My son, and I will be his Father and I will establish the throne of his kingdom forever!"

There was a long silence and then David spoke, "What you say is indeed awesome and bewildering to me. I am grateful that God should build my house. But why must I not build a temple to His glory?"

Slowly Nathan relaxed, opened his eyes and looked at David. "God gave Moses definite instructions for the Tabernacle. And He will do the same when His temple is to be built. It must be built by a man of peace, and the son He has promised to you will be a prince of peace."

David shook his head in puzzlement. "I already have many sons. How can it be that a son yet unborn, named Solomon, is to follow me on the throne?"

The two men were silent as they pondered the strange prophecy. Then Nathan spoke, "The message is as strange to me as it is to you. I didn't want to tell you for fear of looking foolish in my lord's eyes. I know well, my king, that you have many sons to follow you on the throne. By all logic my message is most improbable. Of only one thing I am sure: this was the message given me by the God of Israel to deliver to you."

"It is true," David said, "that I am a man of battle who knows nothing of building a great and beautiful temple. It is more fitting that I collect the materials and gather the gold and precious stones that will be needed." He paused thinking. "I will go to the Tabernacle by the Gihon and fall upon my face before the Lord so that I might know His will."

The two men moved swiftly down the dark steps to the stables where donkeys were saddled for them. Together they rode through the city and out the Dung Gate to the Tabernacle beside the Gihon. Quietly Nathan informed the priest there that it was indeed the king who wished to spend the night in prayer before the altar of incense in the holy place. The king embraced Nathan, then turned and followed the priest into the Tabernacle where he knelt alone to keep his vigil before the golden altar of incense.

The priest backed from the small, tented room and left the king alone with the light from the seven-branched candlesticks casting a soft glow on the curtain before the Holy of Holies. The golden table of shewbread glittered in the shadows, and the altar of incense gave off clouds of perfumed smoke that rose to the jewel-like inner covering of the tent. Looking up, David could dimly see above him the wings of the cherubim embroidered in gold. "In the shelter of Thy wings I shall take refuge," he said, "and in Thy presence I will offer my thanksgiving and praise."

3

EARLY ON THE DAY Mephibosheth was to arrive in Urusalim, Ahithophel went to the house of Uriah to check the final arrangements for the king's visit and the evening's festivities. Finding everyone busy, he turned down the long dark hall and went up the stairs to Bathsheba's room.

She was sitting near the window stitching bright threads on dull brown cushion covers. When she jumped up to welcome him, he noticed that she looked thin and pale. He wondered why, after a year and a half, she had not borne a child to Uriah. To cover his uneasiness he laughed. "It seems you have nothing better to do than sit at your window all day. No doubt you even see the king from time to time."

Bathsheba nodded, surprised at how the mention of David sent her pulses racing.

"Would you like to come to the feast and meet him?" Ahithophel sat down beside her but failed to notice her sharp intake of breath at the mention of the king.

"Yes, oh, yes, Grandfather, I would love to come."

"If it would please my little girl I will see that you are invited. I have asked Michal and. . ."

"Could Jessica come too?" Bathsheba interrupted.

218

"If Michal comes, I'm sure Jessica would be with her. However, don't depend on it. David has refused to see Michal since she denounced him before his men for dancing before the Ark wearing only the ephod." Ahithophel always raised his eyebrows when mentioning some scandal or misdemeanor.

"I saw him dancing too, but I was proud of him."

"You were proud of him?" Ahithophel stared in disbelief at his granddaughter.

"You wouldn't understand, Grandfather. It is something I feel but can't explain."

"It is indeed hard to explain. So much emotion over a box that is obviously not holy. If it were holy, how could it have been taken by the Philistines?"

"If it were not holy, why did Uzzah die when he touched it? I'm sure the king thinks it is holy."

"David is always reading some spiritual message into everything. When he was down at Adullam and his men risked their lives to bring him a drink from the family well in Bethlehem, he turned it into a spiritual event. It was foolhardy of his men to risk their lives going through the Philistine guards, but to treat it as a sacrifice to God is ridiculous."

"I can't agree with you, Grandfather. I have never heard of anything more beautiful. To see him riding home smiling and triumphant after a battle you would never suspect he had this gentler side."

Ahithophel snorted. "Posh! You women are all alike. Half the women of Israel are in love with him." He stared out the window down toward the king's palace. "But it is difficult for a king to find love."

"It is difficult for anyone to find love," Bathsheba said looking down at her sewing.

"It is not only in love he has been disappointed. Now it seems he is not to build the temple he had dreamed of. Nathan has brought a word from God that the temple must be built by a man of peace, and David, he says, is a man of war. Such foolishness. I don't believe a word of it. It is perfectly clear that this Nathan does not want the temple built for some private, selfish reason of his own."

Bathsheba was shocked. "Grandfather, God might punish you for speaking this way about His prophets."

When the caravan of Machir arrived and Ahithophel had greeted his grandson properly, he hurried off to notify the king. David listened eagerly as Ahithophel outlined the plans for the evening's meeting with the son of Jonathan, but he was very firm in stating that Michal would have to wait and see her nephew later.

He started to dismiss Ahithophel, then paused. "Will the women of Uriah's house be present this evening?"

"It is possible," Ahithophel replied. "There is only his old mother and my granddaughter. And the servants, of course."

"Your granddaughter? Uriah is married to your granddaughter? Will she be there also?"

"Yes, my lord, she will be there." For a moment he wondered at the king's interest in Bathsheba but quickly forgot as he bowed and left to make final arrangements for the reception.

ImAshtah did not give Bathsheba permission to greet Machir when he arrived but assured her that he would visit her that evening before the reception. Bathsheba was disappointed and frustrated. She yearned to confide in Machir, but she was learning to be cautious and patient. She realized that if Im-Ashtah knew how badly she wanted to see her brother, she would find a way to keep her from seeing him at all.

In the months that had passed, ImAshtah had become more and more hostile toward Bathsheba. She had told Uriah false stories of ways in which his wife had mistreated her while he was away fighting, and Uriah had believed them. Many times he had called Bathsheba to him and berated her for her treatment of his mother. If she tried to defend herself, he accused her of being worthless in that she had not given them either a son or daughter.

ImAshtah had also become more insistent in pressuring Bathsheba to consult one of the priestesses in the Canaanite fertility cult. When Bathsheba refused, ImAshtah herself spent hours with the women who were versed in occult charms. Month after month she had brought Bathsheba to Uriah at the exact hour and moment she felt the charms were most likely to work. But Bathsheba had not become pregnant.

As Bathsheba waited for Machir to arrive she sat dressed for the evening, studying her face in a small, brass mirror. She noted with displeasure that her face was pale, and her eyes were too big. She put the mirror down impatiently. She could not imagine why she cared so much what David would think of her. He might not even notice her.

When at last Sara opened the door to Bathsheba's room and she saw the kind, concerned face of her brother, she ran to him, threw her arms around him and sobbed. Machir was taken aback. He wanted to know what was wrong.

Bathsheba quickly dried her eyes and attempted to smile. She was determined now to reassure him. "How is Noha? And Reba? The servants and the animals?" But as he answered her questions, she became more and more homesick.

When word came that David had arrived with several of his sons and a small band of men, Machir escorted Bathsheba down to the reception hall of the house. Seeing that men from the tribe of Benjamin were standing near a raised dais with Uriah, Machir went to join them while Bathsheba stood with ImAshtah in the dark shadows at the far end of the hall.

Within minutes voices were heard at the outer door, and David's standard bearer appeared followed by several of his captains. Bathsheba watched expectantly as David himself entered the room. In his royal robes of state, jeweled crown, and close cropped beard, he was in striking contrast to the buoyant man who had danced with joy before the Ark of God. He looked relaxed as he took his seat on the raised dais and glanced around the room.

From a nearby room, Mephibosheth was brought forward by his kinsmen. The young man limped badly but made his way to the king and knelt before him. Quickly, David lifted him by his hand to a sitting position beside him and asked him questions which Bathsheba could not hear.

Then to her surprise he called for Machir. "You have been faithful in caring for the son of Jonathan when even I forgot him. You are a man I would like to have here in my court. There is something about you that reminds me of my friend Jonathan."

"You could not pay me a greater compliment," replied Machir. "My father knew Jonathan well. I have always admired him."

The standard bearer whispered in David's ear that Machir was the grandson of Ahithophel, and David immediately summoned Ahithophel. "You are blessed to have such a fine young man as a grandson." Then casually David asked, "Is your granddaughter also here?"

Ahithophel was pleased to be singled out in this way, and he motioned to Bathsheba to come forward. David's face lit up to see the mysterious lady of the window moving out of the deep shadows toward him in a shimmering Egyptian garment of the substance of moonbeams and wearing jeweled ornaments that flashed and sparkled in the dim light. Her dark hair was lustrous, her face even more lovely than he had remembered it, but hauntingly sad.

She did not drop her eyes as most women did in his presence but looked at him as though she already knew him and was interested in him as a person. He reached out his hand to her.

When Bathsheba placed her small, well-shaped hand in his, David impulsively kissed it. She looked startled, then confused, and immediately knelt before him.

When Bathsheba rose David held her hand in his for one brief moment until she looked at him and smiled. Her eyes were shining with pleasure and her mouth curved ever so slightly at the corners. It was as though they shared some wonderful secret unknown to others in the room. She bowed and disappeared again into the shadows.

David quickly turned to Ahithophel to cover his own confusion. "I was moved to so honor your granddaughter because she is the image of all I imagine Rebecca, the bride of our patriarch, Isaac, to have been," he said smiling. The slight tension of the moment was dissolved as everyone laughed.

As the evening wore on, David turned often to Mephibosheth, looking for the response that would have been Jonathan's. Each time the young man seemed too eager to please or too ready to laugh. Mephibosheth did look like Jonathan, and yet, there was nothing in his personality that even slightly resembled the vibrant, warm son of old King Saul.

David rose to leave. He thanked Uriah and reminded Ahithophel that Mephibosheth must be presented at court the next day in a more formal fashion. He paused before turning to go. "You, Mephibosheth," he said, "son of my dear friend, Jonathan, shall eat at my table as long as you live."

After all the guests had left, Ahithophel led Machir off to his own chambers where he was to spend the night. "How ironic, that with Mephibosheth sitting there beside him, David should turn to you and say that you remind him of his friend Jonathan." Ahithophel shook his head in disbelief. "I'm afraid he sees old Saul in all of them."

Machir was silent a moment. Then he asked the question he had been mulling over all evening during the feast. "Grandfather, is Bathsheba unhappy?"

Ahithophel looked surprised. "What makes you ask?"

"She seemed withdrawn and sad as though she wanted to tell me something but then thought better of it."

"She certainly didn't look sad when she was presented to the king."

"That's true," admitted Machir, "and the king was quite impressed with her, too."

"I can assure you I see Bathsheba quite often, and she has everything she could ask for. Uriah has showered her with gold and jewels, and she has no work to do."

"Perhaps I am wrong." Machir hesitated for a moment, then he said good-night to his grandfather.

224

Back in her darkened room, Bathsheba sat looking out the open window at the bright shining stars and the low-hanging moon that cast an almost magical light over the kings palace. Her heart was still fluttering with excitement. She could trace with her finger the very spot on her hand the king's lips had touched. She would never forget how he had looked at her.

Her gaze wandered out toward the palace. Lights flashed along the parapet and there was a soft glow from one of the lower windows. She heard laughter and the soft strumming of a harp. It was easy now to imagine David sitting with his men laughing and singing together.

She sat at her window until lights went out, the laughter faded and the moon disappeared. A cold wind sprang up and banged her shutters closed. Bathsheba felt a sudden chill and pulled her woolen robe close and then lay down among the cushions. She had the strange persistent feeling that something momentous was soon to take place.

4

IT HAD BEEN A full year and a half since the Ark had been brought back to Urusalim and placed in the Tabernacle near the Gihon spring. Once again the people had begun to observe the morning and evening prayers, the Sabbath and the special feasts. With fall came the full moon of the autumnal equinox, and many families in Urusalim looked forward to the fifteenth of Tishri, the Feast of Succot. All of Urusalim was to enter into the celebration in a way that had not been done for years.

In the house of the Hittite, Uriah ordered his servants to build a small Succot booth of palm branches on the roof of his house. It had little or no meaning to ImAshtah other than that it could be seen from the house of David and would prove how devoted Uriah was to the traditions of Israel. Since Uriah had gained a reputation among David's men for his loyalty and devotion to duty, he intended to take all such religious observances seriously.

ImAshtah was nettled by Bathsheba's interest in the booth and her eagerness to be involved in constructing it. "I used to help in making the Succot booth at home in Lodebar," she said. "We would sit in it every evening for a week remembering all the difficulties our ancestors endured as they fled across the Sinai, living in tents and booths much like this."

ImAshtah stiffened. "I'm sure I will feel strange sitting on my own roof pretending to be an Israelite slave fleeing from Pharaoh, but if this is what Uriah wants I will not object." She walked over to the edge of the parapet to see if the booth could be observed from the king's roof. Satisfied that it was in full view, she turned and went down the stairs.

That evening Uriah and his mother were already seated when Bathsheba returned to the roof. They looked uncomfortable and strange sitting under the fringed palm roof decorated with bright gold citrons. "My dear," ImAshtah said, "the evening prayers have been said, and we have been sitting here waiting to eat." Accustomed to ImAshtah's ill temper, Bathsheba sat down next to her mother-in-law, raised her hand and kissed it respectfully. ImAshtah curled her lips in a forced smile and motioned for the food to be served.

All through the meal Uriah's brooding silence

made Bathsheba wonder if there had been bad news. She ate slowly, choking down the foreign food so alien to this feast. Tears came to her eyes as she heard laughter and singing coming to them over the rooftops of the houses around them. She glanced first at ImAshtah and then at Uriah and thought how far they were from any real understanding of this feast.

The silence was broken suddenly by the sound of the gong at the front gate, announcing a visitor. ImAshtah excused herself to answer it leaving Bathsheba alone with Uriah. Uriah hardly looked up. He did not seem to notice that his mother had left. Bathsheba was suddenly very self-conscious. Taking an orange from the silver bowl, she started to peel it for him. He watched her neatly pull off the yellow layers of skin, but when she handed him the orange all spread out in petals, he looked surprised and refused it.

Bathsheba let the orange roll from her hand, glanced at him with genuine puzzlement and asked, "Why do you dislike me so?"

He looked from her to his big hands that were resting on his knees. "I don't dislike you," he said. "If only you would do your duty and have a child . . ."

Bathsheba stared at her husband, stifling the anger that surged inside her. "My lord," she said, "I have kept all of the laws of my people. What more would you have me do than I have done?"

Uriah did not look directly at her but seemed to focus his eyes on some point beyond and over her head. "I do not know the ways of Yahweh with women. Surely you know how to entice Him to do your bidding. Unless it is as my mother says, that He is not concerned with women."

"You are angered that I have not gone with your

mother to the fertility rites on Olivet?"

"This is a matter for you to settle with my mother," Uriah said impatiently. "My mother is right. The God of Israel is a God of battles. He is a God for men and nations. If you want children you must ask the earth goddess."

Bathsheba choked with frustration. She could hear the shouts, laughter, and beating of the drums from the roofs below them, and she felt desperately homesick for her people and the familiar mountains of the Gilead. Silently she stared out into the darkness until ImAshtah returned to the roof.

"Uriah, there is bad news." ImAshtah was twisting the large ring on her first finger nervously. "The messengers sent by King David to congratulate the new king of Rabboth Ammon have come home in disgrace. The Ammonites cut their beards and chopped their robes off to their buttocks. There is talk of war and Joab has sent for you to come."

Uriah was on his feet immediately. Bowing to his mother, he hurried toward the door and then paused and turned to Bathsheba. "Do as my mother advises and you will be with child." He did not wait for an answer but turned and was gone.

ImAshtah ran after Uriah, and Bathsheba was left alone to ponder Uriah's words. She pulled one of the palm fronds to her and ran her fingers along its smooth surface. Uriah's statement that God was concerned with men and their affairs disturbed her. At her home in Lodebar she had been taught to pray and say the blessing. "Is it not Yahweh," she reasoned, "who has given the women of Israel the rituals of the mikvah to cleanse themselves from defilement?"

She could remember as a very small girl going with her mother to the mikvah in Giloh. They always went just at dusk on the twelfth day of her mother's period of uncleanness. Her mother had not gone to bathe physically. She was always careful to wash her hair and bathe before she entered the pool. This was one of the mysteries. Going to the mikvah had nothing to do with the outer cleanliness of the woman but with something far more elusive.

Her grandmother had explained that an unclean woman should not presume to pray, and she should not touch a man during this time or he would become defiled also. Bathsheba dimly remembered hearing the older woman whisper of disasters that had befallen a house where the women had been careless about this. The children were born deformed, and the husbands did not prosper. They had also hinted that such unclean houses were childless or produced only girls, with none to carry on the father's name. Her grandmother had insisted that she had never known a family in Israel that had kept the rituals of the mikvah and was not blessed with children. "God had told Abraham that his descendants would be as numerous as the stars if they kept the covenant," Reba explained. "Our God is not just the God of battle, but He is also the God of a woman's longing."

She looked up at the gently swaying palm fronds and saw the stars so close they almost seemed to be caught in the weaving of the little booth. She felt reassured and strangely comforted. ImAshtah was not right. The God of Israel was a God of all His people, the women as well as the men. She would continue to resist ImAshtah's pressure to bow to the earth goddess.

In the days that followed, every fighting man in Israel gathered in tents out on the hillsides around Urusalim to prepare for the coming battle with

Rabboth Ammon. There were tribesmen from the north and men from the Gilead. Every village was represented with their banners bristling on the hillsides and flapping in the breeze over their goat-hair tents. Spearmen oiled the leather on their shields and polished the brass with wet sand. The bowmen cut new arrows of reed and fitted them with bits of sharpened horn or choice metal, while the left-handed slingers from Benjamin gathered on the wall of the city and practiced shooting at targets in the valley of the Kidron.

Since this battle was to be fought in the mountains of the Gilead where no chariot could find a path, every man who was handy with a sling or bow would be needed. So that Urusalim would not be left defenseless, David left Beniah in charge of his foreign mercenaries—the Cherethites and the Pelethites. But the other cities and villages would have only the old men, young boys, and women to defend them.

Enthusiasm ran high, and when the signal finally came, David and his soldiers marched off in their tribal groups shouting battle cries to each other. When the men of Israel approached Rabboth Ammon, they found the Ammonite army assembled in front of their main gate, while the Syrian mercenaries they had hired were on the hillside to the north of the city. Seeing that there were armies facing him in all directions, Joab, as commander, chose his best swordsmen and his sharpest bowmen to fight against the Syrians. He placed his brother Abishai at the head of the men who would fight the Ammonites closer to the city. "If the Syrians prove too strong," he counseled Abishai, "you must come to my defense, and I and my men will do the same if the children of Ammon prove too strong for you."

Then Joab attacked the Syrians with such strength that they retreated, leaving their dead and dying men to be trampled under the feet of the oncoming swordsmen. When the Ammonites saw that the Syrians had been routed, they fled into their city and barred the gates. The Israelites then returned to Urusalim where great celebrations were held.

Many of the men wanted to return immediately to the gates of Rabboth Ammon and lay siege to the city, but David resisted this. He wished for his mother's sake, who now resided in the city, that there might be peace. Furthermore, the time of year for fighting battles had almost passed. "If we must fight Ammon," David said, "it would be better to wait until the spring."

The war had left scars. When the Syrian armies had swept down from the north, they ravaged Lodebar, stealing food and supplies, butchering sheep, and carrying off firewood. A messenger from Lodebar brought especially sad news to Ahithophel and Bathsheba. "Reba has died," the messenger informed them. "She had not been well, and with the lack of food and warmth, she developed severe pains in her chest, a high fever, and a wracking cough. Her death was sudden but peaceful."

Bathsheba wept, and Ahithophel was prostrate with grief. He thought of the lost years and the separations. "She never lived to see Giloh again," he moaned. Once more his grief hardened into resentment.

The winter was one of the worst that ever swept down upon Urusalim. The days were dark and cold with rain or snow, and most of the people stayed close to their small fires. David's men sat in the common room recalling past triumphs and planning new battles for the spring.

Uriah now spent almost all of his time with Joab and his men, much preferring them to the company of the women in his house. These days his mother was constantly urging him to divorce Bathsheba and take another wife who would respect the old fertility rites. Uriah was reluctant to divorce Bathsheba lest he lose the close relationship he enjoyed with both Ahithophel and Joab.

Such was the situation in the house of Uriah when spring came and it was time for the army to march against Rabboth Ammon once more. ImAshtah grew desperate. She pleaded with Uriah to force his wife either to worship at the shrine of the goddess with a young pig or at least to keep the small image of the goddess in her mattress.

Bathsheba was summoned to Uriah's room late one afternoon. As she entered, Bathsheba noticed the torches were lit, but the old woman of the bath was nowhere in sight. She was alone with Uriah.

He stood before the dark curtains of the bed holding in his hand a small silver image of the goddess Astarte. "My wife," he began, in his usual impersonal and serious vein, "there is a duty which a wife owes her husband. Do you agree?"

"Yes, my lord," Bathsheba replied wearily. "I have told you, and I have told ImAshtah, that I will do whatever you desire. But I cannot go to the grove of Astarte, nor will I have her likeness in my room."

Uriah stood looking at her, clenching and unclenching the hand that held the small silver likeness of the goddess. His eyes grew hard and pinched, and as a consequence his nose seemed to grow larger while his scar became a dark, fiery red.

There was a shuffling sound outside the door. Suddenly, without warning, it was flung open and ImAshtah swept into the room and stood beside Uriah. "Surely the women of Israel wish to please their husbands," she said to Bathsheba. "It is a disgrace among any people for a woman to be barren. Therefore, I have arranged for you to visit the mother goddess of our people in the grove on Olivet. A small pig killed at the right time, with the right charms intoned and its flesh eaten, will always bring a man child."

Bathsheba shrank in horror from the idea of sacrificing an unclean animal such as a pig before a pagan idol, and the thought of eating the meat was as repulsive to her as if she had been told to eat the flesh of a human. ImAshtah had threatened this many times during the four years Bathsheba had been married to Uriah but had not pressed it further because of the difficulty in obtaining a pig.

"Your mother does not understand, but you know our religious customs." Bathsheba's eyes flashed angrily at her husband. "It is unlawful for a woman of Israel to worship any god or goddess but the one true God, and to eat the flesh of a pig is forbidden by our law."

Uriah clenched and unclenched his fists in frustration. "By the gods, woman, it is also your duty to give me a son."

Bathsheba had always accepted the blame for her barrenness as justified, but now she voiced the question that always lingered in her mind unanswered. "There have been wives before me in this house, and they were all barren. Does this not seem strange to you?"

ImAshtah's face twisted with fury while Uriah drew himself up with indignation. "You have tried your own way long enough. Now take this image to your room and see if it will not bring forth the son we all desire."

Bathsheba held her hands behind her back and edged toward the door. "It is no use. I am a daughter of Israel, and even if I should kneel to the Hittite goddess and kiss her feet, I would only be forced to repent of it when I said my prayers."

Uriah moved angrily toward Bathsheba, holding out the small silver goddess. "It is just a simple thing . . ." He clenched his fist so tight the silver head of the small statue broke from the body and rolled out upon the floor toward Bathsheba.

ImAshtah gasped at the evil omen. "Go! Go to your room before you bring more bad luck upon us," she cried. "There will be no more ritual baths at your mikvah until you learn to respect the gods and goddesses of our people too."

Bathsheba opened the door and fled down the long hall. Back in her room she realized that she was shaking all over, and her teeth were chattering. She did not light the lamp but sank down on her mat in the darkness, overwhelmed by despair.

A loud pounding at the front gate woke her. It was dark outside. She threw open her shutters and leaned out. There below her in the courtyard, the bright moonlight revealed Uriah dressed for the battle against Rabboth Ammon, walking toward the guardhouse of the king's men.

If Uriah does not come back, she thought, *he will be without a son to carry on his name.* She could still hear the words ImAshtah had flung at her so often. "It will be on your head forever if the house of Uriah has no heir."

The shophar was blown, the sacrifices made, and finally, chanting and singing, the army of Israel marched out behind the Ark of the Lord to fight the Ammonites. Without saying good-by to her, Uriah

234

marched with the men of Israel out over the Mount of Olivet to whatever fate awaited him before the gates of Rabboth Ammon.

It was the month of Tammuz, and the days were hot with the terrible, oppressive heat that comes with the khamsin. The wind blew off the southern desert like the blast from a baker's furnace and the people of Urusalim sat indoors waiting for the evening when they could hope to catch a cool breeze from the sea on the roofs of their houses. ImAshtah felt it beneath her dignity to sit on the roof "like a common peasant," so she spent the days in her room with one of the servants fanning her with peacock feathers.

On the fifth evening of the terrible heat and the twelfth evening of her uncleanness, Bathsheba knocked on ImAshtah's door as she always did and asked permission to go to the mikvah to perform the rites of purification. ImAshtah laughed at her scornfully. "Your husband is not at home, and so the ritual is not necessary. Besides I have decided that until you go to the high place of Astarte, there will be no more trips to the mikvah to carry out the rituals of your people."

"But my lady," Bathsheba said. "I must go or all that I touch will be defiled. Nor can I pray until I have been cleansed."

"I'm sure," ImAshtah said, smirking at Bathsheba's seriousness, "the God of Israel does not concern Himself with either a woman's washing or her prayers." With that she waved off further conversation.

Frustrated, Bathsheba went back to her room pondering what she should do. Without ImAshtah's permission she could not leave the house nor could she see any way to carry out the ritual cleansing inside the house. The water must be pure: either rain water or water from a spring.

An idea came. "Sara," she called, "run to the roof and see if there is still rain water in the large basins used by the women who wash the linens. If there is, I will bathe there and you will help me."

When Sara returned to report the rainwater was available, Bathsheba handed Sara the alabaster bowl from her small bath and filled it with ointments, towels, and combs. Then Bathsheba gathered up the linens from her pallet, which also would have to be washed, and followed Sara to the roof.

The moon was rising over Olivet full and bright, but there was no breeze and the air was still and oppressive. Sara has set the bowl down in the shelter of the Succot booth that was still standing on the far side of the roof. Bathsheba noticed that many of its palm fronds were missing, and those that remained were dry and brittle.

Bathsheba ran her fingers down the spine of one of the palm branches watching the dry fronds fall to the floor. "It isn't much shelter from prying eyes," she said, looking up at the roof of the palace that rose behind her, dark and silent in the evening shadows.

"The king must be gone with his men to battle," said Sara pouring water into the bowl and arranging the toilet articles on a clean piece of linen.

"I'll not worry about it," Bathsheba replied, untying her sash and lifting her dress over her head, leaving nothing but the linen shift to cover her. "Let's wash my hair first." When Sara finished rubbing salt into her wet hair and rinsing it with lemon, Bathsheba pulled off her shift and stepped into the alabaster bowl Sara had filled with fresh water.

She stood naked in the bowl and let Sara pour

the fresh water over her and scrub her vigorously with the interior of a wiry goard. "That hurts," Bathsheba said with a grimace and flipped water at her maid from the water jar until the two of them were overcome with laughter.

The sound of a small object hitting the stone roadway below startled them. Bathsheba grabbed the linen towel and wrapped it quickly around her while Sara ran over to the edge of the parapet and looked out toward the king's house. All was dark and quiet just as it had been all evening. Bathsheba shrugged and sat down on the small ivory-inlaid stool and began to rub fragrant oil into her skin while Sara combed her hair.

"You can leave now, Sara," Bathsheba said. "I will carry out the purification by myself."

Sara hesitated. "But you are clean."

"Sara," Bathsheba said, searching for the right words, "uncleanness before God is not just dust or dirt that water can wash away, but it is a matter of God's command and the intent of the heart." Sara still looked puzzled as she backed away and walked down the stairs to fix Bathsheba's pallet with new linen.

David had not gone with his fighting men to Rabboth Ammon. Months before he had promised Joab that the city should be his to conquer, and Joab had held him to his promise.

As the days went by David regretted his decision. He became restless without his captains and their daily counsel. When he imagined all that was taking place before the gates of Rabboth Ammon, he became discontented. Even the thought of flies, heat, and poor food could not spoil the adventurous picture in his mind of men prepared for battle, standing together before the gates of the City of Waters.

He missed the excitement and planning. Worst of all, when the men would sit around the fires next winter, telling of their battles, he could have little part in it.

On this particular evening David could get no relief from the heat of the khamsin winds, and so he walked about his palace roof in the darkness. He had no reason to light the torches; they would only create more heat. Finally in total boredom, he strode into his curtained pavilion and flung himself down on the lion skins.

Gradually there drifted in on the night air the sound of women merrily laughing. Intrigued, he rose, went out through the curtains into the moonlit night and looked down onto the roof of Uriah the Hittite. He was instantly alert. There in the partial concealment of the Succot booth was his beautiful maiden of the window. She was standing in an alabaster bowl of water while a servant dipped water with a gourd and poured it over her. Bathsheba stood without embarrassment even though she had nothing to cover her nakedness.

Ordinarily he would have turned away, but it was all so unexpected and lovely that he continued to watch. With growing admiration he studied her loveliness as only half seen through the dried palm branches. Her hair clung in damp curls to her full breasts, and her tiny waist accentuated the pleasing roundness of her hips. He saw her reach down into the brass jar, cup water in her hand and flip it at the servant girl, making both of them laugh.

As he watched she stepped out of the bowl and tossed her hair back making the curve of her back visible. He thought he had never seen anything so beautiful or so graceful in his life.

Leaning over to get a better look he dislodged a small stone which fell with a dull thud in the courtyard below. He moved back quickly as Bathsheba looked up startled and reached for a large towel to cover herself. When he looked again the serving girl was gone and the maid stood pouring water over her hands and feet. After she repeated it for the third time, he knew she was carrying out the purification ritual of the women of Israel. He watched transfixed as she let the water slowly pour from a wide-mouthed jar down over her head and shoulders. For a moment she stood out from the shelter of the booth with her hands upraised in the bright moonlight, and then she lowered them, obviously saying the words of blessing that were as old as his people.

Impulsively he turned and went down to the guardroom and woke the guard. The man rubbed his eyes and jumped up to stand at attention. "Do you know of the young woman in the house of the Hittite?" David asked.

"She is the wife of Uriah, the daughter of Emmiel, son of Ahithophel."

"Go, bring her to me. I have news that I dare not entrust to another." He hesitated and then added crisply. "I will see her in the pavilion on the roof. Go quickly and see that I am not disturbed while she is here."

David turned and walked from the guardroom astonished at what he had done. He was also excited that at last he would be alone with this woman who had haunted his dreams for so many months. Maybe it would amount to nothing. Probably she would be disappointing. But instinct beyond reason told him that this would be no casual meeting and that he would not be disappointed.

5

"HURRY, SARA, and see who it is at the front gate," Bathsheba urged. "If they bring news of Uriah, listen carefully for the details and then come tell me."

Sara arrived at the door just as ImAshtah was admitting the king's guard. "They are asking for Bathsheba," she sniffed. "Bring her here and be quick about it." Sara rushed back up the stairs and returned with Bathsheba, round-eyed and astonished that she should be called by the king's guard.

"Bathsheba," ImAshtah said, "it seems the king has sent for you. At first I thought they had come with news of Uriah, and I insisted on going myself, but it seems the king wishes to see you about something quite personal." Here she stopped and looked sharply at Bathsheba.

"I did not know the king was here in Urusalim," Bathsheba replied.

"He is here and he has asked to see you alone!"

Bathsheba pulled her robe tight against the dampness. "I am honored by the king's invitation," she said. "However, I must beg a few moments to change into something more suitable."

The guard's eyes were frank and flattering. "If it is necessary," he said. "I will wait with my men here in the courtyard."

With a start ImAshtah realized that for whatever reason Bathsheba was going to the palace, she must be dressed in such a manner as to bring honor to the house of Uriah. "There is no time to spare," she instructed the servants. "Do something with her hair, paint her eyes, dress her in one of the gowns from Phoenicia, and I will bring the family jewels for her to wear."

Bathsheba was hurried to ImAshtah's rooms where chests were opened and garments spread out around the room. The hairdresser followed her about twisting and rolling her long dark hair into the most fashionable style. Then ImAshtah came from the storeroom with two servants who were carrying boxes of gold and silver jewelry. Pushing aside the gaudy, more fashionable jewelry, Bathsheba selected several pieces of older, more elegant craftsmanship. She chose a simple gown of soft, woven material, and then with a quick shake of her head and flying fingers she let down her rich, dark hair, undoing all the careful work of the hairdresser. "Now," she said, "find me a simple headpiece."

Soon they came up with one that suited her, plus a sparkling gold necklace of delicate design. She let them slip beaded sandals on her feet and then quickly caught up her fragile mantle and hurried out the door and down the steps to where the guards were waiting at the gate.

Her heart was pounding with excitement as she realized that within moments she would be ushered into the king's chambers. There was a moment of anxiety when it occurred to her that the reason she was being called to the palace might be that Ahithophel had become suddenly ill. This fear was dispelled when she met Ahithophel at the foot of the stairs leading to the palace roof. He called her to one side and commanded the guards to wait.

"My dear," he said looking down at her approvingly, "do you know where you are going and why?"

"No, Grandfather," she said, searching his face. "I only know the king has summoned me here."

"My sweet, innocent child." Ahithophel's eyes grew pinched and crafty as he leaned toward her. "Lead him on until you see his intention. Be coy, but give him nothing of yourself. That could come later—but in the proper way and at the right time."

Noticing that the guards were impatient, Bathsheba decided not to question Ahithophel as to what he meant. She simply kissed him dutifully and then turned to follow the guards up the stairs.

Coming out onto the roof, Bathsheba was surprised to find it lined with flickering oil lamps which cast enormous shadows and outlined the flowers and small trees around the edge of the parapet. In the center she saw the pavilion covered with the finest, purple-dyed linen through which she saw the soft glimmer of newly lit lamps and smelled the sweet odor of amber being burned as incense. David was obviously at home. Forgetting the guards, she walked to the parapet to see if her roof could be seen from that point. To her astonishment, it lay below her with every corner clearly visible in the moonlight. *Is it possible,* she wondered, *that the king was here all the time, only in the dark? Could he have seen me bathing?*

"Don't worry about it!"

Bathsheba swung around to see that the guards had departed, and she was standing before the king. And he had been reading her thoughts! Overwhelmed at being alone with this man she had envisioned in her dreams so often, she reached behind her for the steadying coolness of the stones of the parapet.

She was totally aware of him: the tunic that showed to full advantage his muscular arms and legs; the thick, gold armbands outlined in rubies; his short cropped hair; the fringe of a well-trimmed beard and the strong, browned hand that held a goblet so carelessly. He stepped toward her and there floated from his person the fragrance of fresh, outdoor hillsides covered with herbs. He smiled, and mirrored in his eyes was the same reckless joy she had admired at a distance.

"I thought you were with the soldiers at Rabboth Ammon," she said hesitantly.

He laughed a happy, boyish laugh and almost spilled the contents of the goblet. "No, I didn't go. Joab considers me too old for battle and has insisted I stay at home. I shouldn't let him manage me this way." He smiled down at her as though he liked very much what he saw. "I'm not too old to fight nor am I too old to admire a pretty woman when I see one."

Bathsheba had regained some of her composure. "I suppose you have called me here to discuss some matter concerning my husband or my grandfather."

"No," he replied, looking down at his drink as though seeking to draw the right words from its depths. "No, this is not a night for matters of state and official business." He looked at her again, and his eyes grew warm with approval. "Come, this is far too public. I have some figs and light wine which I think you will enjoy."

As he led the way into the pavilion Bathsheba was entranced by the richly decorated interior with its red carpets and wild animal skins glowing in the soft light. A couch piled with cushions circled the outer wall of the room while a large raised dais opposite the doorway was obviously reserved for David. It was covered with skins. The lions' heads were stuffed and placed so that their open mouths with bared teeth were actually frightening. Small wisps of incense floated from a tall brass burner. A flickering light was cast over the dais from a hanging oil lamp.

He motioned for her to sit on a velvet mat among brightly colored cushions and served her personally from a tray of fruit and small cakes. He sat down beside her, resting his arm carelessly on the side of the cushion between them. "Now to answer your question as to why I sent for you." Again there was the boyish smile. "I was bored and unhappy, and I had written a song that I wanted someone to hear." Seeing approval in her eyes, he reached for his harp.

The notes from the strings were sharp and distinct . "My men were all gone," he said, bending his head toward the strings. "Only the servants and the older tribesmen stayed at home. Then I heard laughter." He smiled and glanced up at her. "And when I went to investigate, I saw a lovely maiden . . ." He strummed insistently and the chords vibrated with feeling. Bathsheba felt the color rise in her face, and her hands grew moist. But when she dared to meet his steady gaze, she was surprised to find only a warm, amused friendliness.

She relaxed and smiled when David shifted to a lively folk song. He ended the song half humming and singing the words and then he threw back his head and laughed. He put his harp down and leaned toward her. "That's not the whole truth," he said. "I did write a song, and I did want to share it, but most of all I was eager to meet you."

Bathsheba liked his unaffected honesty. Her mouth parted into an amused smile. "I didn't think a king would ever be lonely."

He was silent and serious then, studying her face and letting his eyes take in the curls that edged out from her headpiece and the tilt of her chin, then back to her eyes. "You would have been right a few years ago. I was an outcast, running from Saul, eating berries as I found them, and living on the

244

back side of the desert. I never knew when to expect an attack, but for all of it I was never lonely or bored."

As she pondered the strange paradox, Bathsheba noted the firm line of his jaw, the mouth that was both sensual and strong, and eyes that could be tender or flashing with emotion. When he smiled at her, Bathsheba saw again the man who had danced so exuberantly before the Ark of the Lord.

Impulsively she reached out and touched the curved edge of his harp. "Will you sing your song for me? I will feel so honored to be the first to hear it."

David put his hand over hers on the harp, and she drew it back quickly; astonished at the rush of feeling that flowed out toward him from even such a casual touch. He flashed her a look of tenderness as he picked up the harp and began to strum idly. Slowly he became absorbed in the music of the harp as he made it fairly weep with lonesome, minor chords. Gradually the music grew soft, then sad as finally he began to sing:

My days are consumed like smoke,
My bones are burned as an hearth,
My heart is smitten and withered like the grass
So that I forget to eat my bread.

He strummed as though trying to remember the words and then began to sing again:

I am like a pelican in the wilderness,
I am like an owl in the desert;
I watch, and am as a sparrow alone on the house-
    top. . .

He hummed for several moments, ending with the words,

And I am withered like grass.

As suddenly as he had started to play, he stopped. "That's the way I felt before you came. I don't feel like that anymore, and I don't even want to remember it."

"A sparrow alone on the housetop." Bathsheba was still remembering the song. "I have felt that way. Perhaps not like a sparrow on the housetop but a sparrow caught in a cage."

"I wouldn't blame any man for putting you in a cage. You're beautiful, completely beautiful."

"I'm not in the cage because I'm supposed to be so beautiful," she said hesitantly. "I'm in the cage because I'm not willing to do my duty."

"What duty could such a lovely flower have but to be loved and enjoyed?" He was not smiling, and Bathsheba was more moved by his seriousness than when he had briefly touched her hand.

"My duty?" she said, trying to stifle her emotion. "It is my duty to have a child, and I have not had one."

"And how are you supposed to have this child when I have been told your husband is here with my men in the guardroom nearly every night he is in Urusalim?"

She was startled that he knew so much. She was even more disturbed that the conversation had become personal. "We should not be talking of these things," she said looking away from his eyes to the swinging incense burner. "I have already told you too much."

"You have told me nothing that I did not already know." There was silence between them, not a

246

tense silence, but one of complete understanding. "I have often noticed you sitting in your window. You seemed remote and mysterious, and I wondered about you."

"And I've always watched for you," she confessed. "I have seen you riding home from battle, talking with your men in the courtyard or dancing before the Ark."

"Aha! So you did see me that time. Were you disappointed in me?"

"I thought it was wonderful. I like to see people doing things impulsively. My grandfather never does anything impulsively. I have a bit of Grandfather's blood in my veins, but every once in a while I do something completely foolish for no reason at all . . . like . . . " She stopped.

David enjoyed her confusion. "It's amazing how you have changed my whole attitude in one short evening. I find myself now thinking how lucky I am not to be with my men looking up at those dark walls of Rabboth Ammon. I feel now that I should reward Joab for insisting that I stay here."

"I've heard often how much Joab and all of your men love you. You must never feel lonely with such friends."

"Perhaps I am like the nightingale. Everyone loves the nightingale too, but that doesn't mean they understand him or his needs or even want him around unless it's during the few moments after sunset when he is singing his sweetest song."

David laughed a bit ruefully, then played several more songs on his harp. They talked about the joy and sadness of music and how it communicates the deepest emotions. On sudden impulse he moved the cushion from between them and laid his head in her lap. He smiled at her embarrassment. "Does this frighten you? You act as startled as the

247

time I kissed your hand the day I came to your home to meet Mephibosheth."

"I wasn't really startled," Bathsheba explained, trying to regain her composure despite her fluttering heart. "It was something else. Something I don't quite understand."

He reached up and tenderly ran his finger around the outline of her face. "You were confused and surprised at feelings you thought you didn't even possess. You are a passionate woman, Bathsheba. It surprised you to find this quality awakening within you."

She knew he was right and scarcely dared look into his eyes lest he know all her thoughts. He understood her, and she found herself flooded with love for him. Slowly she lowered her eyes to look at him and found she could not turn away. Gently, David reached up and pulled her down to him and kissed her.

His kiss released a frozen, silent spring within her. Suddenly she was filled with an ecstatic joy she had not known was possible. All the love she had felt for him since the first time she had seen him riding home from battle flooded up and around her. It was a wild, uncontrollable love, and for one dizzy moment she wanted to give herself to him in total abandon as his eyes were asking her to do.

Then she pushed him from her, covered her face with her hands and jumped up. "I must go," she said. "It is late and they will be wondering where I am."

David rose and pulled her to him with gentle words of endearment that melted her resolve.

"My lord, David," she said impulsively calling him by his familiar name. "I want to do what is right even though my whole being pulls me in the opposite direction." There was silence between them, but their emotion flowed back and forth, questioning and answering feelings too deep for words.

"Your grandfather, Ahithophel, has reminded me many times that I am king, and whatever I do is right," David said quietly. "Whatever I want is right, he told me. I love you, Bathsheba, and all I want to do is show you how much I love you. Can this be so wrong?"

Bathsheba drew away from him and bit her lip to keep back the tears. "Grandfather also believes that no one does what is right if it is not to their advantage. He says that everyone, if they are really tempted, will do just what they want to do no matter what God's law says."

"Bathsheba, what are you trying to tell me?"

"It is simply that what we want to do is wrong. We are doing just as Grandfather says everyone does. I want to be different. I want to do what is right."

David stared at her, amazed but deeply moved. "We may never meet again as we are tonight. I will see you in the window again as remote and unattainable as the evening star, and you will see me with my men or hear the strains of my harp drifting over the wall, but this moment is not likely to come again for either of us."

All of Bathsheba's fine resolve began to crumble. "It is not that I feel any loyalty to Uriah or to his family," she said. "It is something else. It is almost as though there is something buried down under everything else inside me that tells me if I stay, I will be doing something very wrong."

David stood looking at her with admiration and love, but he did not move to hold her again. "I am sure I will never spend another night such as this nor will I ever again desire a woman as I desire you. But it is for you to choose. I will not hold you here against your will."

Bathsheba did not answer him. She knew that she should bow and kiss his hand and beg to leave, as it was late. But still she lingered. She tried to remember what Ahithophel had told her on the stairs; she visualized the anger of ImAshtah and Uriah; she tried to recall the wording of God's law against coveting and adultery. She built up walls of resistance only to feel them crumble. With trembling fingers she smoothed her hair and straightened her gown. She could not dismiss the thought that she would soon be back in the dark, lonely house of the Hittite, back to the harsh words of ImAshtah and the indifference of Uriah.

Slowly she turned and looked at him with all the pent-up longing of her loveless existence. Then calmly she held out her hand and without further hesitation walked the few steps to where David stood. "I seem to have forgotten all my fine resolve," she said.

David took her hand but did not move toward her. He stood looking at her, searching her eyes to read in them her true feelings. He let her small hand lie in his larger one and still he did not move to draw her to him. "Are you sure that this is what you want?" he asked, his voice breaking with emotion.

Bathsheba did not answer but let her eyes move from the wavy strands of hair down to the well-trimmed beard and up to his mouth. His face was now familiar and each portion was a new discovery of perfection. The air was fragrant with the odor of spikenard and rich ointment that surrounded him.

She raised her eyes to meet his and nodded, watching the flame behind his eyes ignite and feeling his strong arms come around her as he pulled her to him and kissed her, gently at first, then passionately. All reasoning and rationalizing was forgot-

250

ten as he picked her up and carried her to his couch.

It was almost dawn before they faced the reality that they must find the way back into their regular routines alone. As they stood inside the door of the tent, David drew her tenderly to him one last time. He could not endure the thought that Bathsheba must go alone to face whatever difficulty lay before her in the house of Uriah and that he had no way to protect her. She seemed to him so fragile and so brave. She had not said a word about the problems of returning to her mother-in-law at this hour of the morning. He searched his mind for some solution to this.

He held her close and bent his head until his cheek touched her hair. "My most dear love," he said, "when you are alone in the house of Uriah you will have much to ponder. I can give you only one thing to carry with you as a shield against whatever you must face because of this night. Look at me, so you will know it with your heart and will not doubt that it is true."

He released her and tilted her chin gently until he was able to search out all the love and sadness that were mixed equally within her eyes. "Remember, I love you. I have never in my life loved anyone or anything as I love you. This was not lust. I have known lust many times, but never before have I known love. I love you with every part of my being, and I would gladly renounce my throne and all that I own if I could save you one small bit of unhappiness."

Gradually he could see a warm, vibrant glow of love replace the sadness in her eyes.

"Don't worry about me," she said. "I am grateful for the treasure of your love."

David summoned the guard. As he watched Bathsheba walk down the stairs, he felt a terrible loneliness descend upon him. Some powerful and unknown depths within him had been stirred, and he knew that he would spend both night and day, for however long it took, finding a way to see her again.

Bathsheba met no one on her way out of the palace except a young man whom she recognized as David's son, Amnon. She did not wonder at the time what he was doing up so early, but she was to think a great deal about it in the years that followed.

As she came to the door leading out into the court, she paused to prepare herself for the encounter with ImAshtah. There was no escape. ImAshtah would demand to know what had kept her at the palace all night. ImAshtah would not be the only one curious about her visit to the king. Ahithophel, too, would not rest until he knew just what had taken place between his granddaughter and the king.

6

WHEN THE GUARD pounded on the outer gate of Uriah's house, Bathsheba could hear voices and running feet as though everyone inside had been awake and waiting for this moment. She pulled her mantle tightly around her and steeled herself for the encounter with ImAshtah. The gate swung open, revealing her mother-in-law, stern and contemptuous, standing in the early morning light. Behind her were the servants and maids, half hidden in the darkness, all waiting to see what would happen when the wife of Uriah returned home from the palace.

Bathsheba did not flinch before ImAshtah's gaze. After a long penetrating look, ImAshtah turned and signaled her to follow. As Bathsheba walked through the dark halls and up the stairway, the house seemed darker and more depressing than ever. The room they entered smelled of stale incense and smoke mingled with mildew. There were seeds in one large bowl and numerous empty brass cups. ImAshtah's sleeping mat was rumpled, but her gown lay spread out on the cushions as the maid had left it the night before.

As soon as the door was shut, ImAshtah faced Bathsheba angrily and spat out the words, "I want to know exactly what you have been doing all this time at the king's palace. Mind you, I can guess what happened but I want you to tell me."

"I'm sorry, ImAshtah. I can see that I have worried you, and I am truly sorry."

"Sorry is not enough. I have a right to know just what you have been doing."

"I can only say that I am truly sorry to have caused you so much trouble."

ImAshtah hesitated then lowered her voice. "I have sent for Ahithophel. I'm sure he will know how to get the truth out of you. I understand that your God does not approve of even a king's flirtation with another man's wife. What have you to say about that?"

Bathsheba winced at the accusation and was about to answer when voices were heard in the hall. Without introduction, Ahithophel appeared in the doorway, looking calm and confident.

"Your lordship," ImAshtah said, "are you aware that your granddaughter has been in the house of the king all night? I'm sure, even among your people, that this is a little unusual."

To Bathsheba's surprise, Ahithophel patted her shoulder affectionately and spoke reassuringly to ImAshtah. "I know all about this situation. I met my granddaughter as she went to see the king. We discussed the possibilities, and I advised her. She has always taken my advice, and I see no reason to doubt that she has done that now."

"But, your lordship: all night! What could she have done that was honorable all night in the king's house?"

"Oh, I have no doubt that the king may have had questionable intentions, but my granddaughter has the wisdom of her old grandfather. I assure you, nothing has happened that should upset either you or Uriah."

"Well, you may be taken in by all of this, but I am not. Sooner or later I expect to have the facts to prove you wrong." ImAshtah glared at them both and then turned and walked from the room.

Seeing that Bathsheba was so upset, Ahithophel did not press for details of her visit with David. He simply spoke comfortingly and led her to her room. He called Sara to help Bathsheba to her bed, promising he would return later.

Ahithophel went back to his quarters less assured than he had appeared to be before ImAshtah. Was there any chance, he wondered, that Bathsheba had not taken his advice? It was obvious that she had not been home all night. He wiped the sweat from his brow. ImAshtah was making terrible accusations, and he had to admit the facts were most awkward.

Finally he tried to dismiss the whole episode with a shrug. "After all," he reasoned, "Bathsheba has not been pregnant in these four years that she has been Uriah's wife. At least that is one thing I do not have to worry about." Yet from time to time he would pause, finding himself again anxious about his granddaughter and with a growing resentment of David that he would put her in such a position.

Two months passed with ImAshtah continually suspicious and vindictive. Over and over again she tried to get Bathsheba to confess to the actual nature of her visit to the king's palace, but Bathsheba would neither deny nor affirm anything. This left ImAshtah more suspicious than ever.

When Bathsheba passed the week of her confinement with none of the usual signs, ImAshtah commented about this darkly. Since Bathsheba considered herself incapable of bearing a child, she thought very little of it at first. However, when the second month went by without the usual signs, she was puzzled and uneasy.

Late one afternoon Bathsheba was sitting by her window tying sweet herbs into a chain when the full realization came to her. She must be pregnant! She dropped the herbs and sat trying to comprehend what it all meant. After years of feeling that she was barren and suddenly to know that she was pregnant caused a wave of joy to flood through her. All the pain and anguish she had suffered in this house, all the guilt she had been made to feel, all the times she had been degraded because she had not borne a child were lifted from her. She was not barren. The fault lay with Uriah, or the will of God, but it was not her guilt.

Her joy was only short-lived, for almost immediately she realized that though rid of one guilt, she would be burdened with another and far more serious one. ImAshtah already suspected the truth. Her anger would be terrible when her suspicions were confirmed. Even Ahithophel, who believed so strongly that she had taken his advice, would be terribly hurt and ashamed before his friends.

When she thought of Ahithophel and his great pride, the immensity of the situation almost overwhelmed her. She would be branded an adulteress by ImAshtah, and as an adulteress she might be stoned. The greatest fear of every father and mother in Israel was that a daughter would bring disgrace upon the family. Fathers and mothers had been known to weep at the birth of a daughter out of fear for what the future might hold for her and members of her family. If her womb was barren she would be considered as a piece of land that lay eternally fallow. But if she chose to grow wild weeds planted by the passing wind, only total destruction could blot out such evil.

Other sins could be forgiven with offerings of a sheep or a lamb, but this sin had no remedy. The law clearly stated that offenders should be taken outside the city gate and stoned until they were dead. In practice it was more often only the woman who was stoned. It was as though the woman herself was evil, and so her seed would be evil. Both must be destroyed or they would corrupt everyone around them.

Bathsheba had always known and accepted this law as proper, but never until this moment had she thought she was evil. For the first time she began to see herself as all of her friends and relatives would now see her. Some of them would draw back in disgust, others who had loved her would be hurt. All that had seemed so beautiful while she was with David, now viewed through the eyes of her friends and relatives, was loathsome and disgraceful. If she had merely visited David's pavilion she would have been the envy of all the women of Urusalim. Now that she was with child she would reap their scorn.

Unable to sit still any longer, she got up and walked back and forth across the little room, torn with anguish and despair. She thought of Ahithophel. How greatly would his bitterness toward God and life be multiplied by this disgrace. Then there was the innocent, unformed child she carried who would be cut off from life if she were stoned. She felt a special tender bond with this unborn little one who shared her destiny so completely.

And David. Her heart constricted with a strange new pain at the thought of David being singled out as the man guilty of this sin. How his enemies would rejoice. They would say that while Uriah was risking his life for his king and his country at Rabboth Ammon, David had been home, in safety, seducing Uriah's wife. They would forget all their love for him and would turn on him with even more vengeance because he had been their king and spiritual leader.

Ahithophel had loved David, but only the perfect David. Now if he should find a flaw, he would be doubly disillusioned.

Vividly she remembered her grandfather standing in the house of Saul at Mahanaim years ago, eyes wild and bloodshot, commanding his grandchildren to be a credit to their dead father. Eventually, because he loved her, he would excuse the wrong she'd done. But he would do all within his power to discredit David and make him solely responsible. She could see it all now: if something were not done quickly he would place the blame on David and not rest until he got his full revenge.

Bathsheba buried her face in her hands and sank down onto the mat, but she did not cry. All fear for herself was gone, even her despair over Ahithophel was nothing compared to the concern she now felt for David. Somehow, he must be warned. He must at least know the danger he was in and not ride blindly into the trap his enemies would set for him the moment they knew the truth.

Sending David a warning message was essential. But how? There was no one in the house she could trust to deliver it. All of the servants reported to ImAshtah and such a message would be sure to reach ImAshtah before it did the king. If she sent a parchment, it, too, would be read by every curious official and guard on the way.

She walked back and forth across the small room, her thoughts flying from one possibility to another. One by one she abandoned them as either being too risky or too impossible. If she were to warn the king it must be by some plan so daring and so bold that no one would be suspicious.

Since Bathsheba had been given access to Uriah's library, she closed the shutters of her room, took the lamp from the stand and sped quickly down the dark steps to the ground floor where the scriptorium was located, hoping she would not meet Sara or ImAshtah in the hall.

She arrived at the scriptorium undetected and found the Hittite scribe, old Tabash, reading at the desk beneath a flickering oil lamp. Bathsheba quickly formulated a plan. "The king wishes to know more of the noble past of the Hittite nation and has asked that a scroll be sent to him," she told the scribe.

The old man smiled a toothless smile as she came into the light and he saw that it was the young wife of his master. "I have many scrolls but perhaps something simple would be best."

He got to his feet with great effort and raised his lamp to illumine the dark corners of the room that seemed a jumble of jars holding minor scrolls and great brass and gold cases for the more elaborate works. He shuffled among them, dripping oil from his lamp and muttering titles as he searched.

Bathsheba fumbled among the rough ends of parchment that had been discarded on his bench, selected one, and while his back was turned, wrote with his brush the words, "I am with child." It was a small piece no bigger than her hand and she held it hidden until the old man returned triumphant with a scroll and unrolled it on the desk.

"Yes, yes," she said. "It is too precious to be sent with one of the guards. I would be grateful if you would deliver it yourself and insist that it be given to the king when he is alone."

While his attention was elsewhere she slipped the bit of parchment into the scroll and rolled it back upon its spindle, tying the leather thongs around it securely. She handed it to the old scribe casually and said, "You need not get permission from Im-Ashtah. Be sure and say that this scroll comes from the house of Uriah. Go quickly. No doubt you will be rewarded for your effort."

The old scribe seized the scroll eagerly and hurried out the door. With great uneasiness Bathsheba turned back up the stairs to her room and flung open the shutters to see if he would safely cross the court and be allowed to enter at the king's gate.

Within minutes she saw him walking stoop-shouldered and bent but with determination toward the king's guards. She felt her heart beating wildly, and she tried to quiet the waves of alarm by clutching her mantle firmly at her throat and shutting her eyes against the possibility that the guards would demand the old man open the scroll for inspection.

They were so far beneath her that she could not hear their conversation, but she saw the old scribe nod several times and then, to her great relief, he passed through the door into the darkness holding the scroll.

Tensely Bathsheba waited in the growing darkness until she saw the old man leave the palace without the scroll. He saluted the guards and walked slowly across the court and out the gate. There was no possible way for her to know for sure whether David had received her message. She had done all that she could do.

As night came on, Bathsheba sat in the darkened window and listened to the voices below in the court. The moon came up, huge and silent. Usually a moonlit night in Urusalim brought great peace to her, but tonight there was no peace, and there would be no peace for Bathsheba for a very long time.

7

IT WAS LATE in the day when David finally saw the last of the foreign ambassadors. Wearily he climbed to his roof pavilion and was about to relax when a guard approached and handed him a scroll. "This came from the house of Uriah," he announced.

Somewhat mystified, David dismissed the guard and then unrolled the scroll. He soon found it to be a rambling dull history of the Hittites. Why should this be sent to him he wondered?

When he unrolled it further a small square of parchment fell out at his feet. He picked it up, read the words and turned pale. He read them over and over again until their meaning almost overwhelmed him. "I am with child . . . I am with child . . . I am with child."

The king called for the guard who instantly reappeared. "Who gave you this scroll?" he demanded.

"The old scribe from the house of Uriah the Hittite."

"What instructions did he give you?"

"He told me to give it to you personally and to tell you it came from the house of Uriah the Hittite."

David did not answer, and the guard withdrew. David hurried out onto the roof and looked down at the house of Uriah. Bathsheba's window was shuttered. Where was she? What was happening to her? Was she feeling alone and frightened?

Since Bathsheba had visited him he had thought of little else. He never tired of remembering her slow, radiant smile, the intelligent way she listened to what he had to say. She had the wisdom of her grandfather with none of his skepticism and craftiness. But it was more than her intelligence that made his heart yearn for her. It was the bond of understanding and openness between them; the way they had given themselves to each other so completely.

He should be overjoyed at the news of their child. It was the first time he had ever really thought of a child as having a direct relationship with its mother. Always before he had thought of the children as his children, and now he found himself thinking of this unborn child as something that was a part of both of them.

He had never had this relationship with any of his wives or concubines. Now he felt that he was close to making a new discovery. Could it be that children born of parents who loved each other deeply would always be the lovely ones? If this were true, then the child Bathsheba carried would indeed be a special child.

Suddenly his mind turned back to the problem

at hand. It would not be long until all of Urusalim would know that Bathsheba was with child. *And since Uriah has not been home for months . . .*

Startled, he jumped up. It was all very obvious after all; there was only one solution.

He walked down to the scriptorium and had one of the novices pen a short message to Joab, asking him to send Uriah home at once. When this was done, David sealed it himself with his wooden seal, pressing it deep into the warm wax, and called for a runner.

In a short time he was back on his roof, thinking again of Bathsheba. He did not like this business of sending for Uriah, but it was time that he needed. Given enough time, he felt that he could certainly think of some way to get Bathsheba away from the house of Uriah, and then it would be simple to marry her himself.

Though he was faced with a problem that was to him, personally, as great as any he had faced on a battlefield, David did not go to Zadok for advice nor did he pray as he usually would have done. Suddenly he had the feeling that there were certain things you never mentioned to God or to priests. He wanted to solve this all by himself and in his own way.

Uriah received his summons home with amazement. The messenger was a relative of the king, and the scroll was sealed with the king's seal. Joab excused him from the guard duty he was to have that night and joined the rest of the men in congratulating Uriah on his good fortune.

Uriah's wonder increased when he reached Urusalim and found David himself welcoming him warmly. He was given the seat of honor beside the throne in the common room and was asked for news of the battle as though he were an old and trusted friend. Finally, in the late afternoon when Uriah was glowing with David's best wine and the unusual attention he had enjoyed, David rose and drew him to his feet. "You have fought well, Uriah, and all Israel is grateful to you. I must not keep you from your home and family any longer."

Uriah descended from the dais, the envy of every person in the room. Their eyes followed him as he strode behind the king's own pages out through the door of the common room. As he passed the guardroom at the king's gate, a man moved out of the shadows. "Uriah," he called.

"Who is it? What do you want?"

"You must not come home, Uriah." The man was one of ImAshtah's trusted servants.

"Not go home? Why?"

"Your mother has sent me to warn you not to come home. She will explain when she sees you at the house of Eban, the goldsmith, just after sunset."

Uriah was greatly puzzled by these strange instructions, but shortly after sunset he arrived at the house of Eban. ImAshtah greeted him warmly as she hurried him inside to a secluded corner. "Listen carefully, my son," she whispered hoarsely. "There has been a fox among your sheep, and we must be clever to catch him."

"A fox?" Uriah spoke so loudly that ImAshtah winced.

"This fox is none other than the king," she cautioned. "The king sent for your wife while you were gone. She went in her finest robes early in the evening and did not return until the next morning. Now Bathsheba is asking for strange food and complaining of sickness in the mornings. You must not come home."

"I don't understand at all. Why must I not come home?"

"Uriah, think! Your wife spent the night in the king's palace and now you have been called home. It is obvious. She is with child."

"Bathsheba? With child? Impossible!"

"Uriah, you must listen to me. I have been a mother and I know . . . the dizziness, the sickness. She has all the signs."

"You think my wife is having a child after spending one night in the palace, when after four years with me she has produced nothing? If you are right I will kill her."

ImAshtah shook her head. "You will not have to kill her. Her own people will do that once she is found guilty. It is for this reason you must not come home."

"But they will ask why I have not come home."

"Of course they will ask. You want them to ask. You can tell them that as long as the Ark and the tribesmen of Israel are in tents before Rabboth Ammon, you cannot go down to your house and eat and drink and lie with your wife. Now be sure you mention that you have no intention of lying with your wife so the king will know that you suspect some treachery. He has already sent food for your dinner to the house."

"The king sent food to my house?" Uriah laughed a hard, bitter laugh. "When kings come bearing gifts, it behooves us to check our money pouches and our bedchambers." Uriah took his mother's hand and raised it to his forehead. "Do not fear, Mother. I would not come home now if the king tied me to his chariot wheels and dragged me there. As for Bathsheba, if it is true that she is to bear the king a child, then I will kill her with my own hands as I would the men of Rabboth Ammon."

Without another word he turned and went out the door into the darkness.

In the days that followed everyone in the palace became aware of Uriah's strange determination to stay with David's men in the guardhouse rather than going to his own home just across the palace courtyard. He explained that it was for religious reasons.

"While the men of Israel are camped in the cold before Rabboth Ammon, I cannot go home and enjoy my family," he said.

Some admired him for his great devotion to Israel, but a few detected an implied note of criticism of the king. David had not gone with the army but had indeed been home, eating and drinking and spending time with his wives.

Nathan, the prophet, was among those who became interested in this Hittite who seemed to have become such a devoted follower of Israel's God. He had heard of Uriah's circumcision and the changing of his name from Uri to Uri-Yah and of his marriage to Ahithophel's granddaughter. He was impressed with all he had heard and yet when Nathan studied him at the king's table, the man had looked rather ordinary, even slow and plodding in spite of his fine clothes and obvious devotion to duty. On an impulse he decided to go to the guardroom and talk to Uriah personally. Nathan found the Hittite at the far end of the dimly lit guardhouse, looking down into the glowing coals of a large stone brazier.

It took Uriah a few moments to recognize Nathan. Then his eyes narrowed. "Has the king sent you also to persuade me to go home?"

Nathan was surprised. "I didn't know the king wanted you to go home."

Uriah unclenched his fists, but his eyes stayed narrow and threatening. "Of course the king wants me to go home. He wants me to cover his sin so you and all of Israel will still think him the anointed one, the pure, good king who does no wrong and so is blessed of God."

Nathan drew back in astonishment. "Those are strong words. I hope you have some evidence to prove them."

"I do not have the evidence now, but I will have it soon." Too much wine had loosened Uriah's tongue. "You will see. All Israel will see. They will say, 'How can Uriah's wife be with child when we clearly remember that he did not even go down to his house while he was in Urusalim?' When the truth comes out then we will see what the righteous people of Israel will do. Of course, the king will be protected, but for her . . . there will be no one who can protect her. She will be stoned."

Nathan was aghast at this jumble of accusations and at the willingness of Uriah to see his wife stoned. "But Uriah," he said, "she is your wife."

Uriah's eyes hardened. "I no longer consider her a wife. For four years she has refused to do the small things asked of her by my mother to befriend the earth gods, and now she is with child by another man."

Nathan could well imagine what the "small things" had been that Uriah's mother had asked of Bathsheba. For the first time he felt real pity for this young girl who had been married to a foreigner. "But Uriah," he said, "you have no proof. It may be only idle gossip. You do not have to lie with her or even speak with her, only go home and she will not be brought to this disgrace."

Uriah looked at Nathan with astonishment. "You are a holy man, and you, too, would urge me to go home and cover her sin? I thought the God of Israel was a just God who would reward a man who did his duty and punish those who did wrong."

Nathan dropped his eyes. He realized that he was indeed speaking strangely for a prophet, but he could not imagine the coldness of this man.

Uriah spat on the floor and swore. "If she is innocent, we will know in a few months. But if she is guilty, I will not be the one who condemns her. She will have condemned herself." Uriah glowered at Nathan, his shaven head set rigidly on his massive shoulders, the scar livid on his neck.

With this disturbing picture in his mind and Uriah's words ringing in his ears, Nathan left the room and went out into the night.

Nathan was not the only one who talked with Uriah that night. One of David's young advisors sought Uriah out to determine how the battle was progressing. He was surprised to hear instead a jumbled account of Uriah's grievance against his wife and vague hints that the king had dealt with him falsely. Being a friend of the king, the young man returned to David on the roof and told him all that Uriah had said.

David pushed aside some drawings he had been studying and focused his full attention upon the advisor. "Did Uriah tell you why he is so angry with his wife that he won't go home?"

"He believes his wife has committed some outrage against him, and if he does not go home, she will be punished for what she has done."

"I see," David said. "He is hardhearted, isn't he?"

"My lord, my concern is not with the wife of Uriah but with yourself. He has made threats against you." When David did not answer, the advisor excused himself and quietly departed.

As he paced the floor a great anger filled the king. Uriah was serious. He would stop at nothing to uncover the truth, expose the sin, and ruthlessly punish those involved. The very qualities that had endeared him to Joab as a soldier were ones that would make him a formidable enemy, even to a king.

Quickly he determined what he would do. He summoned a young scribe to bring him pens and ink with parchment and then dismissed him. He wrote hurriedly, instructing Joab in several small matters. Then he concluded with the words, "I regret to write that your captain, Uriah the Hittite, has threatened not only the kingdom but also your king and uncle. I suggest that you put Uriah in the forefront of the battle." Then writing slowly and deliberately, he added, "so that he may be killed."

There. It was at last written out boldly on the parchment. Deliberately he rolled the scroll, sealed it and placed it beside his dais to be given to Uriah in the morning.

The night air was fresh and fragrant with spring blossoms, and David was reluctant to go down the stairs to his dank and musty room. He stretched out on the dais and tried to sleep. He dozed lightly, tossing and turning until finally he called the guard and ordered him to remove the lamp and smoldering incense. He lay down again and tried to sleep, but now he was aware of every step and movement outside on the parapet. He turned on his back and cupped his hands under his head so that he could watch the slow billowing movement of the side curtains in the evening breeze. The moon was high, and he saw with annoyance how the young guard's shadow spread up the side curtain, tall and menacing like one of the giants of Gath.

The lion's skin gave off a musk-like odor, and he

flung it from his pallet impatiently, then turned his face to the wall, his arms up over his head, and tried again to sleep. There in the darkness he seemed to see the narrow, questioning eyes of Uriah. He could see Joab reading the message, eyes bulging in surprise and the lines of his mouth setting in a firm line of disapproval. Joab would be angry. He liked Uriah; he had said the man was disciplined and faithful.

He sat up and called for the guard to bring a light. The young man came rubbing his eyes and squinting in the wavering light of the lamp. "Bring my writing ink and quills," David ordered. He would have to change the bothersome note by taking out the phrase, "so that he may be killed." That was too harsh. Joab would never let it go without a question.

Slowly he rolled out the new parchment and dismissed the curious guard. His quill formed the letters evenly. He finished with a flourish and quickly rolled the scroll together with an abrupt twirling motion and then held it in midair as he remembered something. If Uriah did not die in battle, all would be lost for both himself and for Bathsheba. She would face public disgrace and maybe even death, while he would find his kingdom crumbling around him.

He rose, unrolled the parchment, and stood pondering the problem. "I cannot change the message after all. Uriah has to die and Joab will have to have the message written clearly. It is a rotten business. The man has served us well."

He sat down on the bare pallet and reached for the old parchment. He stuffed it under the mat and pinched out the single flame of the lamp. "I'll have to give it to him in the morning," he told himself as he hardened his heart into acceptance. "It is not certain that he will be killed. If God so wills he may still live despite our intentions." He felt along the pallet until his hand touched a corner of the scroll still protruding. He pushed it firmly under. "Uriah knows something is amiss. Someone has warned him and now he wants to trap his wife to punish her. He's had his chance. If only he'd gone home." With that thought easing his conscience, he wrapped his mantle around him, as he had done so often as a shepherd boy in Bethlehem, and was soon asleep.

When morning came, he sent for Uriah and gave him the parchment to be delivered to Joab in Rabboth Ammon. David noted that his eyes seemed dark and questioning. He also noticed the casual way Uriah held the parchment in his big, blunt-fingered hand and wondered briefly if he'd open it and read the message. It was unlikely. Uriah was too well trained, too disciplined. If he did? David shrugged inwardly. That would be a chance he would have to take.

He dismissed Uriah and saw him turn and walk quickly from the room, obviously eager to be back with Joab and the men before the gates of Rabboth Ammon.

Twinges of guilt and regret clouded David's day as over and over again he pictured Joab's reaction to the message and then the battle with Uriah left alone while the others pulled back. *Uriah will realize too late that treachery is afoot,* he thought moodily.

8

LOUD, INSISTENT knocking on the outside gate awoke everyone and brought ImAshtah with a lamp.

"Where is my son?" she demanded as she opened the gate and saw two soldiers holding several battered pieces of armor she recognized as having belonged to Uriah.

"We must come in off the street," the young captain said, moving through the gate with his companion and past ImAshtah to the middle of the courtyard. There the two men spread out the armor on the rough stones. "Uriah was my friend, and you have reason to be very proud of him."

ImAshtah clutched the arm of the captain and gestured wildly toward the armor with the lamp. "Something has happened. Something has happened to my son!"

"Your son . . ." the captain said hesitantly, "your son fought right up to the gates of the city. If he had not been so outnumbered. . . ."

"He's dead! You're telling me my only son is dead!" ImAshtah screamed the words, glaring wildly at the men who had brought Uriah's armor. "What do I care for bravery or glory if it means my son is dead?"

Bathsheba, standing in the shadows, was paralyzed with shock. She stared numbly at the familiar armor, now twisted and broken on the ground, then at the anguished ImAshtah.

Uriah is dead! The thought reminded her of the note she had sent to the king. Uriah had died in battle, and yet with some deep, inner instinct she feared his death had somehow resulted from that fatal note.

She turned and felt her way in the darkness back up the stone stairs. The noise in the courtyard grew faint as she entered her room, closed the door and leaned against it, breathing deeply to still the wild throbbing of her heart.

The sound of shouting and weeping now came

more distinctly through the open window. She rushed across the room and pulled the shutters closed, bolting them securely. Trembling, she sank down upon her sleeping mat. "He died in battle," she told herself aloud. "There is no reason at all for me to think it had anything to do with the note I sent." She leaned back and breathed more easily. "Israel has lost many men in battle fighting Rabboth Ammon."

She lay down in the darkness, listening to the wind blowing about the house and rattling the shutters, but sleep would not come.

Nathan had been gone from Urusalim when the news came of Uriah's death. When he returned a week later the city was still buzzing with reports from the battlefront. Along with Uriah, two of David's closest friends had engaged in what appeared to be a senseless sortie to the very gates of Rabboth Ammon. There the archers had killed them. "Why did Joab order such a raid?" the people asked.

Reports from the army were confusing. While it was known that Joab was jealous of the king's two close friends who had been killed, it was also true that he cared a great deal for his own Hittite armor bearer. It was unthinkable that he would deliberately send them all out on a mission of certain death.

Nathan heard the news from a young priest in the Khan of the prophets and probed for details.

"The king is deeply upset," the priest replied. "He tore his robes and lamented bitterly over the needless death of his friends. He feels that Joab deliberately placed them in a dangerous position because they were not men he himself liked."

"Joab is a vengeful man. He might do that if he didn't like the men himself," Nathan replied. "I am surprised, however, that he dared to move against the friends of David."

"I was surprised too. But I was there myself when the king questioned the messenger. He answered simply that Joab had asked him to give these words to the king: 'Uriah, the Hittite, was also among those killed before the gates of Rabboth Ammon.' "

Nathan drew in his breath sharply and grasped the priest's arm. "What did the king say to that?"

"It was strange. He turned pale as though he had become suddenly ill, buried his face in his hands and then rose and left the room."

To the young priest the news of Uriah's death meant nothing but the loss of a fine soldier. But to Nathan, remembering Uriah's accusations against the king, it came as a great shock. *Uriah may have been right,* he thought. Was it possible that his death came as a result of his refusal to go home and cover for his wife?

For a long time, Nathan sat alone in the arched doorway of the Khan, pondering all he had heard. Nathan had felt great pity for Uriah's wife when he had talked to Uriah in the guardhouse. But this new information made him wonder. *Now that Uriah is dead, if the king should decide to marry Bathsheba, it would be most suspicious. And if Uriah's wife is actually with child . . .* Nathan stood up and squared his shoulders. *It is conceivable,* he thought, *that justice could be forever buried with Uriah.*

He left the Khan and walked down the steps toward the Dung Gate meditating on what should be done. "Evil is like the thread on a distaff," he mused soberly. "Once you start to unroll it you can't stop."

With the news of Uriah's death, ImAshtah had plunged the whole house into deep mourning. All shutters were closed, all doors barred, and professional mourners were hired to weep and wail in the sunless receiving room. ImAshtah roamed up and down the dark halls of the house tearing her hair and digging her nails into her face until she appeared to be weeping blood. She refused to eat anything brought to her, all the time muttering wild, unintelligible accusations against the king.

At times she flung open the shutters and leaned far out, shouting curses in the direction of the palace; at other times she swore by all the earth gods to wreak her revenge on Bathsheba. The servants tried to pacify her, but no one took her accusations seriously. "Poor one," they said, "she is out of her mind with grief for her son."

For Bathsheba sitting alone in her shuttered room it was like living through a terrible nightmare. The climax came suddenly, just at sunset after the Sabbath when Sara burst into her room, her eyes wild with fright. "My lady! Come quickly," she gasped.

Bathsheba followed Sara down the long halls and into the darkened room which was so familiar. At first she could see nothing until Sara opened one of the shutters. Then Bathsheba drew back in horror. There in the shadows she saw ImAshtah lying among the pillows on her pallet. Her face was blue, her eyes staring as though she had seen an apparition. Her hands were clutching her neck, and her mouth hung open with black rivulets of the poison she had taken running slowly down her chin.

Bathsheba picked up the golden goblet and saw the black mixture still coating the bottom. She turned from the scene, holding her mantle over her nose and mouth to keep from breathing the fetid air. She closed the door behind her, reminding herself that never again would she have to enter that room where she had suffered so much anguish. She also knew that the blue face and staring eyes of ImAshtah, dead among the cushions, would haunt her for the rest of her life.

9

TEN DAYS AFTER the news of Uriah's death, David called for his old friend and counselor. When Ahithophel entered the pavilion, David noticed that he appeared to be ill at ease. It had been months since he had called him for a private meeting, and Ahithophel was undoubtedly nervous.

"My old friend and good counselor, are you well today?" The king's voice was strained though he was trying to be as casual as possible.

"Well enough to serve your majesty," Ahithophel answered. David noticed that his eyes were alert and questioning as he bowed slightly and came to sit in the seat beside David on the dais.

The king engaged in light conversation with Ahithophel while he decided on the words to use. Finally, he leaned forward and spoke directly. "My friend and wise counselor, I have a very special request to ask of you. I have come to admire your granddaughter, Bathsheba, very much, and I wish to marry her."

When David saw Ahithophel's look of genuine surprise, he continued. "Her time of mourning for her husband will be ended in another twenty days. I propose we plan a wedding that will do justice to her status as your granddaughter."

David paused to study Ahithophel's reaction. Well aware of his counselor's ambitious nature, he counted on this trait to overcome any doubts or apprehensions that may have built up inside Ahithophel due to the suspicious circumstances of the past weeks. As he watched his counselor's facial expressions change rapidly from caution to surprise to speculation to an alive interest, David knew he had judged Ahithophel correctly. Casually, David brought out a key from under one of the cushions and handed it to Ahithophel.

"Though we must wait for the mourning to end, you may begin making plans immediately. I will trust everything to your discretion. This key is to my private storerooms. There you will find all that you will need to make this a memorable occasion. Spare no expense. I want the richest carpets, coverings, serving trays, and hangings to make the banquet hall and my rooms ready for my bride."

Ahithophel's eyes glinted with satisfaction as he rose to leave. He hid the key in his wide sash and bowed hurriedly. "Ahithophel," David called to him again, "order the maidens of the city to weave garlands of flowers and the bakers to bake sweet cakes for everyone in Urusalim." Ahithophel nodded and hurried from the room, walking with his head high and his long robes trailing behind him.

Clenching the golden scepter in his hands, David stared after the retreating figure of his counselor. He was pleased to have won Ahithophel's approval and support, but he was also uneasy, knowing that his counselor would be angry and vengeful if he knew the true situation. When Bathsheba's child was born three months early, there would be much speculation and conjecture. Ahithophel already knew too much. He knew that his granddaughter had spent a night in the palace and also that Uriah had refused to go down to his house. Fortunately, he did not know the circumstances of Uriah's death. Ahithophel was so proud it would kill him to be involved in a scandal. He would scoff at the idea of love and see only that his granddaughter had been taken lightly, as a common servant is taken for a night's pleasure.

David shook off his apprehensions and tossed the scepter down among the cushions. *The wedding would silence any gossip,* he thought. *No one need ever know. And who would dare speak out against the favorite of the king?*

As the days passed, the word circulated throughout Urusalim that the king intended to take the widow of Uriah as his bride. In the palace the news was not happily received. One night David learned this himself through old Mahat. Having been with David since his youth, the old servant was often blunt and outspoken. This night she shuffled into the room with an air of sullen defiance.

"Come, speak your mind, old one," David asked. "What is the problem?"

"My lord," Mahat said hesitantly, "there are many problems."

"You don't even know the new bride, and yet you are looking with disapproval on all the arrangements. Speak up. You are too old to fear even death. What trouble is there in the harem now?"

Old Mahat smiled a toothless grin, "Your wives will be unhappy if this new one has all your attention. You no longer call Michal, and if you act the same with the rest of your wives, you will have the other tribesmen as angry as the men of Benjamin."

"My wives only want to be called so they can ask favors for their families and friends."

"Maacah is beautiful, and Abigail is witty," Mahat countered defensively.

"Maacah is only to be looked at. When she came to me a week ago, she looked beautiful and flirtatious as always but begged me not to spoil her coiffure or rumple her gown."

Old Mahat cleared her throat to cover her embarrassment. "But my king, Abigail . . . "

"Abigail, ah yes, Abigail, the beautiful woman with the head of a chief counselor. She always wants to arrange things. Not just my room or personal belongings or my private life, but the whole kingdom."

Mahat sighed with quiet resignation. "They mean well."

"Don't worry, old mother, I understand. I must remember to visit them more often."

"Not just visit them. You must call them to you as before, or they will be angry. A woman's anger kindled to a blaze is hard to quench."

Mahat left the room with the same shuffling gait, and David stood thinking of his wives and wondering why he had encumbered himself so. Each wife had brought him some loyalty from her tribe or some gold for his treasury, but none of them had brought him the love and affection he had received from Bathsheba.

David turned and went up the stairs to the roof. Soon Bathsheba would be here in the palace where he could see her as he pleased. He looked toward Uriah's house and noticed her window was closed. "It is strange," he murmured, "that Ahithophel has not asked the usual bride's price." David determined to reward him doubly and to give Bathsheba the dowry of a princess.

When Ahithophel left the king his mind was whirling. He had entered the king's presence reluctantly. He had spent the last three months striving to suppress his anger at David for compromising his granddaughter, and he was not eager for a confrontation. Even if Bathsheba had resisted David's advances, the fact that she had spent most of a night in the king's quarters could set tongues in Urusalim wagging if it were ever found out. It had caused enough unpleasantness with ImAshtah and would have no doubt led to a divorce if Uriah had lived.

Now his feelings of hostility had been blunted by the king's intention to marry Bathsheba. That he had not expected. With both pleasure and satisfaction he recalled the eagerness and extravagance with which David had made plans to marry his granddaughter.

When Ahithophel told Bathsheba of the elaborate plans for her wedding to David, she was stunned. She had been in complete mourning, her hair tangled, her feet bare, and wearing her oldest garment, dusted with ashes, hanging about her in shreds. Such was the custom, and she felt in some slight way, alone in the darkened rooms, that she was paying her due to the house of Uriah.

David had sent her a message secretly, assuring her that when the time of mourning was over he intended to take her as his bride. But she had expected to go to him quietly, causing as little disturbance and interest as possible. Now that she saw how honored and pleased Ahithophel was with the idea of the wedding, she did not want to disappoint him.

She moved through a sea of conflicting emotions. Love and joy at the thought of being married to David, relief that the wedding would take place before her pregnancy became evident, and worry over what Ahithophel would think or do if he ever traced her pregnancy to the night she spent in the palace. She blushed to think again of how she had thrown aside her grandfather's advice and had deliberately given herself to David without restraint. For a moment, fear welled up within her as she thought of the future, and then just as quickly she dismissed it. *When I am married to David, everything will be all right.*

In the few days before the wedding Ahithophel surrounded Bathsheba with sewing women, beauticians, merchants, jewelers, and perfumers, all seeking to have their wares chosen by the king's new favorite. To Ahithophel's discomfiture, Bathsheba would have none of the more ornate robes, and she sent away the beauticians with their palettes of heavy rouge which would have made her look like a pagan goddess. Ahithophel argued and pleaded, but she remained firm in her desire to go to her husband dressed simply as one of the country women of Bethlehem.

It was evening when David sent a gilded palanquin surrounded by dancers and singers to bring her to the palace for the wedding ceremony. Quickly Bathsheba went down to the courtyard and stepped into the curtained interior, pulling the drapes closed after her. Immediately the band of dancers and singers began chanting and playing traditional wedding songs as they led the way before her out the gate and up the narrow street. On every side Bathsheba could hear the steady beat of the drum, the jangling of tambourines, and the high-pitched singing and yodeling of the young maidens.

Suddenly quite close by Bathsheba heard a childish voice say, "Mother, look! What is in that funny box?"

There was a pause, and then the mother's answer could be heard quite clearly. "Why that is an adulteress, my son, by the name of Bathsheba. It is rumored that her husband was killed so the king could marry her." There was the sound of scuffling as one of the guards drove the woman away, and then the procession moved forward again.

Bathsheba's hands flew to her face as she stifled a cry. She turned crimson as she was overwhelmed by such a wave of horror that she could hardly breathe. She had never thought of herself as an adulteress or of David as planning Uriah's death.

Now that the words had been spoken she could not shrug them off. She remembered everything too vividly: the night in the palace, her frantic message to the king, and Uriah's death so soon after. It was obvious to her now that Uriah's death could hardly have been a chance happening. How it had been managed she did not know. Nor did she want to know.

A new and chilling thought almost paralyzed her. How could she step from this gilded box and walk through all those happy, joyful people, knowing that she, the new bride, was probably responsible for the death of her husband and carried in her womb the child that had brought it about?

She thought of praying as her grandmother had taught her to do, but there was no prayer she had ever learned that would fit such a situation.

Now the procession had entered the palace grounds. There was no turning back. She must go on for her child's sake and for David's. In the house of Uriah she had learned to live with dignity and courtesy in the midst of hostility. She must now draw on this inner strength to carry her through the difficulties that lay before her.

From the moment the wedding had been announced, David's wives had talked of nothing else. Michal recounted in detail her visit to Lodebar. "She is young and beautiful," she warned them, "just the kind of woman the king would find interesting."

"It is just possible he is really infatuated with her," Maacah said with a toss of her head. "If so, it could change everything for us."

They all began to talk at once until Michal signaled them to be quiet. "I have lived in a king's court all my life, and I know how it is with a king and his harem. If we band together against her, she will become unhappy and melancholy. Then David will tire of her and either come back to us or find someone new. She won't last. We can break her."

Kindhearted Rizpah, who still grieved over Abner's death, hesitated to join them, but finally even she agreed to be distant and cold to Bathsheba.

After some discussion, the women sent old Mahat to the king with the message that they could not come to the wedding. Almost immediately, she returned with word from the king that he would not permit anyone to miss the wedding. Secretly they were glad, for they had gone to a great deal of trouble to have new and elaborate dresses made for the occasion, and each one had sought out her favorite hairdresser and beautician. Maacah even sent for one of the temple women to paint her face and dress her hair.

When David's wives entered the banqueting hall on the evening of the wedding and took their places near the throne, they looked at one another smugly, thinking that Bathsheba could not possibly rival any one of them in appearance. From his throne, David greeted each of his wives and children as they entered, checking to see that they were all there.

He noticed that one of his small sons was clinging to the skirt of his mother, obviously frightened by all of the people and the dignity of the occasion. David singled him out and encouraged him to come stand beside him near the throne. He bent down and asked him a few questions. The little boy hung his head, putting his finger in his mouth and hurried back to his mother, who was one of David's concubines.

Ahithophel stood next to the throne, dressed in rich robes of fine linen, pleasantly conscious of the envious eyes of his friends and enemies who marveled at his good fortune to be the grandfather of the king's favorite. The scribes read the terms of the marriage agreement in loud, sonorous voices, and the king descended from his throne to affix the royal seal on the parchment. Ahithophel followed, placing his seal in the space beside that of the king.

David reached out and took Ahithophel's hand in recognition of the new bond between their two families. Again the trumpets were blown and a steward entered, bringing the symbolic mohar, or bride's price. Behind him came servants bringing gifts from the king to the house of Ahithophel which far exceeded anything the assembled group had ever seen. Satisfied that Ahithophel was impressed with his generosity, David signaled for the rest of the ceremony to begin.

The ram's horn blew, trumpets sounded, and dancers appeared, singing the ancient marriage songs and performing the wedding sword dance.

Their shining blades slashed a path through any evil influence that might hinder the happiness of the bridal couple. Next came the drummers and acrobats and finally the harpist and singers. All came to the dais, bowed low before the king, and then clustered around the canopy waiting for the coming of the bride and the start of the feast.

Bathsheba stood in the doorway for a moment with the torches of her attendants turning the white of her dress to dazzling brightness. As she moved forward with regal dignity, the faint hint of jasmine filled the air and the guests whispered to each other, "She's beautiful. How can it be that she is so beautiful, and yet she is wearing something fashioned so simply?"

David's wives were soon glancing sideways at each other, comparing the heavy layers of paint hiding their true features with the simplicity of the bride's dress and flowing hair. Their discomfort increased as they noticed the open admiration for Bathsheba in the eyes of the foreign dignitaries.

As Bathsheba walked down through the softly chanting dancers and singers, she began to feel wild, uncontrollable panic rise within her. If that woman on the street had dared to call her an adulteress, then all of these people could be secretly thinking the same thing. As she came further into the room, she saw David. He was smiling at her as though no one else was in the room. She walked to where he stood, looking only at him, and knelt.

The drums beat softly and the singing came almost to a stop. David lifted the edge of his fringed tallith and placed it over her kneeling form as a symbol of his protection. He then reached down, took her hand in his and raised her to her feet.

The drums sounded a harsh, staccato beat and cymbals clashed as David led Bathsheba to the seat of honor under the canopy. As soon as they were seated, the groomsman signaled for the servants to drop the curtains around the bridal couple, enclosing them within the fragrant bower of soft gauze. Immediately the guests found seats along the wall where the stewards had prepared low tables on which they now began to serve the wedding feast.

While the guests ate, David took advantage of the few moments alone with his bride to comfort her and to reassure her of his love. Seeing that she was almost faint from tension and fatigue, he poured some juice into her small goblet and urged her to drink. She sipped like a small child who obeys an order without enjoyment. Concerned, David tilted her chin so he could look into her eyes. For the first time that day she really looked at him and under his tender gaze her face brightened and relaxed.

The drums began to beat a loud staccato, and the dancers came bringing gifts for the bride. A gold necklace was fastened around Bathsheba's neck, earrings placed in her ears, rings put on her fingers and toes, and robes of the finest cloth presented. When the king himself placed a great emerald on her finger, the members of David's court burst out with clapping and shouts while David's other wives tried not to show their displeasure and envy.

The festivities lasted until the king signaled that he was prepared to retire with his bride to the bridal chamber. No one was too disappointed, since the wedding feast would begin again the next evening and last the entire week.

As soon as David was alone with Bathsheba, he pulled her to him and tilted her chin so he could look into her eyes. He was puzzled by the look of anxiety he saw there. Gently he kissed her. He could tell that something kept her from coming to him with all the joy and abandon of the night they had spent in his pavilion on the roof.

He picked her up and tenderly placed her on the bed, piling cushions behind her. He reached down and removed her shoes, still watching her with a questioning, puzzled look. "My love, something is bothering you," he said sitting down beside her. "I can feel a deep sadness that wasn't there before."

Unable to answer, she reached out and touched his face, tears welling up in her eyes.

"Bathsheba," he said, "we are together, and I love you. That is all that matters. Do you understand? I love you."

Her chin trembled, and she hid her face in her hands and wept.

David stared at her helplessly. He stroked her hair, noticing how it curled like a small child's around her face. Then he reached down and kissed the place on her sleeve that was spotted by her tears.

She laughed a shaky, tearful laugh. "I'm sorry. It's nothing. I'm all right now."

David smoothed her hair, pulling her to him until she was cradled in his arms, and then he gently kissed both her eyes. "I don't believe you cry easily. Something has hurt you."

Hesitantly she reached up and drew his head down to her until she could feel his beard on her cheek. "When I was being carried here, I heard a little child ask his mother who I was. She answered that I was an adulteress . . . "

"Oh, my darling," David whispered in her ear. *How helpless I am to protect her,* he thought. *But she must never know the details of Uriah's death.*

He reached out to extinguish the wick on the

286

small oil lamp and plunged the room into darkness. His arms tightened around Bathsheba, and he could feel that at last she was responding to his love.

10

FOR ONE HAPPY week the celebration and feasting continued. Bathsheba stayed with David, never leaving his rooms until the time came for her to move to the Court of the Women. Bathsheba remembered her last encounter with Michal years before in Lodebar and wondered if the other wives of David would prove to be so forceful and disagreeable. "I am no longer the frightened young girl I was in Lodebar," she reasoned. "I'm almost nineteen and have learned much from living in the house of Im-Ashtah."

When she arrived, old Mahat led her down the several flights of stairs and through the hallway that opened into the Court of the Women. Bathsheba entered a broad, open-tiled courtyard shaded by a few flowering figs. Since the women had taken their children for an outing to the vineyards of Bethlehem, it was silent and deserted. Bathsheba was greatly relieved. She had not fully realized how very much she had dreaded the encounter with David's other wives, especially Michal.

Mahat was shuffling toward a door at the far end of the court. "Jessica has gone with the women," she said, "but she took time to tidy your room herself before she left." The old servant stopped and gave Bathsheba a hard, calculating look. She wiped her nose on her sleeve and motioned Bathsheba to follow.

Bathsheba walked slowly, noticing every detail including the servant's aloof manner. *It will not be easy to win the respect of these women. Even this old servant looks at me with some hidden malice.* David could not help her here, and if he were like most men, he would find complaints about his other wives tiresome. In the time it took to walk across the courtyard to her room she determined that she would not stoop to that.

David had ordered that no expense or effort be spared to make her rooms beautiful. The bed was large and inlaid with ivory, while the floor was covered with soft fur. In one corner was a dark chest with a delicately-worked vanity of carved alabaster sitting on the top. Most of the wives shared one large bath and lounged in the open court; but both Michal and Bathsheba had small courtyards of their own.

Mahat explained all the conventions and habits of the women's court. "The wives usually gather in the large room with their small children. On occasion, when there is a big family festival, they will eat with David in the main room. Each wife has her own set of servants who prepare her food in the kitchen and wash her clothes or clean her rooms. Some of the wives have special beauticians from Philistia or Egypt supervising their baths and arranging their hair. The king often calls one of his wives to have dinner with him. In a court such as this, each wife must be perfumed and ready by late afternoon, just in case she should be called by the king."

"I should think they would be very unhappy getting ready day after day and never being called."

Bathsheba felt a great wave of pity for these women she had not yet met.

"They get used to it," said Mahat, "but they are a quarrelsome lot."

The next few hours passed slowly for Bathsheba until finally laughter and scolding signaled the return of the women and their children. Hungry youngsters rushed into the dining area and elbowed and shoved each other as they settled onto the cushioned mats for their evening meal. The mothers pushed in beside their own children and were just getting settled when Mahat came and whispered something to Michal.

Michal looked astonished. "The old one says the new wife will be eating with us."

There was silence, and then Ahinoam said rather stiffly, "If she insists, let her come. It doesn't mean we must speak to her. Let her come and see just what she is up against."

"It may do her good to see that we are not all old and ugly," said Maacah.

"Where will she sit?" asked Abigail.

They all looked around the room, and Michal spoke firmly. "We will put her at the end, near the concubines. If she talks to us, we will try to act as though we did not hear; but if that is impossible, we will answer her only briefly."

"Will she go immediately to David and complain to him that we haven't accepted her?" Ahinoam asked.

Michal laughed harshly. "Let her go to David. We will tell him we have treated her quite well but that we are all too busy to wait on her. Just let that go on for a while, and David will grow tired of her. It will be fun to watch."

One mother whispered to the children, "Not a word out of you to the new wife. She hates children." Their eyes grew big and round as she added, "She stuffed all her babies down the well just because she can't stand to hear them cry." The littlest boy started to cry from fright then put his hand over his mouth so the new wife wouldn't hear him. All the women laughed. At that moment Bathsheba entered the room. The laughter stopped, and they stared at her coldly.

"Where shall I sit?" she asked Mahat. The women were disappointed that she didn't ask one of them so they could ignore her and enjoy her discomfort.

Bathsheba went to her assigned place on the mat and sat down, seemingly unaware of the hostile, jealous glances and planned silence. They watched her daintily nibble small fragments of bread, then sip a bit of warm broth. They stared, fascinated, as she deftly peeled the tough outer skin from two figs and ate them. All this time she did not say a word. When she was finished, she wiped her fingers on the damp, rose-scented towel the maid passed. Then she looked around at all of them and smiled as though they were the best of friends. She rose, excused herself, never seeming to notice that nothing had been said in return, and left the room.

"Well, what do you think of that?" asked Maacah.

"She doesn't care now; but you wait. She will break sooner or later," said Michal with great assurance. "This is going to be very interesting."

Bathsheba had brought Sara with her from the house of Uriah and was relieved to find that she had lit the small oil lamp and had laid out her robes which she would wear to meet David later that evening. She wondered what the other wives would be saying about her. From their hostile looks tonight they would be capable of stoning her right here in the women's courtyard if they ever found out the truth about her child.

Bathsheba moved out of the shadows of her room to stand in the doorway of her court when suddenly she noticed someone sitting on the small bench near the palm tree.

"Jessica!" Bathsheba joyfully raced forward to embrace the maid she had thought was lost to her forever.

"You are no longer my little Bathsheba," Jessica said warmly, holding her at arm's length. "You are a woman, a very beautiful woman, but you are too thin."

"How good of you to prepare my quarters, Jessica." Bathsheba radiated happiness at seeing her friend again.

"I cannot stay but a moment. I have just come to warn you that the other women are going to try to wear you down. Trust no one, not even Sara, your maid. Michal has been questioning her."

"You must not worry about me, Jessica. I know they do not like me now, and it will be worse when they know for sure that I am already three months with child."

"Does the king know?"

"Yes, the child is his."

"Then all is well. You are married to the king, and who would dare to question anything he does?"

"I'd like to think that you are right, but everything is not that simple. Sara and the servants and friends of ImAshtah have heard all her accusations. She told them I was pregnant by the king and the cause of Uriah's death."

"But ImAshtah was out of her mind with grief. Surely no one would listen to her."

"But when the child is born early . . . " Tears

sprang to Bathsheba's eyes. She could not continue.

"You blame yourself too much, my dear. Everyone will simply say, 'He is the king. How could any woman refuse him?' and as for Uriah, I wouldn't worry about it. He died a hero and like most heroes will soon be forgotten."

A gong sounded. Jessica was instantly alert. "That is Michal. I must go to her. Be careful, especially around Sara. Say nothing to anyone. I will help you whenever I am able."

Bathsheba stood alone in the small courtyard with her arms folded across her stomach as if she would protect the treasure it held. She felt no concern for herself. If they should all turn on her tomorrow and condemn her, she could endure this, but when she thought of the unborn child she carried, fear gripped her with a startling intensity. Whatever was to happen in the days ahead, she must guard this innocent one from harm.

11

WHILE BATHSHEBA was encountering jealousy and hostility in the Court of the Women, David was having his own problems. His men were not nearly as open and friendly as before, and some of his oldest friends had grown critical. Nothing he did seemed to please them anymore. Joab expressed resentment that the wedding was at a time when it was impossible for him to leave the siege at Rabboth Ammon. Others were critical of David for holding such a lavish ceremony when so many of Israel's men were enduring hardship on the field of battle.

As the weeks passed and it became obvious that Bathsheba was with child, Ahithophel was at first overjoyed and then thoughtful. He was so accustomed to thinking of his granddaughter as being barren that it was hard to believe what he saw with his own eyes.

Being a proud old man, he would not entertain the thought that his own "little girl" could possibly bring shame and disgrace upon him just at the moment of his greatest triumph. However, despite his outward appearance of smug assurance, there was the constant, repressed fear that he might sometime have to face the fact that David had not dealt honorably with either his granddaughter or Uriah. "I am foolish to let such thoughts spoil my good fortune," he reasoned to himself. "She is married to the king. No matter how it came about, who would dare to speak against the king?"

With this thought he comforted himself, and yet his doubts intruded like a curtain between himself and David. He was critical of everything the king did and found he much preferred to spend his time with David's young son Absalom. The boy was much to Ahithophel's liking. He had all of David's charm but none of his mysticism. He made decisions as Ahithophel liked to see men make them, using his head and not resorting to the mystery of prayer.

Some of his resentment toward David crept into his conversations with Absalom. He would admonish the young man, "Did you see your father today, excusing the thief because he was hungry? This is not wise. You must mark this, and when you come into power harshly punish the thieves. If you don't, our merchants and honest men will soon be living in fear, and they will blame you for being weak."

Sometimes he would say, "Your father shows his humble origins. He talked about shearing sheep in front of some foreign emissaries yesterday. They will think him a rough shepherd instead of the exalted king of Israel."

Bathsheba was well aware of Ahithophel's struggle, and she understood why he avoided coming to see her. She reassured herself that he need never know the truth; yet there was the ever-present fear that somehow the whole thing might come to light. To face such ridicule and scandal would be the final tragedy of Ahithophel's life. She dared not think what might happen when the child was born early.

As the time approached for the baby's birth, Bathsheba spent most of her time sitting alone in her room off the main court, making small garments and brooding over the carved box with the ivory and gold inlays that would be the baby's bed. She was aware that the women of the harem were watching her intently for any sign of weakness. Though emotion churned within her she managed to remain calm and serene on the surface so that only Jessica imagined her true feelings. She could see that Rizpah and Abigail were drawn to her in spite of their intentions, but the others were angry that she was able to ignore so completely their slights and scathing remarks.

While Michal led the women in stirring up trouble for Bathsheba, Ahinoam supplied most of the information. "My son, Amnon, has reported to me," whispered Ahinoam to the women, "that there are now people in the court who have heard the accusations against Bathsheba and who feel someone should speak out and denounce her."

Michal was immediately interested. "We must find out who these people are."

"Amnon can find out anything. He is a clever boy

who says very little but is always listening to what is being said around him."

Michal leaned over toward Ahinoam and spoke more confidentially. "We must pick the right time. If it is done too soon, people will feel sorry for her. They will say we have no proof, that this child could be the natural result of Bathsheba's marriage to the king."

"But Sara has indicated that Bathsheba was pregnant before Uriah came home. She also says the mother-in-law blamed David for her son's strange death."

"If this can be proven it will certainly take the pious look from the king's face." Michal smirked, relishing the thought.

"I suppose Bathsheba could be stoned?"

"Or sent home in disgrace. I'd like to see that grandfather of hers hanging his head too."

"Whom will we confront first?"

"We must be sure of our facts before we make a move." Michal's expression grew hard and cynical. "Once sure of all the facts, we'll tell the king we can no longer shelter such a woman in our court."

"Do you think he'd listen to criticism of his new favorite?"

"If he does nothing, then we'll take our information to the priests. They dare not take it lightly."

In the month of Abib, before the last of the latter rain, Bathsheba was taken in labor. Usually it was the custom for the women of David's harem to sit with the one in labor and offer advice and comfort. However, as they discussed the situation, they callously decided that none of them would help her.

"It has been less than seven months since the wedding," said Ahinoam, "and now all Israel will know what kind of woman she is."

295

Rizpah spoke quietly but firmly, "Let us be sure that she has done something wrong before we side against her. Is it not possible this child could be Uriah's?"

"Sara has told us that Uriah did not go down to his house when he came home from the fighting," said Michal emphatically.

"Do we know for sure that he did not go home?" questioned Rizpah.

"We have it on the best authority," said Ahinoam. "Amnon was sleeping in the guardhouse, and he saw that Uriah did not go down to his house. He also observed Bathsheba early in the morning about nine months ago slipping down the back steps from the king's quarters on the roof. She had obviously spent the night there."

There was a piercing scream that seemed to echo and reecho through the court.

"It won't be long now," said Maacah.

"Who is with her?" Rizpah asked.

"Only her maid, Sara," said Abigail. "I suppose we should call the old women who deal with such things."

Michal started for her room. "I'm sure it's none of my business."

"Whose business is it?" asked one of the new concubines shyly.

"I suppose it is our honorable king's business, if it is anyone's," snapped Maacah.

"Really!" The concubine was obviously astonished.

"No, not really," said Rizpah. "Don't listen to her. It is actually our business to help each other and to call for outside help from some of the women of the city if necessary."

Just then a door slammed, and David strode into the room with a group of toothless, old women following behind him. He insisted Bathsheba be moved to his rooms and the best of care given her.

The women looked at one another angrily, each one remembering that no such special treatment had been afforded any one of them in similar situations. Abigail spoke first. "My lord, it is already too late." And then winking at the others, she added, "And yet it is too early, is it not?"

Motioning the old women to follow him, David went to the door of Bathsheba's room and pulled back the curtain. In the dim light he could barely see the form of the woman he loved so intensely. She was now bloated, clutching the sheet to her mouth to stifle the cries of pain. Quickly he knelt by her side and grasped her hand. "I love you, my darling," he whispered.

Bathsheba, only dimly aware of his presence, felt his protective strength. Her pain increased, and her thoughts turned inward, flashing out between the intervals of pain with startling clarity. Stark awareness of the little life struggling with such difficulty to be born into a cold and hostile world filled her eyes with tears. David, seeing them, thought they were from the pain and bent to kiss her gently.

Now wave after wave of intense pain tore through her and reaching out she grasped David's arm, digging her nails into his flesh, leaving marks that would be visible for days.

A cry broke the tenseness of the moment, and the oldest woman, with a toothless smile of triumph, held high the wriggling, red shape of a baby boy.

David's joy knew no bounds. Never had he seen a child that won his heart so quickly. He wrapped the newborn baby carelessly in his royal, purple cape and eagerly carried him out to the common room to show his men. The men laughed and jested, admiring his small son. But when he'd gone they whispered to each other, "The child appears to be large enough, and yet it was only seven months ago that Bathsheba was married to the king." A wave of criticism began to circulate against David. People who before had not dared to speak against the king became more open in their comments.

When David announced he was holding a great feast on the occasion of the child's naming, the criticism grew as people questioned the child's birth, the virtue of his mother and now even the integrity of David himself. David was completely unaware of the gossip and speculation revolving around him. He was so happy he did not even notice when his counselors fell silent in his presence and his friends grew distant. He did not sense the lack of respect shown him by his wives. Still worse, he did not know that some who had regarded him as their great spiritual leader were now disillusioned enough to turn to the worship of Baal and the old earth gods.

He made plans for the feast, tending to many of the details himself. Fish were to be sent from the Great Sea and one hundred lambs killed and stuffed with cracked grain. The tenderest herbs were brought to the kitchen, and the ovens burned night and day preparing the sweet cakes which would be given to everyone in Urusalim. This time, not wanting to repeat the slight he was accused of before at his wedding, David invited Joab and the chief captains personally.

David's wives were again reluctant to come to the feast. They didn't want to miss such a festive occasion, and yet they did not want to do honor to Bathsheba in any way. Michal and Ahinoam were angry that David would flaunt this child before all of them so brazenly and talked of nothing but ways that David should be confronted and accused. The men of Benjamin agreed with Michal but disagreed as to who should do it and where it should be done.

David's sons heard the rumors and rejected them as court gossip, except for Amnon who believed them because of what he had seen. Feeling rejected by his father and jealous of the king's attention to Absalom, he did not hesitate to encourage the rumors. Watching his father's indifference to the growing criticism, his cynicism grew. If you were strong enough, he reasoned, you could do just as you pleased.

Ahithophel dreaded the feast. After the baby's birth he had gone to the women's court to confront Bathsheba about the gossip. He had finally found her in David's apartments with the baby and several nursemaids but had stayed only a few minutes. In that time he had noticed that the child resembled his own family, and for a moment he forgot his anger. In a confusion of emotions, he left without saying a word.

When the day of the feast arrived, everyone who had been invited came, even though many had insisted they would never attend such an affair. David's wives were all present, as were his sons, the captains of his guard, Joab, the thirty mighty men, the heads of various tribes, and many foreign dignitaries. After everyone was seated, David entered with Bathsheba and a nursemaid who carried the baby.

Bathsheba looked pale and drawn, but David was at his best, waving to his friends, calling out to his favorites and even at one point taking the baby from the nursemaid and carrying him around to show him to his mighty men. "Already his right arm is unusually strong for a newborn babe," he said proudly.

The food had been served and cleared away, and the guests were more relaxed while waiting for the entertainment when suddenly, without warning, the great door to the room was thrown open. Everyone stopped talking and turned to the entrance, expecting to see dancers and musicians. Instead, there was just one man entering the hall: Nathan, the prophet. David was the last to notice, but when he looked and saw it was Nathan, he stretched out his hand in welcome. Nathan came slowly down the long hall until he stood in front of David. A deadly silence filled the room. All eyes were held by the majestic figure who not only had come to the feast late but was dressed in sackcloth covered with ashes.

David broke the silence, "What is it, my friend? What great sorrow has come to you at this time? Speak, and if there is anything we can do to help, it shall be done as you say."

"O my king, a great injustice has been done in Israel that needs to be set right."

"Let us hear it then," said David, "and I will pledge to bring it to justice for your sake."

"Not for my sake, O king, but for the sake of Israel," Nathan intoned.

"Then for the sake of Israel it must be made right. Come, tell us the tale."

"My king, in a certain city there was a rich man and a poor man. The rich man had great flocks and herds, but the poor man had only one ewe lamb. This lamb had become such a pet that he ate with the poor man's family and slept with his children. One day a visitor came to the home of the rich man, and he decided to honor the guest with a feast. He ordered his servants to leave his own sheep and to take the lamb of this poor man. This the servants did. The poor man's one ewe lamb

300

was taken from him, killed, and baked and served to the traveler. Now, O king, what should be done to this man that justice may again reign in Israel?"

Angrily David said to Nathan, "As the Lord lives, the man who has done this thing shall surely die, but first he shall restore the lamb fourfold. He shall be punished not only for his theft but also for his lack of pity. Who is this man?"

A moment passed, tense with feeling. Then Nathan leaned forward and said in a voice that could be heard plainly. "You are the man. I would that God had chosen one who loved you less to bring this message."

David was stunned as though the words of Nathan had stabbed him in the heart. "If God has sent you with a message to be given to me, speak on," he said. "I must hear it though it condemn me and my entire house."

"Thus saith the Lord God of Israel to His servant David." Nathan spoke in a voice that echoed in the hall like thunder and yet at times was broken with emotion. " 'I, the Lord thy God, the Lord God of Israel, am He who anointed you king of Israel. It was I who delivered you out of the hand of Saul. It was I who gave you your master's house and your master's wives. I have given to you the house of Israel and of Judah, and I would have given you all that your heart desired. But you did not hearken unto Me. Why have you despised My commandments and done this evil in My sight?' "

David's face turned crimson. He grabbed the table as if for support, but Nathan continued in the same terrible voice. "You have killed Uriah the Hittite and have taken his wife to be your wife." Bathsheba, who had been staring at Nathan with wide startled eyes, suddenly moaned and hid her face.

"The Lord saith," continued Nathan, "that the sword shall never depart from your own house, 'because you have despised Me and have taken the wife of Uriah the Hittite to be your wife. Behold I will raise up evil against you in your own house, and I will take your wives from before your eyes and give them to your neighbor, and he will openly lie with them. For you sinned in secret, but this thing will be done before all Israel.' "

As Nathan said these words a great sadness swept over David. "Nathan," he said, "I have sinned against the Lord, and surely you are warning me that He has rejected me like Saul. Tell me, Nathan, what is my punishment? Am I to die?"

Nathan looked directly at David, and his voice was full of compassion. "The Lord has put away your sin, and you will not die. Nevertheless, because you have given the enemies of God occasion to ridicule Him, this child who has been born unto you will surely die."

Nathan turned and walked from the room just as he had come, while everyone sat stunned and shaken.

Bathsheba was the first to move. She rose slowly as in great pain. For a moment only the face of Nathan registered on her consciousness as though it were the face of God—unsmiling, pained, accusing. Then she turned and saw the face of her grandfather, Ahithophel, staring at David. His look of outraged indignation would be forever etched upon her mind. She wanted to run to him and plead with him to have mercy. To forgive. Then her grandfather turned his head and for a moment looked at her with recognition. His eyes, wide and questioning, were raw with hurt.

With a great sob she turned from all she had seen in his eyes and groped toward the nurse who held her small child. "This child shall surely die," thundered and crashed around her. Tenderly she lifted the little bundle from the nurse's arms and ran through the nearest door and up the stairs, shielding him from the curious bystanders. Only in David's room would they be safe. She hurried, sobbing all the while, until inside the room she sank down on a mat and held her baby close.

David slowly turned to find Bathsheba gone. His remorse turned to alarm as he strode past the astonished guests, down the long banqueting hall, seeing no one until he came to the door leading to the stairway. There Amnon and Absalom stood, their faces bold with contempt as they stared back at him. Later David was to remember their faces vividly and to mark from that moment the break with his sons.

12

DAVID HURRIED to his room and was relieved to find Bathsheba sitting on a fur rug beside the carved box that served as the baby's bed. He had not noticed before, but she had decorated the little bed with sweet-smelling herbs and tiny wild rosebuds, a custom followed by the country women. She seemed not to see him now but sat rocking the baby gently in her arms. Such a look of love and concern he could not remember ever having seen on any other face. He stood watching her, trying to comprehend all that she must be feeling at that moment.

Perhaps being childless in the house of Uriah for so many years intensified her feelings for this little one. He remembered how proudly she had carried it in her womb and how sure she had been that it would be a boy. He recalled her faraway, tender look whenever she had mentioned the baby, almost as though already it were a real person. With a shock he sensed that she would prefer to have some harsh punishment fall upon herself than upon this little one.

David closed the door quietly and came to where she was sitting. He dropped to her side, pulling back the linen so he could see his son. The baby's hair stood up in thick tufts of black; his little eyes were closed and his mouth pursed into a round circle, ready to cry or to eat. He noticed that she had placed fragrant herbs and flowers in the swaddling bands, leaving one small hand free and unbound to curl around her finger.

"Bathsheba," David said gently, "perhaps Nathan was mistaken. The baby is so healthy and strong. . . ."

She didn't answer him but held the baby more tightly. Slowly the tears welled in her eyes and dropped unhindered on the small hand she held.

David watched her, his heart torn by her pain. He knew there would be other children, he knew this grief would pass, but he could not say this to her now. *Nathan did not say "he will die,"* David rationalized to himself. *He said, "surely he will die." Surely does not mean for sure. It may be that the Lord will have mercy and turn away from this harsh judgment. I cannot undo what I have done, but I can go and plead this small one's case before the Lord.*

David knelt beside Bathsheba and the baby, overwhelmed by the suffering in her face. He put his arms around her and held her for a moment, then gently turned her face toward him.

"Sheba, my darling, I shall not give up until God Himself tells me there is no hope. I am going to leave you here while I go plead for this small one's life."

He kissed her gently, then held her to him as he said, "It is necessary for me to go, but remember that I love you. In taking you I was wrong, but I loved you then, and I love you now; nothing can change that." He waited until she put out her hand and touched his arm with a slight pressure to give him a sign that she understood.

Outside David found Beniah, the captain of Bathsheba's personal guard, with some of the men. The king took Beniah aside and commissioned him to guard his chamber, letting no one in but a few women to help his wife. The guard was silent as though disapproving.

"Beniah, you must not think ill of my wife. The fault is mine before God, all mine."

"It is not that, my lord, it is only that there are no women who will come." He stopped in embarrassment.

David was trying to understand the meaning of Beniah's words when he heard the sound of footsteps on the stairs. Then Rizpah and Jessica appeared. Rizpah spoke, "My lord, we have come to wait upon Bathsheba."

She paused a moment until she saw the relief and gratitude on David's face then led the way into the room to comfort Bathsheba. David turned from them and wound his way alone up to the pavilion on the roof. He bowed himself to the floor and cried out of the depths of his heart to God.

Oh, God, You have always answered me when I
  have called You;
You have built walls about me so that my enemies
  could not reach me.

Now, O Lord, see my heart and know that I intend
  no evil.
Forgive me and heal my child.

I was foolish, Lord;
I thought because I was king I could make my own
  rules.

I forgot that this was Your world;
This was Your kingdom and I was but Your servant.

David rose and stood silently looking out at the
setting sun as he had seen it so many times as a
shepherd boy in Bethlehem. Always before when
he had stood and prayed in this manner he had felt
the presence of God. Now he felt nothing. It was as
though the sky was empty and God had retreated
into some remote corner of His world. He remembered old King Saul. Saul had not stooped to such
blatant sin, yet God had rejected him. It had been
terrible to see the suffering of Saul. He had never
admitted he was wrong. To the day he died he argued and justified himself.

"Lord," David knelt in prayer again, "I'm not so
foolish as to try to tell You I'm right. I know I did
wrong. Every day I judge men harshly for taking
things that do not belong to them. I have meted out
death to those who took their neighbor's wife or
their neighbor's life and now, O Lord, I am guilty of
both. You are my Judge. Take my life, but oh, my
God, spare my little son!"

While David stayed on the roof, no one dared
come to him except old Mahat, who insisted upon

bringing him food which he always refused. Each time she would turn away, grieved at the haggard face and rent garments of her king. Sometimes she found him pacing back and forth, head tipped back as if listening for some message of reprieve for his son. At other times she found him kneeling on the bare floor, his head cupped in his hands.

Once he came down the long stairs to his room to see if the baby was still healthy and well. Inside the door he met Rizpah who drew him aside. "My Lord, the child has taken strangely ill. He cannot live much longer unless he can take the milk we give him. My lady has plenty of milk, but the child cannot keep it down." Rizpah wrung her hands in despair.

David's face paled as he saw Bathsheba. She was rigid with concern and totally unaware of anyone in the room. The baby lay limp and feverish in her arms. He could sense the desperation with which she raised the little head and applied cool cloths to his fevered brow. Her beautiful hair hung in damp dishevelment; her clothes were wrinkled and unkempt. If he had not known this was his lovely bride, he would not have recognized her. Yet, surprisingly, he found his love for her was more intense than it had ever been. He desperately wanted the little one to live for her sake. He turned and walked out of the room and back up the steps to the pavilion. He did not kneel as before. Instead he slumped down upon the dais, his face in his hands.

He remembered how lightly he had called for Bathsheba to come to him. It had seemed so right, so beautiful. How had he not seen beyond the moment? How could he have been so blind?

Now he remembered the last time he had seen Uriah. How could he have given him the message of death so callously? He groaned as he imagined what Uriah must have felt when left alone to die before the walls of Rabboth Ammon. Then he prayed:

Oh, my God, don't keep looking at my sins;
Erase them from Your sight.

Create in me a clean heart,
A clean heart filled with clean thoughts and right
    desires.

Don't toss me aside,
Don't take Your Holy Spirit from me.

Oh, my God, make me willing to obey You.
I know You don't want penance;
If You did, how gladly I would do it.

You aren't interested in offerings,
Burned before You on an altar.

It is a broken spirit You want,
A broken and contrite heart, O God, You will not
    ignore.

There was a slight stir near the opening to the pavilion and David looked up to see old Mahat standing in the doorway. She could not speak but stood shaking her old head and holding her mantle to her quivering lips. David, seeing her grief, knew that Nathan's words had come true and that his son was dead. He slowly rose from the dais and ordered his servants to bring fresh garments. When he was dressed as befitted the king of Israel, he left the pavilion and went down the stairs.

He paused for a moment outside the door to his room and listened to the sad keening of the women for the dead. He opened the door quietly and saw the women gathered around Bathsheba and her child. The child was lying on a square of costly linen. Bathsheba, thin and worn, her dark hair falling over her shoulders hiding her face, was gently washing each small hand, each lifeless arm, and the small, motionless face. The keening sound of the women grew louder as she bent and laid her own cheek against the baby's soft hair.

The time came to wrap the baby in linen with pungent spices. Jessica and Rizpah held open the carrying cloth and Bathsheba, seeing their intent, lifted the small lifeless form wrapped so tightly in the coarse grave clothes and for the first time wept freely.

David stepped forward out of the shadows and lifted the small form from her arms, placing it tenderly in the carrying cloth. "When did Bathsheba last eat?" David asked Jessica.

"My lord, she would not eat."

Mahat appeared at the door, and David called to her, "Go, old one, and prepare food for us that we may be strengthened. I must journey with my men to the family tombs at Bethlehem before nightfall."

Mahat looked bewildered at the change that seemed to have taken place in her king. Seeing her astonishment, David explained. "While my son was alive, I fasted, hoping that God would have mercy and spare the little lad. Now there is no more reason to do this. Someday I will go to my son, but he will never come back to me."

Hearing his words, Bathsheba began to cry again softly. David motioned the women to leave them alone. When the door had closed behind them, David stooped down and gathered Bathsheba up in his arms as though she were a small child. With swift, sure strides he carried her to the great bed of Hadadezer that he had taken in battle and gently placed her down among the soft skins. He sat down beside her and brushed the damp hair from her face so he could see her eyes. "Don't cry, my love," he said softly. "I will carry our little son myself to Bethlehem, and with my own hands I will place him in the burial cave with Boaz and Naomi and all my people."

At the mention of the cave she drew in her breath sharply, and suddenly he was filled with an over-whelming tenderness for her. "He's gone back to the God who made him," he said, watching her closely. "We'll see him again, I promise you."

She tried to speak, but the words would not come. Only the keen-sound of deep and wrenching loss flowed through her parched and swollen lips. Her anguish was untouched by his words of comfort, and nothing he could do or say would lift the weight of guilt from her soul.

She clung to him and let him brush the damp tendrils of hair from her face and kiss the tear-streaked cheeks. He wondered at the bitter pain that held them closer than passion. He pulled her to him until her trembling form was enveloped in his great, rough cloak. He wondered briefly if indeed she could conceive again. Another child would speak to her of God's forgiveness and ease her pain. A child born, not of lust or fleshly desire, but of this deep, aching need to comfort each other.

In the women's court Michal called Jessica to her and demanded to know all that had happened. When she heard that the baby had died, she called for Ahinoam and told her the news and the two women rejoiced together. "Now my nephew will sit on the throne of his grandfather, Saul," gloated Michal.

Ahinoam stiffened, "Amnon will sit on the throne of his father, and if your nephews learn to respect him, I'm sure they will be well treated."

The two women who had been such close friends a short moment before were now wary and hostile. "It will be the sons of Saul who will rule in the future. David and the house of Jesse are finished." Michal's eyes flashed and her long nails dug into the pile of the cushion at her side.

"If one from the family of Saul is to rule, it will not be from your nephews but from the sons of Rizpah." Ahinoam rose from the dais and drew her robes around her. "The sons of Rizpah are the only true sons of Saul," she taunted.

"I still control the tribe of Benjamin, and what I say, they will do." Michal leaned back among the cushions and tried to look composed though her drumming fingers betrayed her annoyance. "David has never been able to claim the loyalty of the northern tribes and now that he is in such disgrace, even Judah will turn against him."

"It's not a matter of the people's choice," Ahinoam insisted. "Samuel, the prophet of God, anointed David as king, and David's sons will follow him on the throne, whether the tribe of Benjamin approves or not."

Michal laughed a hard, mirthless laugh as she rose and came to stand before Ahinoam. "My father was anointed by Samuel too. He believed all that foolishness about the oil, and it drove him out of his mind." She threw her head back defiantly. "I don't believe in anything but myself. My nephews will rule after David, not because some old man puts holy oil on them, but because I have laid careful plans. I can see now that everything is going to work out even better than I had thought."

Fear glinted in Ahinoam's eyes as she turned to

face Michal. "What do you mean?"

"However you choose to look at it, David is finished. He has committed far greater sins than my father. If he had not tried to be *soooo* good, *soooo* innocent and *soooo* noble, the people could have understood. If you could search through all Israel you would not find a man who has committed worse sins than David."

"Do you really think the people will turn from David?" Ahinoam's eyes were filled with alarm.

Michal ignored the question as she sank down among the cushions on the soft mat and leaned back smiling, a smug look on her proud face. "I can hardly wait to see it happen. I know these people. I saw it happen to my father. First they will whisper among themselves. Then they will laugh at him behind their hands and ignore his commands. He will find his armor unpolished, his cup unfilled, his bath cold, and always their eyes unsmiling and disdainful. Finally, they will taunt him openly and plot his overthrow, and I will be there to laugh and laugh and laugh."

Dark clouds rolled in from the east. A hot wind stirred the dust, and a few large drops of rain fell on the warm stones of the court. The sunshine of the morning hours had turned to the threatening gloom of afternoon showers when David rode into the palace courtyard with his guards. It was a man's business to bury the dead, and Bathsheba would not be going to the burial caves at Bethlehem. The child lay in a carved box on a cart garlanded with wild flowers. Curious bystanders crowded and pushed to get a better look at the object of all their gossip.

Beniah rode into the courtyard with the Cherethites and took his place behind the king, but David gave no signal for the procession to move. He was silent and withdrawn, waiting and looking toward the Valley Gate for the tribesmen of Judah, his brothers and his sons.

"They are not coming." Beniah was at his side speaking softly so the gathering villagers could not hear. "None of them will be going to Bethlehem."

When David looked at him questioningly, Beniah spoke hesitantly, not wanting to hurt the king further. "They have vowed among them . . ."

"All the tribesmen . . . my brothers and sons? Why? What reason do they give?"

Beniah shifted uneasily. "They say you desecrated the burial cave to place this child with all the noble men of Jesse's tribe."

David said nothing, but his hands gripped the reins more tightly, and his back stiffened. He turned from Beniah and pulled his cloak around him to ward off the rain. He started to give the signal for the men to move out of the courtyard when he noticed someone standing in the shadows. With a start he saw it was Bathsheba.

She walked toward them as in a trance, neither seeing the crowds that parted for her to pass nor feeling the rain that fell. She stopped beside the cart and gently fingered the dripping flowers and ran her hand over the damp surface of the carved box that held the body of her child. David dismounted and came to stand beside her. He placed his hand over her smaller hand and drew it from the box, speaking to her in quiet, comforting words that could not be heard above the sound of thunder and stirring wind. She nodded, and the drops of rain that clung to her tangled hair ran down her face like giant tears giving even the most critical observer a twinge of pain.

Bathsheba seemed unable to turn from the cart that carried the body of her dead baby. It seemed to bother her that the rain was falling and on impulse she pulled her shawl from her shoulders and carefully placed it over the box, tucking it in at the sides as though she were putting a child to bed for the night.

A clap of thunder sounded to the west and lightning split the sky in two, but she noticed nothing of the weather or the people crowded around her. With a sigh, she turned at last and walked alone, back to the open door of the women's court, unmindful that her hair was blowing loose in the rising wind, and her skirts were dragging behind her in the mud of the courtyard.

David did not mount until she vanished from sight. "We are going to Bethlehem," he told Beniah. "This child has done no wrong. It is I who stand accused and rightly so." Without another word he sprang into the saddle and led his men out the Valley Gate.

The wind tore at him, and the rain pelted down, penetrating the tightly woven cloth of his cloak. In places the low-hanging fog obscured the path and wet branches of the pines that edged the road brushed against him. He could hear the steady creaking of the cart as it bumped along and the clipping sound of the mule's feet on the stony path, but his men were hidden from him by the fog. He felt nothing but a great sense of loss. It was not the child lying in the carved box riding behind him that burdened him but a loss deeper than anything he could express. He felt bereft, separated, alone. Even his brothers had not stood by him. Only the palace guard and his Philistine mercenaries would be there when he carried his son into the family cave.

He remembered other times—times when the

family of Jesse had stood together and wept, locked in each other's arms at the mouth of the cave. They had always been a loyal family, standing together against their enemies and even against the other tribesmen.

At the cave he let his men pull away the sod and roll back the stone, but he alone went into its dark depths with the small box still covered with Bathsheba's shawl. He found a niche prepared for an infant and he wedged the box into place. The tomb was fetid, dank, and silent with only a distant sound of the rain falling outside and the low murmur of voices coming from a great distance. On a sunny day with all the men of Judah to pray and chant and weep together, this cave had been a fearful place. But now in the gloom and silence the very walls of the cave seemed to close over him. Untold numbers of his tribesmen and family lay wrapped in their decaying shrouds, all honorable, all righteous. In the larger niches lay Ruth and Boaz, parents of Obed, grandparents of Jesse. Would they, too, resent his bringing this small one to lie here with them?

As a young boy, coming here with his shepherd's crook to bury Obed, he had believed this cave to be the very antichamber to the house of God. Now as a grown man, jeweled and perfumed, he waited to hear the voice of God. He heard nothing but the sound of rain and his own imagination again forming distinctly the ominous tones of Nathan's dire predictions:

The sword shall never depart from your house . . .
Behold I will raise up evil against you in your own house . . .
And I will take your wives from before your eyes. . . .

It was not over. There was more tragedy to come. Where would it strike first? Who would be the victims?

He backed from the cave toward the opening where his men waited cold and wet in the early dusk. He did not speak to anyone nor did he wait for his men to roll the stone back across the cave's opening. He mounted his mule and rode alone ahead of his men, back towards Urusalim.

13

In THE DAYS that followed the death of her baby, Bathsheba stayed in David's quarters, ill with fatigue and fever, and so heard nothing of the verbal battle that raged over and around her. The men of Benjamin, encouraged by Michal, had been the first to insist that Bathsheba must be punished. Then David's tribe of Judah, his brothers and his sons, refused to come to court as long as she was in the palace. David listened patiently to them all, and finally, fearing for Bathsheba's life, agreed that she should move to one of the new houses being built along the western ridge.

Within the week Bathsheba was strong enough to sit upon a donkey and make the short journey through the Valley Gate out to the small stone house David had prepared for her. She was relieved to be away from the confining walls of the harem and out of its hostile atmosphere. Hearing she was gone, the men of Judah and David's sons returned to stand beside the king, silent and morose, their presence restoring to the court some semblance of its old routine.

But the whispering and conjecturing did not stop, and there was a new rebelliousness among the princes. Some of David's close advisors, like Ahithophel, now turned from him. They had been annoyed with what they'd called "his old perfection," but now that he had shunned the usual human frailties to indulge in sins they carefully avoided, they were enraged.

Of them all, Ahithophel had suffered most. After Nathan's denunciation he had ridden to Giloh where he bolted all the doors and sat alone in the gloom of his old home. Over and over again, Nathan's thundering words pounded in his temples. He paced the floor and cursed the king and the cruel fate that had dealt him such a blow.

Since the bitter night in Mahanaim so long ago when Abner told him that his son was dead, he had thought himself impervious to further hurt. But now, experiencing a mental anguish so intense it made him ill, he quickly sank into a bleak depression. He could not forget the smug remarks and open slights cast his way, nor the eyes glistening with delight at his confusion, nor winks of amusement at his plight.

"All this I could endure," he muttered, "but not the thought of her betrayal." He had trusted Bathsheba completely. He wondered how she had gone so easily from his advice to give herself to David's lust. He saw Bathsheba's smiling face, her open, honest eyes and felt again her baby arms around his neck. All that he knew of her and loved was slipping from him in this monstrous tragedy.

"I cannot let her go," he groaned. Along with Giloh, she had become one of the desecrated treasures of his broken heart.

Gradually his illness passed, and once again he opened all the doors and walked with measured steps about his courtyard. Again he felt the sun upon his back and watched the storks fly overhead. He noticed how his hands looked old and gnarled, the flesh upon his arms no longer firm. "I am like olive trees on Olivet," he grimaced, "with silver hair, rough bark, and at the center, hard as a round pit."

The outcome of his anguished vigil was to find Bathsheba innocent of any wrong. She had no choice, he reasoned. It was the king he blamed for everything, this king whom he once worshiped almost as a god and who repaid him with such treachery and inexcusable deceit. All that the king had done to make the wedding glorious had only added to his misery. "I'll have revenge," he vowed. "I will not rest until I've had revenge. The first step will be to go and bring Bathsheba home."

It was late afternoon when Ahithophel rode over to the western ridge and found his granddaughter outside her small stone house, weeding among her herbs and pink thicket-roses. There was a moment of uneasy silence as Bathsheba looked up from her work and saw him standing in the shadow of her wall. She was aghast to see how old he looked, how hard his mouth and chin were set, and how defiantly he bore himself.

He has been hurt. So badly hurt, she thought. *He trusted me. And I betrayed his trust.*

"Bathsheba," he said quietly, "I've come to take you home." There was no anger in his voice or hidden blame. She dropped the digging tool, ran to him, threw her arms around his neck and cried.

He would not come inside, and he refused the fruit her servant brought him. He was intent upon his purpose, to rescue her from David and take her home with him to Giloh. "There you will grow strong again, and all this trouble will be forgotten."

It seemed a monstrous thing to tell him no, to

318

disappoint this fine old man who loved her so. "Grandfather," she said hesitantly, "I cannot leave the king."

She spoke the words softly, and yet Ahithophel drew back as though he had been struck a fatal blow. "You cannot leave?"

"Grandfather, I love my lord, the king, with all my heart."

"Love. I do not doubt you think it's love you feel, but let me tell you what it really is you're choosing: an occasional tumble in the king's bed and then a lonely life with his forgotten wives. Come home with me. There you'll be safe."

"Grandfather, I cannot leave the king." The tears ran down her cheeks, her eyes begged for his understanding.

Ahithophel looked at her helplessly, angry that David should have such a hold on his granddaughter. "Then stay, but be assured that this king, this man you say you love, will pay and pay and pay for what he has done. I'll have revenge." He turned without another word and walked out through the postern gate, leaving Bathsheba pale and shaken.

David often came to visit her in the evening. She watched for him, sitting at her low window facing toward the city so she could see the first dim glow of his lantern as he passed through the Valley Gate. Quickly she would prepare the rooms for his visit. Rose water was sprinkled over the cushions, incense lit in the alabaster urn; coals were fanned in the brazier, and she would be dressed in one of the new robes he had given her.

When he arrived she always sent Sara and the other servants away, removed his sandals and bathed his feet herself, anointing them with warm, fragrant oil. She served him tea and small cakes made by her own hands as he watched, piled the pillows for his comfort and sang for him the village harvest songs he loved. There was never any mention of the battle of Rabboth Ammon or the hostility he encountered at court. She wanted these evenings together to be small islands of peace in the midst of the storm that raged around them.

Though the subject of all their heartache was not mentioned, it hung heavy in the air between them until late one evening a month later. "My lord," Bathsheba said, "can you tell me what it is that bothers you most? Was it the pain of having Nathan denounce you publicly or the predictions he made of trouble yet to come?"

"Neither," he said thoughtfully. "It is something more subtle. I know God has heard me. I had that assurance as I prayed on the roof for our son's life. It is something different. It is as though some glory has departed; some bright joy is gone."

"I'm not sure I understand."

"I don't understand it myself," David said. "When Samuel came to my father's house long ago and chose me to be king, I knew God loved me. I thought He loved me and chose me because I was perfect and upright in all my ways. If I had died on Gilboa instead of Jonathan, I would have died believing that I was incapable of any evil deed. I walked in righteousness, delighted in the law, and was hard on men who were weak and sinful. Now I find that within my heart, all this time waiting to show itself, was both adultery and murder. You see, I never was perfect."

David paused, looking at Bathsheba for understanding, but she was silent.

"Don't you see?" he said in anguish, his head buried in his hands. "The sin in me was there all the time. I now consider myself not as better than other men but as much worse. With this knowledge, the glory has departed."

Bathsheba took his hand reassuringly as he continued. "After I was anointed by Samuel, I feared nothing. God was with me. What could man do to hurt God's anointed? I knew I could not possibly lose. Even to fight a giant was not difficult. Whatever I attempted I knew that God would bear me up. But now I've lost that sureness. My life has been spared, I am still king of Israel, but the glory is gone. If the giants should walk again in the Valley of Elah, I would not dare go out against them. I'm afraid I would sit in my tent as Saul did years ago. The power is gone. The glory has departed. Do you understand?"

Bathsheba nodded. "Yes, I remember seeing you come home from battle joyous and confident. There was something special about you. I think it was this glory that I saw. There was no fear in you, no fear at all."

"It is not just the glory that is gone," David said quietly. "I can no longer find God. For the first time in my life, I am anxious and fearful. If the Philistines should come up against us as they have in the past, I would not know the outcome of the battle. I have become apprehensive enough to ask Joab to number the men of Israel."

Bathsheba was as shocked as David's men had been. Over and over she had heard Ahithophel insist that Israel would never have a proper army until the tribesmen were numbered and conscripted into service. In the past David had laughed, telling Ahithophel not to worry; God would send men as they were needed. "My lord," Bathsheba said, "what does Joab think?"

David shrugged. "He is annoyed. When the battle

321

of Rabboth Ammon is over, we will discuss the numbering of Israel again."

There was silence between them as each tried to dismiss all that Rabboth Ammon called to mind. When David spoke again it was without enthusiasm. "At any moment now, Joab will send for me to come and take part in the capture of this city."

"Perhaps if you defeat the Ammonites, you will know that God is with you again."

"I wish before God that it was really that simple. But I have done far more evil than Saul, and he was never restored."

Bathsheba reached out and touched David's clenched fist. "My darling, remember this. Saul never admitted his guilt nor sought forgiveness."

David stood up. "The water jar that is broken may be put back together again, but the cracks are there and always will be. Perhaps I cannot endure the thought that I am but a mended jar, unfit to hold God's holy oil."

Bathsheba answered hesitantly, "In the hands of a skillful potter, a jar can be mended. Maybe it cannot hold water, but it can hold grain. Does it matter which it holds so long as it is useful again?"

The stillness of the night was broken by the steady *plop, plop* of mules coming up the slope from the city. Quickly David moved to the window and in the light of the lantern he recognized two soldiers from Joab's camp.

"What is the news?" David called out impatiently.

"Joab requests your presence at the capture of the city of Ammon. If you can ride back with us, you will arrive in time for the final attack."

David stopped only to kiss Bathsheba good-by and then hurried out to join the men. When he was mounted, the older of the two men spoke urgently.

"There is bad news as well as the good."

"If there is bad news," said David, "I would have it first."

"The Philistines are ready to march again. Therefore Joab has urged his men to take the city of Rabboth Ammon as soon as possible."

"Where are the Philistines?"

"We have heard only that they are gathering for attack. Whether they intend to attack Joab's men at Rabboth Ammon or sweep down upon Urusalim while he is gone, we do not know. Joab has sent a division of his bravest men down to the plains to try and intercept the Philistines."

David nodded in agreement. "That should hold them for a time. Let's be off." He slapped the mule sharply with his riding whip and started down the narrow path that led back to Urusalim.

After he had gone, Bathsheba sat at the open window thinking. She was glad they had spoken frankly to each other, and yet, perhaps it had not been frank enough. She was again with child and wondered if she should have told him. She had hesitated, not knowing whether this news would make him happy or add to his sorrow. For herself, she knew it made all the difference. Another son, perhaps; a special child born out of their compassion for each other. This child would thrive and grow.

It was late the next day when David arrived at Rabboth Ammon. He had ridden most of the night and was tired and dusty from the road. Worse, he had spent the entire journey haunted by the figure of Uriah, who months before had marched along this same road, carrying the message that assured his death.

When greeted heartily by his men, the king smiled at them wanly and went sullenly into Joab's tent. Joab embraced him and bade him be seated.

"My lord, I dared not wait any longer. We have already taken the city. We have made slaves of the men as you ordered, and many of the women have been taken by our men as wives or servants. We did not kill them, as they are our relatives. Only the young king, Hannun, was killed. We have taken his crown and the men are waiting now at the gate to place it on your head."

David said nothing but sat down exhausted and moody. His feet were washed by a servant. He did not want to see the city, and he did not care to appear before its gates or have the crown placed on his head. He wanted nothing to do with the ill-fated place.

When Joab led him out before the shouting, jubilant men, David greeted them, but he could not share their joy. Before him was a path that had been cleared for the occasion, leading to the towering gate of the city. David noticed that Rabboth Ammon was built on a great pinnacle of rock, and this path was the only approach. On each side of the narrow roadway the ground fell away leaving steep cliffs, explaining why the city had been so difficult to take.

As David and Joab walked side by side toward the city gate where his army captains waited with the jeweled crown, David turned suddenly and took Joab by the arm.

"How did he die, Joab? I have to know. How did Uriah die?"

Joab looked startled. He was a man who fought hard, did whatever he felt had to be done, and then forgot about it. He met David's piercing, steady gaze and shrugged.

"I obeyed your orders. Every day the men of Rabboth Ammon marched out of that gate up there with their shields and spears. Then as our men advanced on them, they drew back, disappearing inside the gate, leaving our men open to the archers on the walls. You told us not to fight close to the wall. And we didn't until your message came."

David said nothing. His whole body was tensed against what he knew Joab would say next. "Every day it was the same," Joab continued. "They would march out, and our men would follow them back to the gate, being careful to stay out of range of the archers on the wall. Finally I suggested that some of our best fighters surprise them by rushing them at the gate for heavy, hand-to-hand fighting. Then, just at the right moment before it became too dangerous, they would be given a signal to draw back. I neglected to tell Uriah about drawing back nor did I give him a signal."

"You also neglected to tell Judah and Elihu, two of the men I cared for more than all the rest put together. They were the ones who risked their lives to bring me water from the well at Bethlehem while it was besieged."

Joab's eyes grew hard. "It grieved me to lose Uriah and in my anger I did not think to tell them. It was not my intention. . . ."

David's voice was harsh. "I know exactly how it happened. Now go on. I must hear it all—in this place and before these gates. And then I never want to hear of it again."

"It all happened just as planned," Joab continued. "The enemy came out of the gate toward us as far as they dared. At just the right time I led a charge of my men which pushed them back close to the wall. When I gave the signal to withdraw, those of us who knew dropped back. Judah and Elihu were killed within minutes, but Uriah . . ." Here he paused and looked at David.

"I must hear it all, Joab. What happened to Uriah the Hittite before these gates of Rabboth Ammon?"

"Uriah looked back too late and saw us retreating. I could tell that he knew. He knew everything."

"I was afraid of that."

"Uriah turned back to the men of Rabboth Ammon and fought so fiercely that they formed a circle around him, all of them slashing out at him with their swords and battle axes until he was wounded and bleeding. But Uriah wouldn't give up. He wouldn't stop fighting. Blood ran from his head and chest in great spurts, but he managed to stay on his feet and fight until, with a rush, they closed in on him."

Joab wasn't through with the grisly story. "When he finally fell before the gate, they dragged his body inside the city." He paused again. "We recovered the bodies of your friends and buried them on the hillside, but Uriah's body was hung from the walls of Rabboth Ammon. It remained there for days."

"Oh, my God, how can you forgive me for such a thing?" David groaned in anguish as he looked up and saw the gate before him.

"Come, there is no time now for regrets," Joab snapped. "Our men have fought bravely. They have looked forward to this moment when they could put the crown of Nahash on your head. You must not disappoint them."

David stared at Joab dully. He saw his men at the gate holding the crown of Nahash, eager to put it on his head. Over and above them was the great, arched gate of the city, and he could imagine vividly the body of the Hittite hanging from the walls. The scene was chiseled on his mind like the stylus writing of the scribe on wet clay. It would haunt him forever.

He squared his shoulders and marched ahead of Joab toward the gate to receive the crown from his friends.

14

SECLUDED IN HER home on the western ridge, Bathsheba had few reports of the final taking of Rabboth Ammon or of the battles that followed with the Philistines. Much of what she did hear turned out to be idle rumors until the day that Ahithophel came riding from Giloh in a terrible state of agitation and fear. "You must flee with me to Lodebar while there is yet time. The Philistines have broken through our lines, and they cover the plains and mountain gorges as far as the eye can see. There is going to be a terrible slaughter."

He refused the drink she offered him and waved away the servant who came to wash his feet. "Bathsheba, you must listen to me," he demanded. "The Philistines have again called out the giants of Gath. It will be a worse slaughter than the battle of Gilboa."

Bathsheba fought down the feeling of panic that surged through her. She remembered with alarm what David had said only a few days before. "If the giants should walk again in the Valley of Elah, I would not dare go out against them." She turned from Ahithophel and walked back and forth across the room, twisting the emerald ring David had given her, trying to fight down the fear she felt for David and for Israel.

"Bathsheba, you must go home to Lodebar while there is time." She could see that her grandfather was genuinely concerned for her safety even though she had disgraced him and brought dishonor to his name.

"I cannot leave my husband," Bathsheba said looking at Ahithophel with great pity.

His face turned red with anger and frustration. Without another word he turned and walked from the room and down the steps, mounted his mule, and rode off.

Days went by, and the summer fruit and grains were being gathered in by women and children working long hours under the bright, cloudless skies. The olives ripened on Olivet, and in Bathsheba's walled garden the herbs were ready to harvest before the news came that the Philistines had been overcome. The army of Israel had gained a great victory.

The people of Urusalim were ecstatic with joy. Windows were flung open and the news shouted across the narrow alleyways of the city. Crowds gathered at the gates to hear over and over again the reports of the battle brought regularly by runners from the coast.

It had not been David who went out to defeat the giants, but rather two obscure young men. One of them was Elhanan ben Jair and the other David's own nephew, Jonathan, the son of his brother Shimea. Jonathan had slain a giant of enormous stature who had six fingers and six toes on each of his hands and feet. The people were mildly surprised that it had not been David who challenged the giants. "He is too much a king to fight giants now. Giant fighting is for young boys," they concluded, laughing at their own bit of humor.

Once the giants were defeated, the Philistine army was totally unnerved and fled before the men of Israel. Victory followed victory, and the Philistines were driven back down the ravine right to the gates of Gath on the plain. David and his men had killed them by the hundreds until those who remained fell to their knees, begging for their lives, swearing allegiance to David and agreeing to pay tribute to him regularly as their overlord.

There had never been a greater victory for Israel. All of Urusalim was in a turmoil of celebration. While Bathsheba was happy to hear of the victory, a pang of apprehension nibbled away at her joy. She could almost envision David's thoughts as he rode home with his men. He would be angry and frustrated that he had not gone out against the giants himself. Perhaps he would even see these two young men as threats to his throne.

When David finally returned to Urusalim, she found that she was right. He did not mention his victories to her but dwelt only on his failures. He told her briefly how Uriah died, not giving in, but fighting with all his might until completely overwhelmed. He spoke slowly as though the very words stuck in his throat and choked him. He did not look at her or touch her but sat with his head in his hands looking down at the floor.

He spared no detail in telling how the giants had come again to challenge Israel while he sat in his tent like Saul, morose and moody.

Bathsheba put her arms around him and tried to kiss away the hurt, but when she looked into his eyes she knew it would not be easy. They stared at her without a spark of tenderness or love, like two cold, burned-out stars that had no message left to give.

David's men had been puzzled at his dour looks and sullen depression. Though they had returned exuberantly from one of the greatest victories Israel had ever won, the king had ridden before them silent and heavy-hearted. He had not played his harp; instead he had spoken sharply to his captains, giving them no word of commendation for all they had done. They remembered sadly the times in the past when they had feasted and celebrated with shouting and singing after far lesser victories. Remembering, they were hurt and puzzled by the unaccountable change in their hero.

Back in his palace among his men, David was driven by unrest. For the first time in his life he was experiencing fear; fear that his enemies would return, and he would be unable to turn them back. Even his prayers did not relieve him of this fear. Finally, reluctantly, he called in Joab and ordered him to number the men of Israel.

"My uncle," Joab said, "with two great victories behind us, we should be entering a time of peace when we will no longer need such a large army."

David was unmoved. He wanted the men numbered. He no longer had the assurance that El Saddai, the Almighty God, was with him. Therefore, he would rely on men and arms to secure the boundaries of his country.

Reluctantly Joab went out to the cities of Israel to number the men of fighting age. Each tribe greeted him with disrespect, not wanting to be controlled in this fashion. When asked in the past, they had gladly given of their young men; but to have this service demanded of them made them angry and rebellious.

When Joab returned two months later, David requested him to give his report before the captains and counselors. Even Ahithophel was summoned from Giloh to meet with them in his pavilion on the roof. "I would not be doing my duty if I did not inform the king that there is much sickness abroad in the land," Joab stated. "Some of the men who fought most valiantly before the walls of Rabboth Ammon have died. The people are asking some dangerous questions."

"What questions are the people asking?" David interrupted. "Though a man is able to survive a battle, this does not mean that he won't die of the summer fever."

Joab shook his head, "My lord, you do not understand. The people are whispering that this sickness has come upon them because the king has ordered the numbering. Every time a young man dies they say, 'See, God is showing the king who is in control.' They say these deaths are a punishment from God."

David turned pale. "A punishment from God?"

Joab hesitated, "It is a delicate subject, my lord. Do not ask me to explain."

"Joab, I must hear what the people are saying. Better I hear it from your lips than from another."

Joab motioned to the rest of them. "Leave us alone that I may tell the king all that I have seen."

"Let them stay," David ordered. "There is nothing secret here. Everyone knows what you are about to say, while I alone am uncertain."

Joab spoke hesitantly. "My lord, the people feel this sickness is a punishment from the Lord because you have numbered Israel and . . . " He paused, but David motioned for him to go on.

"They say the king is not as he used to be before the Lord. . . ."

Everyone was silent and embarrassed until David burst out angrily. "I'll tell you what they say. They say that David the giant killer sat in his tent cowering while the giants of the Philistines walked in the valley. They are saying that their king no longer dared fight the giants. They say. . . ."

"No, no, that is not what they are saying," interrupted Joab. "It may be that a few of the men of Benjamin have joked that way with Jonathan because he killed one of the giants, but that means nothing."

"Then what are they saying?" David demanded.

Joab cleared his throat and ran his fingers through his hair. "They are saying this punishment has come upon Israel because you took Bathsheba and knew her when she was another man's wife. And then you had Uriah killed because he would not cover your sin. Now you have numbered Israel because you fear that God is no longer with you as before."

As Joab said this, Ahithophel rose, his face pale and drawn. He started toward the door, then turned and faced the king. "Will I never hear the end of the disgrace you have brought upon me and my house? First my granddaughter became the scorn of all Israel, then my only great-grandson died, and now I find the tongues are still wagging over the dishonor that you have brought upon my house. Tell me no more of your prayers. You do not know God any more than I do. You have been among us as a holy man, but now we see that you are worse than any one of us. Speak to me no more of God. If there is one, He has ruined me and now sits laughing at my stupidity."

Ahithophel turned and stalked from the room.

No one spoke. David sat silent, his head in his hands, while one by one his men got up and left, not daring to see the look in their king's eyes.

Joab was the last to leave. He stood for a moment with the tent flap in his hand, looking back at his uncle and his king. To see the golden one, the lion of Judah, speechless with some deep, wordless depression frightened him. Joab dropped the flap and went down the stairs and out toward the guardhouse to sit with his captains.

It was there that Joab heard a slight disturbance at the gate. Gad, a prophet and a seer, was asking admittance to see the king. Joab instructed the guard to take him to David. As he watched the barefooted prophet, dressed in coarse cloth, his beard untrimmed, walk with long, sure strides to the stairs, Joab muttered to himself, "God of Israel, let him have some message for the king to bring him some comfort."

Gad stopped before the curtains of the pavilion and listened. The muffled voice of the king praying could be heard:

My God; oh, my God; night and day I am crying
    unto You, and You do not listen.
I remember all the days of my youth,
All of them gone.
You were as a shepherd to me;
I was one of Your sheep.

Now I am as one lost among dark caverns;
Or as one fallen into a deep pit.
Is there no end to this darkness?
Is there no way back into the light of Your love?

When David paused, the prophet opened the curtain and walked in. Gad was a man of quiet

333

self-assurance, a man who felt it quite natural that he should live among humble people and yet associate with the king. He walked over to David with outstretched hands and helped him to his feet. "God has sent me to you with a message," he said with simple directness.

He closed his eyes, and when he spoke again it was in the manner of the prophets. "So saith the Lord God of Israel: Choose you this day which of these three evils shall surely befall you. Either you will flee before your enemies for three months, or there will be seven years of famine in the land . . ." He paused a moment before giving the final choice. "Or there will be three days of pestilence with the angel of the Lord destroying throughout the land." The prophet stepped back waiting for an answer.

David stood there shaken, accepting the message as valid and pondering the choices. "It is a hard decision," he said thoughtfully, "but it seems better to fall into the hands of God than to fall into the hands of men, for great are the mercies of the Lord."

"So it shall be the last one then," said Gad as he turned to leave. Quickly David reached out to detain him. "I know I have displeased God and have done evil in his sight; but tell me, Gad, why is it that I and I alone am not punished?"

"It is not for us to question the ways of God any more than it is for your servants to question your will." Gad moved toward the door as if the subject was closed.

"Gad," David said with enough command in his voice to stop the prophet again, "has this punishment come upon Israel because I numbered its men? Is not this a cruel punishment for such a small thing?"

Gad thought for a moment. "I have been a prophet and a seer since my youth, and there is one thing that is plain to me. Physical death is normal and natural. It must come to all of us. This is not to be feared. Spiritual death is the real death, and if the threat of physical death brings spiritual life, then it is justified." With that he lifted the curtain and was gone.

15

IN THE DAYS that followed, David did not leave the pavilion but spent the time in meditation and prayer for his country. The first two days he heard nothing but sounds that were normal to the city. On the morning of the third day a wind that had sprung up over night seemed to weep and wail as it circled the palace. When David heard below him at the palace gate the sound of people weeping and shouting, he sent for his two priests, Abiathar and Zadok.

They came quickly and reported in hushed tones that from Dan to Beersheba a pestilence had struck the people of Israel. They were dying by the thousands.

"Have any died in Urusalim?" David asked anxiously. They shook their heads. "It is strange," they told him. "It seems to move across the land from north to south. Hebron and Bethlehem have been smitten, and we are fearful that Urusalim will be next."

"Go quickly to the gate," David instructed them, "and tell the people to put on sackcloth and ashes and to repent of all their sins. It is still possible that

God will spare the city." Then David sent for the elders of Israel to come to him on the roof dressed in sackcloth, that they might pray together.

When Abiathar and Zadok returned with the elders, they found the king out on the ramparts of his palace looking toward the north where the huge projection of rock known as Mount Moriah could be seen rising beyond the wall of the city. He stood with his feet apart, bracing himself against a wind that tore at his hair and tugged at his robes of sackcloth. He stood as though unaware of their presence as they crowded together and waited for him to speak.

When David turned and saw them huddled before him, clutching their cloaks of sackcloth against the wind, he moved toward them. "As I walked up and down on the roof," he said, "the Lord opened my eyes so that I saw the angel of destruction standing on Mount Moriah with a drawn sword stretched out over the city of Urusalim. Look now to the north above the mount and you will see him too, for he stands there still, just as I first saw him."

The elders looked where he pointed, and many of them fell to their knees in awe, saying that they, too, saw the angel with the drawn sword. Such was the emotion of the moment that even those who could see nothing also fell down and wept and prayed that God would have mercy on them and spare their city.

Then David came to stand in the midst of them and prayed in a loud voice that could be heard over the roar of the wind. "O God, God of my fathers, it was I who did evil in Your sight. Let Your hand be on me and my father's house, but spare these sheep for they have done no wrong."

No one saw Gad enter, but suddenly the weeping

subsided. Gad raised his hand for silence, then turned to David and shouted over the sound of the wind. "The angel of the Lord has sent me again to you with this message: 'Your prayer has been heard. Go now to the threshing floor of Araunah, the Jebusite, and set up an altar before all the people. Here you will offer burnt offerings and peace offerings and your prayers will be heard and your city spared.' "

The great wind continued to blow as David and the elders did as Gad had instructed them. They passed through the court and out the North Gate in silence, with the wind howling and tearing at their cloaks. Then, as they climbed to the gray stone threshing floor of Araunah, the wind slowly began to die down. Finally, as David stood before Araunah and asked if he could buy his threshing floor to build an altar, the wind became a gentle breeze, fragrant with the smell of new-mown hay.

Araunah insisted on giving his oxen for the burnt offering and the threshing sledges for wood. David thanked him but refused. "No, I must buy them for the full price. I will not take for the Lord that which is yours or present a burnt offering which costs me nothing." Araunah accepted 600 shekels of gold for the threshing floor, the oxen, and the sledges. Then David and his men built an altar to the Lord.

The priests and elders and all the people who had followed them out to the threshing floor stood in silence before the altar. Each man looked within himself to find the sins of deceit, malice, envy, covetousness, blasphemy, lust, greed, murder, cruelty, pride, adultery, and hatred for which they stood guilty before God and their fellowmen. Then as they had been taught by their fathers, they brought their sins and failures up out of the secret places of their hearts where they had hidden them and laid them on the oxen before God to be sacrificed.

David stood before them, silent, lost in meditation. Now that he carried a greater weight of guilt than he had ever known before, this sacrifice for sin had new meaning. "Surely I have sinned more than these my brethren," he prayed. "How can the blood of these oxen take away the guilt and shame that I carry in my heart? As a king I have often pronounced the death penalty on men who have sinned as I have sinned."

Then he heard in the deep recesses of his heart the voice of God speaking gently to him. "You are guilty, and I have decreed that sin must be punished. But because I have loved you with an everlasting love I have provided a substitute for death if you will take it. See now these oxen. I have decreed that every sin placed on these oxen will no longer rest on you. You will go free. The Lord your God does not mean for you to be forever burdened with this guilt."

A great joy filled David's heart. He pictured all his wrongdoing, not just his taking the wife of Uriah or plotting Uriah's death, but all his frustration and anger, doubts and fears, the depression he had suffered and the losses he had borne. He brought them all out and placed them on the sacrificial oxen before him. Now for the first time he grasped the overwhelming truth that God had forgiven him and did not intend that he carry this burden of guilt forever.

Nor did it matter that he did not understand how the sacrifice of these oxen could take away his sin. What mattered was that God loved him. He loved these people clustered around him and those afar off. He loved them enough to plan a way by which a man could be free of his sin and guilt.

Tears ran down his face as he prayed:

Purge me with hyssop, Lord, that I may be clean;
Wash me that I may be whiter than snow.
Rescue me from blood-guiltiness, O God.
Create in me a clean heart,
And renew a right spirit within me.

He watched the priests bind the animals to the altar and kill them with one swift stroke. He saw all of the sins and doubts and failures of his past bound on that altar with the oxen. God had planned it so that he could see and hear and feel the weight of his burden lifted from him and placed on these oxen and then burned in the all-consuming fire of God's altar.

The fire leapt up, and the men stood watching it as the sacrifice was lost in the roaring flames and smoke. No one spoke. Each man stood alone, and yet all were bound together.

Suddenly an old man pointed to the clouds that hovered above the pinnacle of the hill. "See, the angel of the Lord has sheathed his sword; the city is saved!" They all looked up and some saw the angel standing above the city with his sword sheathed; others saw nothing. But they all rejoiced together.

The rest of the day David was with his people as he had been before he became king. They sang praises unto God, and David played again on his harp as he had not played in months. Finally as the sun sank low over the mountain, David rose and spoke.

"Men of Israel, we are on holy ground. Our father, Abraham, when he was a stranger in this land, brought his son here and built an altar on this same spot and placed his son on the altar as a sacrifice to our God. God spared Abraham's son then as he has spared our lives today by providing for us a fitting sacrifice. The sword of death was seen by many of us. We deserved to die, for we are all men of evil deeds and thoughts. There is none righteous among us, none without sin. But God has heard our prayers and has accepted our offering and healed our land.

"We are crude men of battle and our hands are stained with blood. Nathan, the prophet, has brought us God's word that we cannot build the temple to our God as we would like to do. But we may prepare and bring together as gifts of love to our God all that will be needed to build a temple to Him on this spot."

The men shouted and laughed and sang, reluctant to leave. One moment their lives had been threatened by the angel of death. Now, suddenly, miraculously, they had been spared. They were farmers and merchants and shepherds. Many were rough fighting men who would be uncomfortable any place but in the open air. They would not have known how to go about building a great temple, but collecting the materials for the building was different. That was something they could do. To cut the stone, make the pegs, hammer the brass, dig in the mountains for gold and precious stones to adorn a temple suited them perfectly.

There was almost a visible bond unifing them as they left the threshing floor of Araunah and headed back to the city. At the North Gate they parted and returned to their homes. While David's men rode back into the city, the king and his armor bearer traveled on down the path leading to Mount Zion.

David did not tell his men where he was going, but they all knew that he must be going to see

Bathsheba. For four days he had not seen her. In fact, during this whole time he had not thought of her nor had he thought of his old counselor, Ahithophel. Now he wondered what had happened to Ahithophel. He had not been with the elders on Mount Moriah nor had he been seen by anyone since leaving the pavilion in such anger.

David knew it would be difficult to win back the respect of his chief counselor or for that matter, the respect of his sons and all of Israel. He did not know how he could ever make right all that had gone so wrong. He did not have any answers, and yet suddenly everything was different. While going up to Mount Moriah with the men of the city, he had felt a great burden of guilt and shame. Now coming back down he realized it was gone. He no longer felt cut off from God and his fellowmen. The terrible hours he had spent in prayer and the solemn, then joyful sacrifice on Mount Moriah had washed his soul.

He was not going to be like Saul. He had admitted his wrong, accepted God's pardon and cleansing, and at last his soul was at peace. Now he was eager to tell Bathsheba.

He left his armor bearer at the gatehouse and climbed the stairs to the roof where he knew he would find her. She heard his footsteps and ran to him, flinging herself into his arms like a frightened child. He kissed her and held her tight with loving reassurance. He could tell that she had been badly frightened. "My dearest love," he said tenderly, "this has been a terrible time for you. I am sorry."

"Never mind, you are well," she said through her tears. "That is all I need to know. Grandfather was here twice, wanting me to go home with him. He said you would surely die of the plague as a punishment for your sins. He insisted that is the way God does things."

"But that is not the way God does things," David replied. "Today, before all the people, I stood on Mount Moriah and offered a sacrifice unto the Lord, and I was accepted by Him. Something wonderful happened there. My eyes were opened and I understood many things I have never understood before. I always thought God wanted us to be burdened with guilt for the wrongs we commit. As a king I have wanted others to feel their guilt and be burdened with it. Now I see that God expects us only to repent for our wrong. He will free us from our guilt that we may be happy and whole again as He created us to be. I never saw it so plainly before. I may never find the glory as before, but perhaps a humble and grateful heart is as acceptable unto God as one that is pure but proud."

Bathsheba smiled and tenderly traced with her finger the line on his cheek where his beard started. "I can see the change in you. Do you think our troubles are at an end?"

David shook his head. "No, there will always be trouble. As Nathan told us, 'The sword will not depart from your house.' That has not changed, but it is as though my God is a king like myself. He has forgotten all that was wrong between us and is welcoming me back to serve Him at His right hand."

Tears of joy ran down Bathsheba's face as she saw the radiance on her husband's face.

"There is something else," David said hesitantly. "Before I stood there on Mount Moriah today, I feared that God would reject me and my sons as He rejected Saul. Now I know that will not happen. I feel God working in my life again, and I know that His promises to me will be fulfilled. My son will build a great temple over the very spot where we sacrificed today. It seems impossible. I have nothing but His word to me that this will happen, and yet, today, as I watched the smoke ascend, I knew it with a deep, inner sureness."

In the dim light Bathsheba reached out her small hand and placed it in her husband's. "My lord, I also have some news for you. I am moving back into the women's court. It is necessary for me to become a part of the life there for my child's sake." She paused, noticing the look of surprised joy on David's face.

"I did not tell you before as I was not sure. But now I am sure. My beloved," she said, looking into his eyes and seeing her own happiness mirrored there, "I am sure this child I bear will live."

BOOK FOUR

SOLOMON

1

DAVID DID NOT plan a big feast for the naming of his second son born to Bathsheba. He had been named Jedediah, "Beloved of Jah," on the day of his birth, and now at his circumcision his official name would be revealed. Bathsheba brought him to the common room where only a small group of close friends and advisors had gathered. No one placed much significance in the event since it was conceded that this child would have no legal right to David's throne.

Bathsheba waited behind the curtain for the last business of the morning to be finished before she entered the common room carrying the small, eight-day-old baby. She walked slowly to the dais where David stood waiting to take the child, and then returned to her place behind the curtain. Women took no part in the sacred rite.

Most of the men looked at her with curiosity, some with open hostility. They were surprised to see that she looked very much like any pretty young mother rather than the painted harlot they

347

had imagined all these months. The most critical among them had to admit that she had eyes only for the baby and for her husband.

Though Ahithophel had entertained the idea of never returning to the court of David, he found at the last moment that he could not stay away. Now as he looked at the two flint-stone knives that would be used for the circumcision, he wondered who would be the one to perform the ceremony and who would have the honor of holding his great-grandson. David was looking at him. It was a questioning look, a look that sought his friendship. Ahithophel inclined his head and held out his arms, and David gave him the child to hold. Ahithophel noted with grudging approval that David was going to honor this son by performing the circumcision himself.

Ahithophel looked down at the small face and found with a start that he looked very much like his own son, Emmiel, had looked as a baby.

The baby was unwrapped, and David swiftly performed the operation while the small bundle let out a vigorous cry that brought tears to the eyes of Bathsheba behind the curtain but smiles to the men watching. "This one is strong," they said among themselves.

David put down the knife and cried with a loud voice the ancient words of his forefathers. "Blessed art Thou, O Lord, who has hallowed us by Thy commandments and commanded us to initiate our sons into the Covenant of Abraham our father."

Now was the time to make public the child's name. David took the child and held him as though offering him to God. He closed his eyes for a moment in silent prayer. There was a feeling of expectancy in every man there, for in the name they would read the heart of the king. Already they knew this child was especially favored by David in that he had refused to let anyone else perform the circumcision.

"My king!" The call came from the back of the room, and a man pushed through the crowd and walked to the dais. David opened his eyes and saw his friend, the prophet Nathan, standing before him. Nathan reached out and took the screaming infant. To everyone's astonishment, the crying stopped.

"My king," he said, looking straight into David's eyes. "The Lord has given me the name for this child."

David had been startled by the interruption, then apprehensive as he saw Nathan stride toward him. Now his face showed complete surprise. "You have a name?" he questioned.

"Yes, my lord, the name of this child is to be Solomon."

"Solomon?"

Nathan continued. "Last night as I lay on my bed, I saw a vision of a temple more beautiful than any that has ever been built. As I watched, an angel appeared and said unto me, 'The child is born who is to build this temple. Get thee to the house of David and tell him the child that is born of Bathsheba shall be named Solomon, the beloved of God. He is the promised one who will rule after his father David, and he will build the temple.' "

Nathan handed the child back to David who stood in stunned silence. Nathan turned and started to walk from the room.

"Nathan," David called out after him.

Nathan hesitated, then he turned and said, "Yes, my lord?"

"I have questions about this that must be answered before I can rest tonight." The child began to cry again, and David handed him to Ahithophel with a quick command. "Take the child to Bathsheba and tell her to return to the women's court."

He walked to Nathan, put an arm around the prophet's shoulders and led him off with not a backward look to the guests who stood speechless at the strange interruption.

When the two men were alone in the king's chamber, David spoke. "Nathan, my friend, months ago you told me I would have a son who was to build the temple of God here in Urusalim. Now, today you have come to say that God has shown you that this son born of Bathsheba is that child. I don't understand this. You were the one who denounced my sin in taking Bathsheba. How then can you say this child of Bathsheba's is to be so honored?"

"I understand nothing," Nathan said. "I did not even want to come to the common room for this ceremony, and yet a strange, inner feeling forced me to come. I determined that I would say nothing. As I stood with the others and saw you circumcise the child I felt nothing. But when you raised the child in your arms, an inner voice said to me, 'You must tell them the name of the child now.'"

"Nathan, this is as strange a thing as I have ever seen God do," David replied. "What do you make of it? You are a holy man. You know that God will not wink at evil and yet. . . ."

"I know, I know," Nathan blurted out. "I also know that God is merciful beyond our comprehension. It is His perfect will to give us only blessings."

"You and I think much alike," David said. "I cannot fathom the mind of God, and yet I have had intimations that He favored me and blessed me above my brothers until. . . ."

"Until you became as other men and committed this sin. Yes, I know. I know also that trouble has not left your house. Once evil has been let loose, it unwinds of itself and weaves a net that traps us again and again. It is not that God thinks up punishment for us, but rather that our actions bear fruit like small seeds planted in the dark which flower in the sunshine and bear fruit in the summer when we have long since forgotten the seed that was planted."

"But Nathan. . . ."

"My king, evil is not one act committed by one man. There is a chain of evil, and the final, open act that all may see comes at the end of many acts by many people."

"I don't understand," said David. "What I have done was done by me and no one else. How can this act have anything to do with others?"

"I don't see it all; but in this instance I have seen more than one is usually able to. First the failure of each of your wives to give you the love you needed. Is this not true?"

"It is true. But what of Uriah? I wronged him, and he did nothing to deserve that wrong."

"I happen to know a lot about Uriah. He only wanted a wife to give him a son to carry on his family name. If he had been a real husband to Bathsheba, she would not have been tempted to return your love."

David meditated on this for a moment. "How do you know Uriah did not love Bathsheba?"

"If he had loved her he would not have wanted her to be publicly disgraced."

"Then what was my sin?" David asked. "I have sinned against my wives, Uriah, and Bathsheba, but now you say that they also have been partially responsible. I have sinned against my people by influencing them to do as I have done, and yet, here too I am only partially responsible. The inclination to sin has been in their own hearts from the beginning. It seems there aren't just two kinds of men, those who sin and those who do not. There are only those who seek forgiveness and those who don't."

There was a long reflective silence. "As I see it now," said Nathan, "there was something behind the act you committed that brought about the act itself. This was the very same thing that brought about the sins of Adam and Eve."

David again struggled for understanding. "Eve took the fruit because she believed the serpent and was afraid that she would miss something, while I. . . ."

"Yes, while you took Bathsheba for the same reason. You thought God had given you success, wealth, fame, even had made you king, and yet you were afraid He would withhold from you the thing you wanted most. So when the opportunity came you took it. When I first brought you the word of God, it seemed harsh. Yet, do you remember that God also said, 'Have I not given you all things, and do you not think I would have given you this also, if you had asked for it?' "

David was stunned. "You think that God may have intended to give me Bathsheba all along?"

Nathan nodded. "It may be; I don't know. And we will never know. But that is how it seems to me. Before you ever saw Bathsheba, God told you that you would have a son named Solomon. Would Solomon have been born without Bathsheba?"

David sank back among the cushions and stroked his bearded chin thoughtfully. "Then it's God I've sinned against. By reaching out greedily like some thief for the thing I wanted, I must have spoiled some great and glorious plan I was too small to comprehend."

Nathan rose and stood for a brief moment looking down at David with a great compassion. "We'll never know just what was meant, but that is how it seems to me." Nathan then turned and left the room.

David sat for a long time pondering the events of the day. Finally he rose and walked to the open window where he fell down on his knees and cried out from the depths of his heart. "Oh, my God, I have spoiled your plan with a selfish one of my own. It is against Thee and Thee only I have sinned."

When Bathsheba left the common room with Solomon and walked down the dark, irregular steps toward the women's court, she felt as though she had not only had a death sentence removed but at the same time had received some special honor. She clutched her little son to her heart with joy and wondered at the strange words of Nathan. That he should someday be king seemed impossible, but that he should be chosen to build God's temple was beyond her wildest imagining.

Now as she turned on the landing she paused at a small slit in the wall through which the sunlight was flooding in a golden stream. It would not be easy to return to all the resentment and hostility in the Court of the Women, but with David's love and Nathan's wonderful promise for her little son she could feel nothing but gratitude.

Out through the slit she could see only the blue sky and gently waving fronds of a palm tree. Suddenly, it was as though the sunshine itself pierced her heart and she was flooded with so much happiness that tears of joy ran down her face.

Off the women's court was a small receiving room where the women of David's harem often entertained members of their families. It was to this room that Ahithophel hurried to see Bathsheba after the circumcision.

When she appeared, he was pacing impatiently back and forth, his jaw squared and rigid, and his eyebrows raised, giving his face the fierceness she had seen on occasion as a child when he was very upset. "Now, my dear," he said, trying to control his voice, "explain this nonsense to me if you can."

"Nonsense?" Bathsheba searched his face, bewildered by his anger.

"This nonsense of David's. Who does he think will be fooled by this drama we witnessed this morning? Does he think the men of Israel are so addled they will not see through his plan?"

"What are you talking about, Grandfather?"

Ahithophel flung his headpiece around his neck in irritation. "How much did David pay Nathan? The whole thing was so obvious. So preposterous. In such bad taste."

Bathsheba was horrified at his accusations. "Grandfather," she pleaded, "David did not pay Nathan nor did he even know that Nathan would be there."

"I don't believe it." He unwound the headpiece from his neck and wiped his brow. "How can David think that people will be taken in by such an obvious ruse? There is no possibility that your little son will ever become king. The harem is bulging with young sons of David, all of whom have more claim to David's throne than Solomon."

Bathsheba stared back silently at her grandfather. Her eyes were filled with dismay at the truth of his words.

Ahithophel's impatience mounted. "Do you think people of Israel will ever forget the name of Bathsheba? 'Bathsheba,' they will say, 'the woman who led David into sin.' " He rose to his feet unsteadily. "That is how they see you—an adulteress. They will never let your son come to the throne."

Bathsheba was appalled at the raw hurt she saw in Ahithophel's eyes and numb with the pain from his words. "Grandfather," she said softly, "if it is true, it will come to pass, and if not, we will see then that Nathan was mistaken."

Their conversation was interrupted by a soft tapping sound. Bathsheba opened the door cautiously and found Jessica standing in the shadows, looking nervous and frightened. "I must talk with you right away," she said entering and closing the door quietly behind her. "This will also concern you," she said as she noticed Ahithophel.

For a moment Jessica leaned against the wall to catch her breath. "No one must hear what I am about to tell you," she whispered. "Michal may have had me followed."

"Michal is plotting something?" Bathsheba asked in alarm.

"Not directly, but she knows about plots. Either you or your grandfather must get word to the king that there are plots within the palace against his sons—plots to take their lives."

Ahithophel looked at Jessica skeptically. "There is nothing new in what you say. There have always been plots against the king's family, but nothing usually comes of them."

Jessica shook her head. "There is a plot to harm Amnon and Absalom and keep them from the throne."

At the mention of Absalom's name, Ahithophel's

whole attitude changed. He leaned forward anxiously. "It is those nephews of Michal's. They always give us trouble."

Jessica nodded. "You are right. Michal's nephews know about the plot and are encouraging it, but I don't think they are actually involved themselves. They say they only want to bring ruin to David's house."

"Ruin to David's house," Ahithophel snorted. "What more ruin can overtake the house of David than he has brought upon it himself?"

"I don't know the details of the plot," Jessica said. "I only know that David's nephews, Jonadab and Jonathan, are at the root of it."

Bathsheba was surprised. She knew Jonadab as a quiet boy who had always been Amnon's best friend, while Jonathan, his brother, was a handsome, ambitious young man who had been a great favorite at the court ever since he had killed the six-fingered giant of Gath. Both young men were sons of David's brother Shimea and have been raised with David's own sons and princes.

Ahithophel stroked his beard and nodded. "Jonathan has been compared to the young David ever since he killed the giant, and he is quite ambitious. But I can't imagine anything that Jonadab and Jonathan could do which would remove both Amnon and Absalom from the palace and bring ruin to David. It is most improbable. However, I will suggest the guards be doubled at the houses of the princes." Ahithophel wrapped his cloak around him and abruptly left the room.

Jessica lingered a moment after Ahithophel's departure. "These are evil days," she cautioned Bathsheba. "It would be wise to take your little son back to Lodebar where he will not be subject to plots and threats as he is here."

"Have the women heard of Nathan's prophecy?" Bathsheba asked.

Jessica nodded, "They have heard, but they don't take it seriously. Michal believes that David paid Nathan well for his prediction."

"Grandfather thinks the same thing. Perhaps that's best. Many years will pass before we will know if it is true or not; for the present my little son will be safe."

"Don't be too sure. There are some in the palace who are troubled by Nathan's prophecy because they think that David wants it to come true."

As they walked to the door together, Jessica hesitated. "Does your grandfather blame you for all that has happened between you and the king?" she asked impulsively.

Tears welled in Bathsheba's eyes. "No, he has chosen to blame David for everything. It is revenge he wants. He will not rest until he brings disgrace and ruin to David."

2

SINCE THE SACRIFICE on Mount Moriah, much of the old joy and camaraderie had returned to the court of David. Once again he sat with his men on the roof in the evening, telling stories of battles, playing his harp, and singing the songs he had written. The days of his dark depression were gone; his faith was strong again, and he led his men into battle without fear.

There had been times when he wanted to tear down the gloomy house of Uriah lest it continue to remind the tribesmen and especially Ahithophel of

357

his dark treachery against the Hittite. Finally he had decided that it should stand just as it was—a bleak tribute to Uriah and a guard station for the army. As with his own graying hair and the newly chiseled lines of aging in his face, he had come to terms with these reminders of the past and was able to accept himself as flawed and imperfect but forgiven and right with his God.

Over and over again he marveled at God's patience and forgiveness. He tried at times to explain this to his men as they sat out under the stars or warmed their hands over the hot coals of his brazier. "God is like a shepherd," he told them. "We are His sheep, and He loves us not because we are perfect but because we are His."

One evening in the month of Kislev, a week after his son's circumcision, he stood out on the roof of his palace, meditating on all that had happened. On the one side he could see the house of Uriah rising square and firm, housing the men of his house guard, then by walking across the roof to the far northern side he could see the great rounded rock of Moriah where he had found his way back to God.

The sky was full of bright stars and a chill was in the air, making him draw his cloak around him as he walked to the western side of the roof. There he looked out toward the pine-covered hillside across the Hinnon Valley where he could dimly see the half-built houses of Amnon and Absalom. He was concerned about these sons of his. They had not been at court lately, and now he'd had this message from Bathsheba concerning some plot against his sons.

The house of Absalom looked closed, the shutters drawn, but there were flecks of light filtering through the loose boards while music and laughter could be heard, faint and light upon the evening air. The house of Amnon was also dark, but there was just the faintest trace of light coming out from under one of the closed shutters.

Nathan had predicted that trouble would not leave his house. He wondered if it was not already at work behind the closed shutters of his sons' new houses. Today, Ahithophel had sent him word suggesting some conspiracy and telling him that Amnon had taken to his bed quite suddenly with some strange illness.

"I should go to him," he muttered. "Someone may be trying to poison Amnon." He called for his armor bearer and guards; within the hour they were riding on the bright, moonlit path across the valley to the house of Amnon.

Two full years had passed since that night when Amnon had become aware of his father's indiscretion with Bathsheba. Ever since, he had been obsessed with a strange lust he had developed at that time. He had enjoyed letting his imagination conjure up scenes of all that his father must have done. Then he had begun to think of ways in which he, too, could take a woman if he chose.

Jonadab, his cousin and close friend, had been the first to notice the change in him. Then his mother and finally his father had observed that he was pale and thin as if from some lingering illness. When the young men of the court were throwing javelins or were out hunting, Amnon stayed home. He said he was not ill, but they noticed he was moody and impatient.

At first his passion centered on several of his father's young concubines. Then he became consumed with desire for Tamar, the sister of Absalom and his own half-sister.

He thought of her constantly and swore to Jonadab that he would never have a moment's peace until he had taken Tamar for himself. In every way possible Jonadab encouraged him, watching the obsession grow until Amnon admitted he was ready to resort to any trick to get Tamar from her brother's house to his own bedchamber.

Cleverly, Jonadab proposed a plan and watched Amnon reach out and grasp it as his own. "Feign a sickness," Jonadab suggested, "and when the king comes to see you, ask him to send Tamar to bake special cakes for you. Suggest that your sickness may come from poison being put into your food or from a charm that had been made against you. Once she is in your house and brings the food to your bedchamber, you can do with her as you please."

When David arrived and saw Amnon lying limp and listless in his bed, he was genuinely concerned. When Jonadab suggested that Tamar come and prepare special food for her half-brother, David agreed and sent word to the house of Absalom that his sister should go the next day to the house of Amnon to bake cakes by her own hands for him.

As David rode back across the moonlit valley and up the slope to the Valley Gate on the west side of the city, he thought again of the warning that had come to him. "A plot against his sons," they had said. He wondered if someone could be slowly poisoning Amnon. *It will do no harm,* he thought to himself, *to have Tamar prepare his food until this threat is past.*

The next morning began with the usual routine. The servants in the women's court busied themselves making bread for the day, and old Mahat swept the courtyard as always with a few broken palm fronds. Some of the younger concubines sat

360

in the open room and sewed while two of their children teased Mahat until she became angry and slapped their legs with the fronds. When the children cried, their mothers jumped up to shout abuse at her, but Mahat paid no attention to them.

In the months that she had been gone from the court, Bathsheba had almost forgotten how quarrelsome and envious these women could be. There was hardly a moment that someone was not either angry and indignant, crying or sulking.

The news Jessica had brought several nights before was not surprising. There were always plots of one kind or another. Every mother sought advantage for her son and every tribal leader had his favorites within the harem who would put his cause before the king. Until now their ends had been gained by subtle trickery and sly maneuvers. If Jessica was right and there was now a plot against the very lives of David's oldest sons, this was indeed frightening.

Bathsheba sat in her own courtyard beside the small crib made of fine cedar wood and decorated with the delicate carvings of the prancing lion of Judah. She looked down at the baby sleeping soundly in spite of the noise from the outer court and shuddered. *If there were threats against the lives of Absalom and Amnon,* she thought, *in time there could be threats also against my little son.*

She remembered the words of Nathan when he had said, "The sword will never depart from the house of David." A sword meant violent death. Since Jessica's secret visit she had felt as though that very sword were raised ready to strike. She reached down and lovingly rearranged the coverings on the baby.

The noon meal was served as usual, and the

women had retired for their afternoon rest, when suddenly there was a frantic pounding on the great brass door of the women's court. The women rushed out into the courtyard while old Mahat shuffled toward the door to open it. "Mother, Mother!"

"It's Tamar!" Maacah shrieked as she rushed to greet her daughter. Tamar was almost unrecognizable. Her brightly colored dress with long sleeves worn by the virgins of Urusalim was torn, and her beautiful, thick, black hair was disheveled. She held her hands over her face and cried hysterically.

Seeing her daughter in such a state so paralyzed Maacah that Michal grabbed Tamar by the arm and insisted she explain what had happened. Tamar sobbed all the harder as she tried to talk. "I went to the house of my brother Amnon. I was to bake cakes for his dinner and . . . and. . . ."

"Go fetch the king," Bathsheba whispered to old Mahat. Remembering the warning Jessica had given them, she wondered if indeed Amnon had been killed or wounded.

At the mention of Amnon, Ahinoam pushed forward and confronted Tamar. "Stop this silly crying and tell me what has happened to my son."

Tamar was shocked into indignation. "Your son Amnon is fine, just fine!" she shouted. "I am the one who is ruined. Your son forced me into his bed. Afterwards he threw me out as though I were some stranger." She covered her face again with a torn piece of her skirt and wept bitterly.

"How can you tell such lies?" Ahinoam challenged her. "My son is a good boy. He would never do such a thing, never! You and your fancy brother have always tried to get Amnon in trouble."

Tamar was like a wounded animal. She threw back her mantle. "Look!" she cried, her dimpled chin quivering and her eyes flashing with anger.

The beautiful robe of variegated silk was torn, exposing one breast. She pulled aside the torn skirt and the women drew back with shock at seeing how her undergarments had almost been torn from her.

Maacah rushed at Ahinoam in a blind rage, pounding her, pulling her hair, and scratching her face. "You have always bragged your son was so good," she screamed. "Who will marry my daughter now? Where will she hide her shame? What use is her beauty to her after what your son has done to her!"

Ahinoam could only groan and sink to the floor beneath her frantic blows.

The door to the women's quarters burst open, and David strode in. He shook off Maacah and pushed Ahinoam from him as he walked over to where Tamar stood with her face hidden in her mantle. David spoke gently to her and tenderly brushed the disheveled hair back from her face. "My wounded dove, can you tell me what happened? Was it truly your brother Amnon who did this thing?"

With sobs and broken sentences Tamar told her father that she had gone to prepare her brother's dinner in his rooms as she had been told to do. With no warning he had grabbed her and forced her into his bed as though she were a common harlot. As if this were not bad enough, she moaned, afterward he had pushed her from his bed and called Jonadab to put her out and lock the door of his bedchamber.

David motioned for Maacah. "Take Tamar," he said, "to Absalom's house and see that he does nothing rash. Assure him that I will see that Amnon is punished."

Ahinoam rushed forward throwing herself at his

feet and clinging to him. "Don't touch Amnon. He didn't do it; I know he didn't do it!"

David looked at her helplessly then called Abigail to come and take Ahinoam to her room.

As Abigail loosened Ahinoam's fingers from David's robe, her eyes met David's. "Our sins are not so pretty, are they," she said, "when we see them committed by our sons?"

David drew back as though he had been struck. He realized that what she had said was exactly what all Israel would be thinking before nightfall. He turned and walked from the room, slightly less determined to mete out punishment to Amnon.

The news of Amnon's act spread quickly through the city and everyone waited expectantly to see how David would punish his son. Finally as weeks, then months passed, it became the gossip of all the small towns and villages, even of the traders and shepherds, that Amnon had defiled his own sister, Tamar, and David had taken no action to set it right.

Ahithophel now became more blatantly hostile to David. He spent his days in Absalom's home decrying the injustice that kept the beautiful Tamar a prisoner in his house, disgraced and alone, and left the offender, Amnon, unpunished. He talked to all who would listen and gathered them to the support of Absalom and his sister. He did not question the strange turn of events that had so suddenly brought both Jonadab and Jonathan to sit with the friends of Absalom, eating and drinking and talking of revenge, when such a short time before they had been constantly seen with Amnon.

Bathsheba knew before anyone else that David would never be able to punish Amnon. On occasions when they were alone together, he mentioned the need for it, but he always ended by saying, "Who am I to punish Amnon? He simply took what he wanted as he had seen me do."

Bathsheba, however, could not contain her indignation. "I have no sympathy for Amnon at all. If he didn't love her, why did he take her? And if he loved her, why did he disgrace her like this?"

David just shook his head sadly. "You have to understand Amnon to answer that."

"Do you understand why he sent her away like a common harlot? He was cruel. Her life is over just as though he had killed her."

"I've asked myself the same question over and over again," David replied wearily. "Amnon isn't an unfeeling monster. He is an idealist. He always wanted the world to be beautiful and orderly. Unfortunately, like the rest of us he is also attracted by things that are wrong. You can't have both worlds. Perhaps when Amnon tried to mix the two, he was revolted by what he had done, and Tamar became something he hated. The thing he loved in her he had destroyed. Trampled flowers are no longer mysterious and beautiful."

Bathsheba was horrified. "I don't understand at all. If he loved her, he should have felt sorry for her."

"I'm not sure he really loved her. Amnon is selfish and soft. He probably came as close to loving Tamar as he will ever come to loving anyone."

"If you love him, you will punish him." Bathsheba said softly as she reached out to David and tenderly ran her fingers through his hair.

There was a long silence, and then David spoke in great anguish. "If I really loved him," he said, "I could punish him." He looked at Bathsheba with such a pleading look she bit her lip and vowed never to mention the subject again.

Months passed, and then two years, and it was evident to everyone that David was not going to punish Amnon. Despite Tamar's tears, Maacah's tantrums, and Absalom's persistent arguments, David did nothing. Tamar spent her days in lonely isolation in the upper rooms of Absalom's house. Each time her brother looked at her and saw her lovely beauty fading, he swore to Jonadab and all his friends that he would seek revenge.

"It's an easy thing to talk about revenge," Jonadab taunted. "But when will you do something? It's been two years since Amnon. . . ."

"I need a plan." Absalom interrupted him impatiently. "I only need a plan, and you will see what I will do."

"I have already suggested the method and the means. A feast when everyone is celebrating would be a perfect time to take revenge."

"And I have always told you I dislike the idea of a feast to carry out such bloody plans."

"You want some quiet poison, a dark and moonless night, no witnesses. That is not revenge. To have revenge, the victim must see his killer and suffer all the torment of knowing why he's going to die."

"All right. I agree. But someone else, possibly one of my men, will have to do the deed itself. I have no stomach for the business."

"You shame your sister with that kind of talk."

Absalom's face grew white and serious. "Then tell me exactly what to do, and by the gods I'll do it."

Jonadab could not hide his delight. "When you plan the feast for the spring sheep-shearing on your land at Baal-hazor, invite the king and all his sons. . . ."

"The king?"

"Of course, the king. You want them all to know

just how you feel and why you took revenge. Don't worry. It will be so simple. Either at the feast itself while everyone is making jokes and laughing, or as they ride back home. But either way, you want to make it plain that you are killing Amnon for revenge."

Everything was done just as Jonadab suggested. Invitations were taken to the king, his wives and concubines, and all his sons. The king declined; there were some traders coming on important business, but he was pleased for all the rest to go, especially Amnon. This meant to him that the brothers would be friends again.

When Ahinoam heard of the invitation, she was stricken with such fear for Amnon that she dressed in sackcloth, poured ashes on her head, and then ran to the common room and flung herself at David's feet.

"Last night," she said breathlessly, "I had a dream in which I saw my son, Amnon, sitting at a feast with all his brothers. They were all laughing and making jests until a servant came and stabbed my son. I saw Amnon dying." Her eyes bulging with terror, she began to weep and beg. "He must not go with Absalom. It is not safe, and you're the only one to stop him."

David was embarrassed. "Ahinoam," he said firmly, "go back to your room and don't be afraid. Absalom's invitation is a sign that all is forgiven and they can be friends again."

"My lord," Ahinoam cried, rising slowly to her feet. "Take heed or there will be still more evil to befall the house of David." In a daze she turned and walked from the room.

Bathsheba decided not to go to the feast. It was a long and dusty ride and would be difficult since she was again with child. Besides, two-year-old Solomon was into everything. However, when her little son saw the carts piled high with food, his eyes grew round and pleading. "I want to go," he begged.

"No, no, my baby," Bathsheba crooned softly to him. "Another time we'll go, but not today."

She felt his plump baby arms go round her neck, his curls against her cheek, and warm, wet tears fell on her shoulder. "I want to ride."

When he would not be consoled, she carried him to one of the carts and placed him in the straw among the serving maids who were to ride with all the food. "There, there, my love," she smiled down at him. "You'll ride to the gate and then you must come back, and we will make some honey cakes for your papa, the king." The little boy nestled down, content and smiling until the cart began to move. When he saw that he was riding off without his mother, he began to cry.

They stopped the cart and waited while Bathsheba ran to pick him up and comfort him. She stood with him a moment waving at the happy party-goers and then turned back into the women's court, holding her little son close.

When the laughing, happy young people with their mothers rode off from the palace, Jonadab was not with them. Instead he sent his brother, Jonathan. "See that Absalom does not weaken in his purpose," he whispered to Jonathan. Then he went into the guardroom to await the result.

David spent the day in his common room, entertaining wealthy traders from the south who came to make a treaty which would give them free access to the king's highway that ran along the far side of the Dead Sea and on to Damascus. In turn, they promised to give him first choice of the incense, dates, and spices they marketed.

There were five separate tribes, and each one wished to seal the agreement by giving David a beautiful young girl to add to his harem. David recoiled at the thought of still more concubines, for each one taken added to his problems, but to refuse them would be a great insult. He wondered uneasily what Bathsheba would think of his taking more concubines. Would she see it as only an agreement between tribes and the king, or would she become cold and distant, thinking he had tired of her?

The decision had to be made quickly. He looked from one face to the other and saw the pride and dignity of these desert dwellers. "Take the women with their slaves to the Court of the Women," he ordered and he thanked the traders for their generosity.

Shortly after he had bid the traders good-by, there was a loud wailing from the palace gate. Adab, a friend of Amnon, rushed into the room, breathless and distraught. "The sons of my lord have all been killed," he shouted.

A gasp went up from the tribesmen crowded around the room. The king rose from the throne in anguish. "All my sons, all my sons slain?" Weeping, he tore his robe.

Friends and servants of the king rushed into the common room, and when they saw their king and heard the news, they too rent their robes and wept with such grief that the women in their court heard the commotion and came running to see what had happened. Only Ahinoam stayed away. She was so stricken with foreboding and fear that she fell across her bed as one who was dead.

3

AHITHOPHEL WAS THE first to recover from the shocking news. He hurried out of the common room to the guardhouse, where he found Jonathan reporting to his brother, Jonadab, on all that had happened at Baal-hazor.

"What do you know about this?" he demanded, glaring at them. "Are all the king's sons dead?"

Jonadab was so surprised he blurted out, "It was only Amnon. Only Amnon was killed."

"Absalom has avenged his sister, that is all," said Jonathan.

"That is all . . . that is all!" Ahithophel repeated the words with a mixture of shock and relief. "I see your part in it now, both of you. Jonadab, you encouraged Amnon to take Absalom's sister, knowing Absalom would have to avenge her. Thus at one blow, you hoped to have two of David's sons out of the way. Then you, Jonathan, as the giant killer would become the most likely candidate for the throne. Well I can assure you, it won't happen like that," he thundered. "You will never sit on the throne of David."

Jonadab cringed before this man who seemed to look into his mind and heart and read his most secret thoughts. "It is true; I sought the throne for my brother. He is much more suited to be king than those pleasure-loving sons of David."

Startled by Jonadab's frankness, Ahithophel turned to Jonathan, who stood with his feet apart and his head thrown back defiantly. "You may have killed a giant just as did your uncle, the king," the counselor snapped. "But that is the only way in which you resemble him. Come with me now to the king and tell him the truth."

370

"We will admit nothing to him," Jonathan said.

"At least tell him it is Amnon who is dead and his other sons are safe. If you do not do this, I will tell the king the whole ugly part you have played in this affair."

Jonadab's eyes glinted. "You will find when the runners come with the news, that Absalom has fled. He will never be king now. Remember, it was by his order and at the hand of his servant that Amnon was killed."

Ahithophel had not counted on this, and his anger flared again. "You have planned well, but you will not succeed. From now on it will be your wits against mine, and I will win. Come along now, both of you. You can't undo all that you have done, but you can at least ease the hearts of the king and the mothers of his sons."

Jonadab and Jonathan glanced at each other knowingly and then went quietly behind Ahithophel into the common room to tell the king.

The murder of Amnon had taken place exactly as Jonadab had planned. After a morning of sheep-shearing, all the sons of David had gathered hungrily for a feast of new barley and roast lamb beside the shearing sheds. They crowded in around the food, laughing and joking to find their places wherever there was room. Absalom sat next to Amnon and kept his cup well filled with wine until his brother's speech was slurred, and his eyes grew bloodshot.

Suddenly, as prearranged, Absalom motioned secretly to his servants. Immediately they moved along the wall behind the guests. There was another nod from Absalom, and then without warning, his servants lunged at Amnon, driving their sharp shearing knives into his heart.

371

Amnon slumped forward on the woven mat, and Absalom rose hurriedly to join his men outside. There were screams and groans and oaths, but within minutes the princes had gathered up Amnon's body in a sheet, placed it on one of the carts and started the grim, four-mile journey back to Urusalim.

As they passed through Bethel and then Gibeah and other small villages, the local people joined them, all lamenting and weeping over the tragedy. By the time the procession came in sight of Urusalim, the king, with members of his court, had all come out to meet them, and together they bore the body of Amnon back to the palace.

The servants removed the rough cloak Amnon had worn to the shearing; they bathed his body and then wrapped him in costly grave clothes. All the time David sat beside his son and watched, tearless and gaunt with suffering.

Each moment brought some new grief. When he first saw the open wound and the still flowing blood, David felt as though he himself had been stabbed. When they closed Amnon's staring eyes and combed his matted hair, the king winced with pain that his son had seen so little of his father and had so rarely felt his father's fingers in his hair.

When they removed his rings, David took them sorrowfully, remembering so well the hand with its blunt, practical fingers that had so recently worn them. He grieved that these rings would never be handed down to the sons of Amnon or to his grandsons. The bitter knowledge that Amnon had been murdered by his own brother jabbed like a knife in David's heart.

Ahinoam was brought from the Court of the Women to look upon her son before they wound his face in grave clothes. She was silent and fearful,

372

but her tangled hair and clawed face were testimony to her anguish. Suddenly, with a wild scream, she flung herself down on the cold tiles and clutched him to her breast, rocking back and forth as she wept.

It was late when the funeral procession left for Bethlehem, and David's heart was heavy. In one day he had lost two sons, one cruelly murdered and the other gone into exile. Of the two, he realized that he grieved more for the loss of Absalom than for Amnon, and this deeply distressed him.

Absalom fled with Tamar to the kingdom of Geshur on the far side of the Sea of Chinnereth where his grandfather was still king. Here he set up his own household and gathered his wives and children, servants and friends around him.

Maacah did not leave the women's court in Urusalim but yearned continually for her son and Tamar. However, while Maacah worked tirelessly to bring Absalom back to the palace, Bathsheba used every means within her power to keep him in exile. She distrusted Absalom. He had always been ambitious, and now, when she saw that he would stop at nothing, even murder, to attain his goal, she feared more than ever for Solomon.

Three more years passed and in this time Bathsheba gave birth to two more sons. She named them Shimea, meaning "famous," and Shobah, meaning "bright." When David offered her gifts at their circumcisions, she had refused each time, saying, "If it should please my lord, grant that Absalom shall not return home to threaten the young princes of my lord." David could refuse her nothing and for three years Absalom remained in Geshur.

Then it was spring again and Ahithophel had come to Urusalim on one of his rare visits to take her with her sons and maids to spend the day in Giloh. Bathsheba had accepted his invitation reluctantly, fearing that her grandfather had planned this outing with the intention of persuading her to change her mind concerning Absalom.

The morning hours in Giloh were pleasant. Ahithophel ignored the two small boys and centered all of his attention on five-year-old Solomon, asking him questions to test his judgment and giving him long lectures on the genealogy of his mother's family. Solomon listened respectfully, but Bathsheba could tell by the way he shifted from one foot to the other that he longed to be free of his great-grandfather.

"Come, Solomon," Bathsheba interrupted, "Grandfather and I will walk down to the olive orchard so you can climb your favorite tree." She saw his face light up, and the three of them walked together down through the village and out into the olive orchard.

"You must conquer this strange fear you have of Absalom," Ahithophel said as the two of them stood watching Solomon kick off his jeweled slippers and begin to climb one of the olive trees. "He is coming home, you know."

"Absalom is coming back to Urusalim?"

"Many of us have been working to bring him home. It is important that you do not stand against him now. He has assured me that when he is king, I'll be his chief counselor."

"I'm sorry, Grandfather. I think he is dangerous and I will do everything I can to keep him from coming home."

"You must accept the fact that someday Absalom will be king. To my way of thinking, the sooner the better."

Bathsheba flushed scarlet with anger. "I know

you don't believe Nathan's prophecy about Solomon, and now you talk as though you wish that Absalom were king in place of David. How can you be so disloyal to my husband and my child?"

Ahithophel became cold and hard. "You want me to forget the past? Wipe from my mind all of the hurt and shame of these last years? God may forgive him for what he did, but I'm not God. I remember everything, and I will have revenge against the king just as Absalom did against Amnon."

In despair Bathsheba realized there was no hope of reconciling the two men who were both dear to her. She called Solomon, and without looking at her grandfather again she said coldly, "It's getting late. We must start home." They walked back to the house in silence.

As she mounted her mule to leave, she spoke one last time to Ahithophel. "Remember, if you fight the king to get revenge, you're fighting me."

Ahithophel was unmoved. "Whatever I am doing or have done is for your good. You cannot see it now, but in the future you will understand."

Seeing that it was useless to argue with him, she said good-by quietly and rode out toward Urusalim with her nursemaids and children, saddened and depressed by Ahithophel's attitude. Solomon rode beside her without speaking until they were out of the village. Then he asked, "Mother, why is Grandfather always angry?"

"I had not thought of him as angry. Why do you ask?"

"Well, he never smiles at any of us, and he is always saying things like, 'All is vanity and vexation.'" Solomon drew himself up and spoke in a pompous voice that sounded very much like his great-grandfather.

In spite of her frustration Bathsheba smiled at

her son. He had captured exactly the stance and tone of his great-grandfather. *Strange,* she thought, *what a child will remember.*

4

IT WAS LATE SPRING when Absalom moved quietly back into his home on the western ridge of Mount Zion. David had given permission for his return but in deference to Bathsheba had denied him the privilege of returning to court. David had also been quick to assure Bathsheba that he would take whatever precautions necessary to safeguard her little sons. Seeing his eagerness to please, Bathsheba could not bring herself to argue with him further.

Though David did not want to go against Bathsheba's wishes, he longed more than ever to see this son he loved so much. At first he sought out Absalom's friends, asking for news of him, and when he walked upon his roof he would look out across the valley toward his son's house in hopes he'd catch a fleeting glimpse of him. Finally, before another year was up, David had been persuaded to bring Absalom back to his court and into his favor.

This time he did not tell Bathsheba. She heard the news first from her maids in the harem, then from Jessica, and finally from Ahithophel. Ahithophel was overjoyed. He told her how he had joined with Joab in promoting David's handsome son among the tribesmen and elders until they had all come to the palace and urged the king to recognize his son. Ahithophel was strutting with pride at his accomplishment and was very boastful of his role in the affair.

Bathsheba did not hide her anger. "It sounds almost treasonous."

"Perhaps it is a little treasonous. But never mind. David welcomed Absalom with open arms, granted his every wish, and swore to make amends for all the injuries of the past."

"Make amends! And for what injuries?" Bathsheba's voice was choked with frustration as her grandfather coldly bid her good-by.

Absalom had not been back in court a month before he was sitting beside David in the common room and at his right hand during mealtime. He had taken over the rooftop pavilion as if it were his own. Though David had been overjoyed to have him back, he was uneasy over Bathsheba's resistance to this new closeness with his son.

Gradually he relaxed. *Bathsheba is a woman who looks to see how things are going and then fits herself into the situation,* he thought to himself. It had happened that way with the concubines the tribesmen had thrust upon him. When he had spent time with them that usually went to her, she had only searched his face with her large, dark eyes, then, seeing no change in his love for her, had shrugged and come to him with no reserve. *It will be the same with Absalom,* he thought. *Now that she sees he is here to stay, she will accept him.*

Late one night when he called her to his room, she came dressed as an Egyptian serving girl with a woven basket on her head full of the most delicate cakes, fragrant bread, and roast leg of lamb.

Until he saw the food David had forgotten he had been too busy that day to eat. He watched her deftly unroll a reed mat and set the food before him. He liked the way she took over his room, opening the lattices and letting in the moonlight, straightening the skins on his bed, and bathing his feet in herbed water.

As he ate, David watched her move around the room. She had been eighteen when he married her and now she was twenty-four. Yet in those years she had only grown more beautiful. Bearing children had filled out her hips and enlarged her breasts, but her waist was still narrow and her stomach nicely rounded so that she looked much more enticing now in the costume she wore than she would have six years before.

A surge of desire rose up within him, drowning out his need for food. Not wanting to spoil her game, he clapped his hands and waved away the rest of the meal. He wiped his hands on the perfumed towel and reached for his harp. "Does this Egyptian maid know how to dance?" he asked.

He saw her eyes sparkle with delight at his acceptance of her role. He strummed the harp and marvelled at how gracefully she danced to the old tunes, flinging back her long hair scented with jasmine and making her bracelets and golden headcoins flash and twinkle in the dim lamp light.

Now he sang along with his strumming, making the steady rhythm throb and beat as he sang the old, old words. He slipped out of his heavy, ornate robe and rose to follow her in the dance dressed only in his short battle tunic. Then together they danced, singing and stomping out the old familiar rhythm until she turned too sharply, and with her hair flying in a cloud around them both, fell laughing into his arms. He flung his harp onto the soft

skins and breathed in deeply the odor of her hair
and skin as he felt her fingers in his hair pulling him
to her.

"Darling," her voice was soft in the velvet darkness,
and he had to rouse himself to answer her.

"Yes, my love, what is it?"

Slowly her fingers moved through his hair and
then traced the outline of his face, touching lightly
his mouth and following the outline of his beard. "A
king has many enemies, and I fear for you."

David braced himself for news from the harem
where all plots were ultimately known and analyzed.
"Be careful of the friends of Absalom," she whispered. "They are not just the jolly fellows they appear."

He laughed at her seriousness, ran his finger
down her face and stopped at her lips to bend over
and kiss her. "I thought I was not going to hear of
Absalom. I want to think of you tonight and not of
Absalom."

"My lord, I am afraid for you and little Solomon,
or else I would not mention Absalom again."

"I know you are afraid but there's no need." He
tried to draw her back to him, but she pulled away
and sat frowning in the center of the skins that
made up David's bed.

"You don't realize the hatred of my grandfather.
He wants revenge. There are already plots and
plans."

"In a king's court there are always plots and men
who seek revenge. I have no doubt that Ahithophel
is angry, and I will try to pacify him. As for Absalom . . . he is my son, and I've forgiven him. Don't
worry about young Solomon. Absalom loves the
little prince. He's always asking for news of him."

Instead of calming Bathsheba, David's words

frightened her. "Yes," she told David, "Absalom had a special interest in Amnon too. Remember?"

"Bathsheba," David said soothingly, "there is no need for you to fear. I will not love Absalom more than your son, Solomon."

Bathsheba felt her face grow red that he should think her jealous. In desperation she tried again to explain how subtly Absalom had united all the factions that had reason to resent or hate the king. It was useless. He did not want to listen.

"My king," she said settling down into his arms again, "if there is ever a real threat to Solomon, would you approve my taking him to Lodebar?"

David smiled in the darkness. He needed only to humor her. "If he should ever be in danger, I'd be the first to say he should be taken to some safe shelter, and I suppose for you that would be Lodebar."

A few days later an incident took place that further alarmed Bathsheba. Solomon had been playing in the courtyard when the clanging gong announced a visitor. It was a young man who said he had a gift for Solomon. Then he left.

Solomon ran eagerly and grasped the woven basket left by the man. "How lovely," Bathsheba cried as she joined him, and they both admired its strange and delicate design. "I wonder what's inside."

Solomon unhooked the latch and raised the lid. There, coiled in some fresh green leaves, was a snake, tail rigid, head raised ready to strike. Solomon reached out to grasp its waving neck.

"Don't touch it," Bathsheba screamed knocking the basket from his hand. From the doorway Mahat sprang forward to crush the snake with a brass pot while the women gathered around shrieking with horror.

When Solomon scolded Mahat for killing the most beautiful snake he had ever seen, Bathsheba gathered him in her arms. "It was poisonous, my son. Someone was trying to harm us."

Though Solomon described the stranger who had brought the basket, no one could identify him. The women shrugged and went back to their various activities, but Bathsheba remained badly shaken. She was sure that someone, knowing how Solomon loved animals and plants, had planned this attack carefully to kill her son.

In the days that followed there was a subtle change in the atmosphere of the harem. Things that had been whispered in secret were now spoken openly, and opinions that had been unpopular were now accepted and even welcomed.

Bathsheba noticed with growing alarm how people like Michal, bitter and resentful against the king, sided with Absalom, bringing to his side the rebels of her tribe. They were finding Absalom's easy morality and youthful leadership exhilarating. "We need less emphasis on prophets, priests, and religious exercises," they would tell each other.

Ahithophel's attitude alarmed Bathsheba most. He boasted how the prince met foreign dignitaries with smooth sophistication, and gloated over Absalom's ability to make David look naive and simple. Ahithophel no longer spent his time at Giloh but was a regular guest at Absalom's table and his small court. He liked the witty conversation, good food, and more than anything else, the prestige of being an important part of Absalom's inner circle. When Absalom ordered chariots and horses with fifty men to run before him, or rose up early to stand beside the Gate of the Tribes to greet the elders and win the hearts of the men of Israel with his charm, or built a mausoleum to himself in the Kidron Valley, Ahithophel and most of the people of Israel approved.

It was on the day that Absalom dedicated his monument in the Kidron Valley that Bathsheba packed her belongings and prepared to leave for Lodebar. To Bathsheba the dedication of the monument was final proof that Absalom's ambition was coming to some sort of dangerous head. It was the fashion to copy everything Egyptian, and Absalom had built his mausoleum after those he had seen in Egypt. Men from Egypt had come to construct it out of native stone, and all Urusalim had watched it being built. "No king outside of Egypt has ever been buried in such a tomb," the people said, admiring the sophistication of their favorite prince.

Business matters kept David from attending the dedication, but he had ordered an elegant feast prepared as though it were a wedding or a coronation. He composed a song in his son's honor and sat by while men of Judah sang and danced, all but hailing Absalom as king.

Late that same night when David returned to his pavilion, old Mahat was waiting for him. "My son Absalom seems to have taken over my pavilion," he complained casually to the old servant, looking around at the wreckage of his favorite meeting place. The cushions had all been moved, fruit peelings were all over the floor, the wine cups scattered carelessly about, and some of the wine had spilled out on the floor coverings.

"Your majesty," old Mahat said, "I have come with a message from Bathsheba."

"From Bathsheba?" David turned to her expectantly.

"My lord," Mahat continued, "Bathsheba has packed her things. She has ordered the mules to be ready at dawn to carry her with her children to the Gilead. She has asked to see you before she goes."

David was startled. "She has packed?"

"Packed and determined to go," Mahat said with a knowing look.

David shrugged. "It's just a threat. Go, old one, and tell her to come. We will settle this quickly and then have a celebration of our own."

When Bathsheba appeared in the open doorway, David turned smiling to meet her serious, questioning look. She was dressed in bright, sunshine yellow with one shoulder provocatively bare and her hair piled under a turban of twisted purple strands that fell carelessly down her back.

He went to her, smiling with pleasure, and was puzzled that she stood before him silent and serious. "I know this is no place to entertain the queen, but. . . ."

For the first time she looked around at the destruction. "Absalom?"

David nodded and laughed. "He seems to have carried his festivities into my most intimate quarters."

Bathsheba did not smile. "Your son Absalom has not only taken over your rooms, he has taken over your heart so that you no longer can see things clearly."

David dropped his joyful banter, came to her and pulled her into his embrace. He felt her stiffen and push against him.

"I have come to ask your leave to take my sons to Lodebar where they will be safe. You promised."

He dropped his arms and turned from her. "Mahat tells me you are packed and ready to leave. Have you completely forgotten all that we have shared of love and heartache and real joy?"

"Oh, my darling," Bathsheba reached out to him and grasped his arm, "you know I love you. But I must think of Solomon, my sons. . . ." She stared at him helplessly.

"Your sons! It is always your sons." David turned from her angrily. "It is never you and me anymore."

"And who have you been thinking of but your son—Absalom?"

David's eyes blazed with cold fury. "Aha. You see? You are jealous. You will not listen to reason because you are jealous."

"It is not jealousy, my lord, but fear. I fear your son Absalom."

"Enough!" David threw up his hand. "I don't want to hear it all again."

They stood for a moment numbed by the hostility that swept between them. "David," Bathsheba said coming towards him, "please let us part as friends."

David whirled around as though he had been struck a blow. "As friends . . . now we are to be friends. . . ." He shouted the words at her. "Oh, my God! All the suffering we've shared, and this is how you want it all to end . . . as friends!" He slumped down onto the dais and buried his head in his hands.

Bathsheba came hesitantly and knelt beside him, running her hands through his hair as she had done so often in the past. "My darling."

"Go! Just go!" He raised his arm and pushed her from him.

She hesitated. Her heart was breaking so that she couldn't speak. "But my lord. . . ."

"Go on to Lodebar. Do what you must. . . ."

She paused a moment, yearning to reach out to him, to make it right. She could not bear to leave him, but she dared not stay. As she backed from the pavilion, she remembered vividly the time years before when she'd left this same pavilion with all her guilt and shame but sheltered in his love. With a sense of utter desolation and loss she felt her way down the long steps back to the women's court.

5

EMBITTERED BY THE KING'S rejection of her, Michal seldom left her own courtyard. But hearing that Bathsheba was packing to leave, she called for Jessica. "My dear, bring out my queenly robes and crown. I am going visiting and want to look my best."

Jessica opened the large wooden chest and lifted out Michal's robes of Phoenician design. Then she brought out the small, gold circlet that Michal wore on special occasions when she wanted to remind people that she was not only the royal daughter of Saul but also David's first wife and therefore queen.

Michal took a long time dabbling in the alabaster pots of glitter for her eyelids and red ointment for her cheeks and lips. She noted with displeasure that she had grown thinner and her breasts no longer filled the gown. Her hips were as narrow as a young boy's, reminding everyone that she had never borne a child. She ran her fingers over her body and touched her hair to be sure it was in order, then smiled a tight, thin-lipped smile of satisfaction. "Now I am going to see Bathsheba before she leaves."

Bathsheba was sitting on a large cushion in her courtyard with the six-months-old Shobab on her lap and Shimea leaning against her knee, while Solomon, now seven years old, sat at her feet and listened as she told them of the journey they would take to Lodebar. She told them of the soft, white lambs that would be frolicking on the new, green, mountain grass and of the strong oxen that plowed the fields behind the village. She described the pigeons that fluttered down into the courtyard to eat the plump brown grain from her brother's hand.

Solomon's eyes grew round and large as he imagined all the wonders of the creatures she described. He was a boy who could spend an afternoon observing the movement of a colony of ants through the courtyard or sit beside the cages where his father kept the lions that were the symbol of their tribe, watching to learn their language and their ways.

There was a knock at the door, and Bathsheba turned to see Michal standing before her in all her queenly array. Startled by the unexpected visit, Bathsheba rose slowly, brushing back the stray wisps of tangled hair and smoothing her rough, loomspun gown with one hand as she held Shobab with the other. "Sara, come quickly. Take the children." Bathsheba motioned for Michal to be seated on the stool near the early blooming narcissus, while she turned the children over to her maid.

Michal declined the stool and stood looking around the small court that was very much like her own only made more attractive by the herbs and flowers planted there. "I have heard that you're going back to Lodebar," Michal said testily.

"Yes, I am leaving tomorrow. My grandmother is

dead, and my mother and brother wish to see the children."

Michal raised one eyebrow. "Only for a visit? My dear, I have it on the best authority that you are leaving us for good."

The color drained from Bathsheba's face, but she did not flinch. "I will not be gone past the barley harvest, and I am leaving Sara here to tend my little garden." Bathsheba saw a flicker of interest in Michal's eyes and continued. "It is a shame she will have no more to do. She was trained in the house of Uriah to cook wild game and pigeons stuffed with wheat. The king is very fond of her honey cakes."

Michal studied Bathsheba's face for any hidden motive. "I could use such a girl," she said hesitantly. "What is her price?"

"What would I ask for her?" Bathsheba tried to hide her excitement. "I suppose now you would have more use for a cook than a hairdresser. I could consider trading Sara for the maid you took from me in Lodebar."

"I don't see how I could part with Jessica," Michal said hastily. She seemed about to drop the subject when she had another thought. "You say David likes her little cakes?"

"They are his favorites."

Michal smiled a slow, subtle smile. "Jessica is no longer of much use to me. I have found other maids. I'll trade with you."

Bathsheba was overjoyed, yet fearful that Michal would change her mind. She added, "As I remember, Jessica is older, and so the trade would not be fair unless you gave me something else of value."

Michal's eyes glinted with delight. Sure now she had made a good bargain, she pulled four gold pieces from off her headpiece and handed them to Bathsheba. "There. This will finance your trip to Lodebar, and Jessica is yours."

It was all Bathsheba could do to conceal her elation. Jessica had been restored to her.

Michal turned to go but then swept back for one final thrust. "It is too bad the king no longer confides in you. You should have known that this is how it all would end."

"Nothing has ended. I am simply going for a visit to my home. That is all."

"The king no longer takes the prophecy of Nathan seriously and now definitely favors Absalom. It has been obvious all along my dear; no son of yours would ever be accepted by the people. The king is glad that you are leaving and freeing him from this embarrassment."

Bathsheba struggled to keep back the tears at the hurtful words. The two women stared coldly at each other. "It is not on the word of the king I base my hopes," Bathsheba said simply, "but on the word of God spoken through the prophet Nathan."

"We will see. We will see." Michal's eyes grew hard. "Once you are gone, it won't be long until the king will have some new young beauty to take your place."

As Michal swept out, Bathsheba watched her go down through the larger court, a proud and remote woman who lived daily with her extra portion of bitterness. Over and over again Bathsheba would hear the echo of Michal's voice saying, "Once you are gone, the king will have some new young beauty to take your place." How well she had known the deep, unmentioned fear that tugged at Bathsheba's heart.

She looked around the crowded court and wondered out loud. "How have I dared to think I would be any different than the rest of David's wives who sit here in this court discarded?" Every instinct warned her to stay and fight for her position, but remembering Solomon, she knew that in the morning before sunrise, she would be on her way to Lodebar.

Back inside her small courtyard she saw Solomon standing beside the bed of lilies, head down, kicking at a loose stone aimlessly. She knelt beside him and gently took him in her arms. "You heard all that she said?"

She felt him nod and heard him whisper, "Yes."

"I'm sorry. I thought you'd gone with Shimea and Shobab."

He looked at her puzzled. "She said we're never coming back. Why did she say that? Is it true?"

Bathsheba tried to keep her voice steady. "I don't know. I really don't know."

To her surprise he smiled. "Don't worry, Mother; we will come back. I know we will."

She hugged him to her and wondered at this child who seemed to have some special gift of understanding.

The next morning in the cold, predawn darkness, Bathsheba's donkeys were saddled and ready to leave. There was nothing left to do, and yet Bathsheba was reluctant to start. She longed for David to appear and tell her he was sorry for his angry accusations of the day before. If he would only come and say he understood why she must go. She looked up at the great, dark bulk of David's house, saw that his windows were all shuttered and dark, and noticed that there was no light along the parapet. A feeling of unutterable loneliness overwhelmed her.

She checked each sleepy little son and the baby, Shobab, held by Jessica. The donkeys were impatient, and she was ready to give the signal to the young men guiding the caravan to move out, when the door to the women's quarters slowly opened. Bathsheba's heart raced. *Of course,* she thought, *he would not let me leave without a good-by.*

A dark figure moved out from the shadows. Bathsheba saw with disappointment that it was not David but Ahinoam. Why was she coming now? She had been sick in bed for weeks.

"Bathsheba," she said weakly, "are you really going back home as all the women say?" Her voice was old and tired.

"Yes, I'm going to see my brother in Lodebar."

"I may not be here long, and I must tell you something."

"Of course you'll be here," Bathsheba encouraged her. "It's just the cold. Everyone feels sick when it's so cold."

"No, no, it's not the cold. I am not burdened by the cold or thoughts of death. It's something else." She paused, and then she spoke so softly Bathsheba had to bend forward to catch the words.

"I'm sorry," she said. "Sorry for the things I said against you. I didn't understand how you must have felt until my son. . . ."

Bathsheba put an arm around her and gently led her back toward the door. "It's all over now. Don't worry."

"But that's the trouble. We don't see things until they're over. I hated you, Bathsheba, because I thought that you were wicked and evil. I resented your tempting David into such open sin. Now I see that you at least loved David, but Amnon didn't even love Tamar. Why did he do it? I was a good mother. I loved him. Why?"

"I don't know why Amnon did what he did. Perhaps he didn't know why himself."

The two women stood in the doorway in silence, and Ahinoam put her hand on Bathsheba's arm hesitantly. "You don't hate him, do you?"

"No, I never hated him."

Ahinoam sighed as though she were relieved of some great burden. She clutched Bathsheba's arm and swayed to catch her balance. "You are right to go to Lodebar. May God go with you and protect your little sons."

Bathsheba mounted her donkey and gave the signal to start. Somehow to know that at least one of the women was now her friend and able to wish her well was comforting. She looked up again at the closed shutters of David's rooms and the unlighted roof. He had not even cared to come and say good-by. She didn't see the figure of David standing on the roof top in the darkness, watching, with a wrenching sadness and terrible sense of loss, the lights of the caravan move down through the city and out the southern gate.

For her own peace of mind it was fortunate Bathsheba was not aware of another figure standing in the deep shadows of a lower palace window, watching the whole proceedings with great interest and noting especially that Solomon was traveling with his mother.

6

COMING HOME TO Lodebar was a strange experience for Bathsheba. She missed her grandmother, but everything else was very much the same as she had remembered it. Noha sat in the sun, carding wool or weaving. Machir walked out each morning to supervise the work in the fields. And now Jessica was with her again to manage the servants and care for the little princes.

Each morning Bathsheba woke in her own familiar room of the court to see the sun shining through the lattice or Jessica bringing the warm bowl of groats for the princes. Just as in the past her pigeons fluttered in through the window, and the door to the bath still hung crookedly on its leather hinges. Over and over again Bathsheba struggled to fit herself back into her old way of life as though the years in Urusalim made no difference, but it was impossible.

Each day she wandered from her small courtyard to the roof and back down again, restlessly waiting for some news, some message from Urusalim. Often she was haunted by the bitter words of Michal. "He's glad you are leaving . . . He is glad that you are ridding him of this embarrassment."

She hadn't really believed Michal, but here in Lodebar, so far from David and hearing no word from him, she began to wonder if Michal had not been right.

While Bathsheba felt lonely and uprooted, her sons went from one delight to another. They skipped and tumbled around Machir, who occasionally took them out to his fields, or they descended on old Phineas and begged for a story. If there seemed nothing else to occupy their time, they could always try to wheedle sweet cakes and dates from Jessica. Bathsheba kissed each little flushed face many times a day and yearned to share all this with David. *How happy we could be,* she thought, *if we were simple peasants living in a small village, caring for our flocks and fields.*

Since there was no one in Lodebar to teach the children, Bathsheba worried that her sons were missing the schooling they must have as young princes. It was Machir who finally suggested Judah. "He is a scholar now and happens to be back here in Lodebar."

Ever since his disappointment in not being able to marry Bathsheba, Judah had lived with a group of prophets in the cliffs above Jericho. He had spent his time as a student, reading the Scriptures and making copies of them on fresh parchment. "I will be happy to teach the young prince as long as I am here," Judah assured Machir.

After a week it was obvious that the lessons with Solomon were progressing well. It gave Bathsheba a sense of satisfaction to look down into the court-yard and see this old friend with her son, bent over a parchment, and to hear the young voice reading to the older man.

It was the middle of the morning on the day before the Sabbath. Bathsheba had been on the roof, aimlessly spinning the wool that lay in soft, cloud-like heaps around her. The twisting yarn made a soft, whirring noise, and soon Bathsheba became aware of the voice of Solomon as he went through his daily recitation in the lower court. Quietly she moved to the parapet where she could look down and see him at work with Judah.

They were directly below her. Judah nodded encouragement as Solomon formed the square-shaped letters with his tapered charcoal on a coarse piece of leather parchment. Solomon sat cross-legged on a woven reed mat with the sun glinting from the dark curls that followed the shape of his head. His royal robes were dusty. He must have followed Machir to the field early that morning.

He held the charcoal suspended while he looked up at Judah with large, questioning eyes. "Judah, how did God know to make things taste good if He never ate anything?" She saw Judah's look of surprise as he cleared his throat while trying to think of an answer. "I don't know, Solomon. I really never thought of it until you mentioned it just now."

Solomon is like Grandfather, Bathsheba thought with a start of apprehension. *He has the same questioning mind.* People had always credited Ahithophel with being a wise man, and yet she realized suddenly that he had used this gift for his own selfish purposes, and it had brought him no happiness.

The idea was disturbing to her. She put the distaff and spindle down and went to the stairs. *Solomon needs his father,* she thought, as she hurried down the stairs. David was wise too, she knew, but it was an anointed wisdom not bound by his own emotions or will.

She reached the courtyard just as Judah stood to leave. Solomon did not look up from his writing, and so she walked to the gate with the scholar. "Judah, is my son progressing as well as you had expected?" she asked. "I've noticed that he is often more interested in watching a butterfly's wings open and close or a colony of ants moving across the courtyard than in making his letters correctly."

"Solomon is interested in everything," Judah answered. "Very often he asks questions I can't answer. He is an extraordinary boy."

"What question does he ask?"

Judah thought a moment. "The very first day he had been out with Machir and the sheep. He wanted to know if animals laughed. 'Are people the only ones who know how to laugh?' he asked. What could I answer except that I had never seen an animal laugh. That's the sort of thing he seems to be puzzling about all the time."

Judah opened the gate and bowed slightly. "Don't worry about your son's abilities. He has the head of his great-grandfather, Ahithophel, and the heart of his father."

Bathsheba walked back to where Solomon sat still absorbed in writing the letters. She noted again the soft dark curls that framed his face, his royal robes torn and dusty, and that his soft jeweled slippers were nowhere in sight. She sighed. *It is foolish to keep him dressed in such clothes here in Lodebar. I must have something made that will let him enjoy this time of freedom.*

She knelt down beside him and looked at his letters. They were as awkward and misshapen as those of any other boy his age. "What are you writing?" she asked.

"Bethlehem," he said looking up at her with the wide alert eyes. "I want to write it really well to surprise my father."

"Do you think so much about your father then?"

"Yes."

She reached out and hugged him tight. "Learn all you can and ask all the questions you like, but never forget there is more to life than what passes through the mind. A man is also emotion and spirit, and he must make room for them to grow too."

"When I grow up," he said turning to look at her, "I want to be just like my father." A butterfly flew past, and the moment of serious thought was gone. She watched him bound off and then kneel almost reverently beside a flower where the butterfly was resting. She sighed and felt again the dark cloud of despair settle around her. She couldn't go back to Urusalim now. She wondered if the time would ever come when she could go back.

Days, weeks, and then months went by and still there was no word from Urusalim. Bathsheba became anxious and more restless. She had not realized how final her break with David had been. She knew he would not send for her; he would never banish his son Absalom from the palace, and she would not go to him as long as Absalom was there. How impossible and utterly hopeless it seemed.

Every day in Lodebar was almost the same to Bathsheba. She tried to keep busy baking bread, grinding the meal, or working at the loom. She rarely left the four walls of the house except when Jessica persuaded her to walk to the well or down by the stream. She hated to leave the house lest some message would come, some word from David or Ahithophel. She yearned for her husband with a longing that was almost an illness.

When she visited the mikvah, old Tiva and others gathered around to ask her when she was going back to court and whether she had heard from David. These questions were like arrows that lodged in her heart, and she could not answer them without tears coming to her eyes.

One day late in the afternoon Bathsheba was sitting at the loom idly pushing the shuttle back and forth when she heard light running footsteps bounding up the stairs to the roof. She glanced up and saw Solomon hot and dusty from the field with a look of puzzlement on his tanned face. "Mother, I saw him. I saw that man again."

She reached out and made him sit on the bench beside her while she tried to straighten his tunic and pulled a burr from his hair. "What man, my son? Who did you see?"

"The man who brought the basket to our courtyard in Urusalim. The one with the snake that Mahat had to kill."

"Oh, no!" Bathsheba could not hide her sudden fright. "You're sure he was the same man?"

"He was the same. He came out to the field to talk to Uncle Machir. He asked about our wheat and barley, and then he asked where we lived in the village."

Bathsheba's face turned white. "Solomon, listen to me. You must not go out alone. You must be either with Judah or Machir or me. Do you understand?"

"But Mother. . . ."

"Just do as I say. Now go down and work on your lessons."

Bathsheba was too distraught to stay any longer at the loom. Instead she walked over to the stairs where she could look down into the courtyard at Solomon as he bent over the parchment. She tried to calm herself, to brush off the terror that she felt, and yet it seemed to settle in around her like a dark cloud.

Several days later Bathsheba was again sitting at her loom, finding it hard to keep up the steady push and pull of the bobbin while her mind was so filled with anxiety. She listened to the sounds coming faintly from the courtyard below her: the soft bleating of lambs; Jessica calling to one of Bathsheba's small sons to get down from the wall.

Suddenly there was pounding of hooves coming up the lane and a voice heavy with a foreign accent calling for the house of Machir. Bathsheba's head spun, and her body tensed. She ran down the stairs and found old Phineas had let in an Edomite trader who stood there rummaging in his pack for a message.

"It's for you." Phineas took the parchment from the trader and handed it to Bathsheba.

Bathsheba trembled as she broke the seal and unrolled the rough parchment. She read swiftly the first line and then looking up and seeing the trader still there, she dismissed him and turned to Judah. "Here," she said handing the parchment to him, "it is too difficult for me to read."

Judah spread out the parchment on the mat before him and began:

Ahithophel to Bathsheba. Greetings to all our family and dear ones.

It is well that you have taken your sons to Lodebar. In the next few months there will be many changes here. Do not worry when you hear David has been deposed and Absalom is ruling in his place.

Absalom depends on me as David used to, and he will see that my family is well cared for.

Tomorrow I leave for Hebron where I will meet Absalom for his coronation. Joab is with me.

A startled gasp escaped Bathsheba. She bent down and ran her finger along the words until it rested on the fateful word, "coronation." She read again, incredulously.

"Mother," Solomon bent over the script, "what has happened to my father? Why is Absalom to be crowned? Why should my great-grandfather want Absalom crowned in place of my father?"

"Revenge," she said. "He wants revenge."

"Revenge?" Solomon's eyes began to show the hurt he felt. "Why should he want to get revenge?"

Bathsheba looked at Judah helplessly. There was no way she could explain the circumstances to her son. This child who already was so wise and asked such penetrating questions; what would he think of her and his father if he knew the truth? Impulsively she reached out and took Solomon in her arms and felt his hard, unyielding young body still demanding answers she could not bring herself to give. "We must not worry my son; the God of Israel is with your father."

"But Mother, Joab has left him and gone down to Hebron too."

"Kings have few people they can trust. Friends are not always true and relatives are even worse. Absalom, Joab, and Ahithophel all have gone against him." Suddenly she felt his arms around her neck, and his hair brushed her cheek.

"Mother, you can depend on me. I would not ever go against you or my father."

Bathsheba hugged her son fiercely, unable to speak for the tender pain that flooded over her.

A feeling of great foreboding hung over her throughout the week. Absalom in his overwhelming ambition was threatening his own father, and if Joab had sided with Absalom there was no way that David could combat such strength. It pained her that Ahithophel could be part of such a plan.

Machir had gone to Mahanaim where he could get more news, and Bathsheba waited impatiently for his return. She could not eat, and Jessica retreated down the stairs with an untouched bowl of warm lentil soup. "She's thinking only of the king," she reported to Noha.

Noha stirred the pot of soup angrily. "I hate that old man for what he's done."

"Ahithophel?"

"Yes. He always thought he was so wise. He loved her best in all the world, and yet he broke her heart. Now he wants to kill her."

"He doesn't want to kill her, it's just. . . ."

"He didn't want to break her heart either, but he wanted to marry her to Uriah, and so he did. And now he wants revenge, and he will have revenge even if it kills Bathsheba."

Again there was the hard pounding of hooves outside in the lane. They could hear Phineas pulling open the wide gate and exchanging a few words with Machir.

"Poor one," Jessica murmured as she looked toward the roof where she could see Bathsheba running to embrace Machir. "No matter the news, it can't be good."

Machir would not tell her anything until she agreed to sit down beside him quietly. "There's no good news," he said looking at her with apprehension.

"Then Absalom was crowned?"

"Yes, Absalom was crowned, but Joab left the coronation and rode back to warn the king."

"To warn the king?"

"David had suspected nothing. If Joab had not warned him of Absalom's treachery, he would have been taken prisoner in the palace by his own son."

"David fled the palace on foot," continued Machir. "He left behind ten of his younger concubines. Grandfather has now advised Absalom to follow David and cut him down before he reaches the Jordan."

"Grandfather and his revenge." Bathsheba was looking at her brother with wide, hurt eyes and trembling lips.

"Bathsheba," he said gently, "there is no way for Solomon to be king. Forget this dream. Forget the words of Nathan. There's not a man in Israel who would accept your son as king."

The anger left her face. There were no tears. No outcry. Her eyes looked out across the parapet, and yet she seemed to see nothing. She took Machir's arm to steady herself. "I need to go to my room," she said.

Machir led her down the steps and to her room, blaming himself for having hurt her so. "I'm sorry," he said, but she didn't hear him.

7

NO SOONER HAD ABSALOM taken over his father's palace, discarding the old olive-wood throne, burning the lion skins of his bedchamber, and installing himself in his father's pavilion, than Ahithophel appeared. Absalom welcomed him eagerly and led him to the seat of honor at his right hand.

Ahithophel was shocked to see that David's fun-loving son was ready to prepare a feast and celebrate his victory. "My lord," he whispered, "you cannot rest now. Did you not see among the shouting, singing people those with hostile looks and somber faces?"

"What do you suggest?" The prince leaned back, holding out his cup for a servant to pour in more wine.

"You must let the people know you are to be their new king and that you will not surrender to your father on any terms."

"You are right, Ahithophel. I'll send off for the

scribe and you will help me word a proclamation. . . ."

"Now is not the time for words. Only actions will tell the people whom to follow and obey."

"What actions?" Absalom asked with interest.

"You have begun well by throwing out his throne and taking over his bedchamber. But all these things David would forgive. He would take you back but punish those who followed you. There is only one thing he will not forgive. . . ."

Absalom leaned forward eagerly. "And that is?"

Ahithophel watched the young man closely and saw that he was overconfident with wine. The time was right. "Sire, when your father fled, he left here ten concubines, all young and beautiful, brought by traders from the south. I would suggest you plan a party here in your father's own pavilion and announce that you intend to send for David's concubines."

Absalom's eyes sparkled. "To take a king's concubines has always meant a challenge to his throne. Was it not even prophesied as one of my father's punishments?"

"Your memory is good, my lord. Announce it now. Gather the people before the palace, then bring in the concubines."

"What an old goat you are, Ahithophel. No doubt you will be glad to see me take them here in this pavilion where my father had his little dalliance with your granddaughter. It is a rather fitting revenge, I'd say." Absalom laughed uproariously.

Ahithophel was taken aback at his frank observation but relaxed when he saw that Absalom was looking at him with admiration. "Tomorrow I will have the people here to witness all that happens," he said. Then with a smirk, "My lord, all ten concubines at once may be too much. . . ."

Absalom broke into raucous laughter. "Don't worry, Ahithophel; you bring the people, and I will manage the rest."

As Ahithophel left the pavilion amid Absalom's laughter, he felt annoyance and disappointment. It was a terrible sin to take a father's wife or concubine while he was still alive; yet to Absalom this seemed to be only another adventure to joke about among his friends.

Ahithophel put aside his qualms and did as he had promised. Word quickly spread throughout the city of Urusalim that Absalom intended to take the concubines of his father, and by late afternoon, at the appointed time, the courtyard before the palace and the roof of Uriah's old house were crowded with people.

Just before sunset the sounds of tambourines and singing came from the region of the North Gate. Slowly the noises became louder until the procession reached the onlookers gathered in front of the palace. The virgins of Urusalim appeared first, dancing with garlands in their hair, singing and playing on harps, lyres, and flutes. Behind them came ten palanquins bearing the concubines of David. The boxes were curtained so the women could not be seen, but the carvings on the boxes clearly bore the prancing lion of Judah. To the followers of Absalom it was a moment of wild triumph. They shouted and clapped, laughed and sang raucously. But to the older men who had fought under David and who recalled the taking of Urusalim and the bringing of the Ark, it was an insolent and unsavory act against the old king.

One by one the palanquins were placed before the palace door, and the women alighted. All of them were dressed in the wedding clothes they had worn when they were brought to David. Servants received them and led them into the palace and up the stairs. The waiting crowd could see them briefly on the roof before they disappeared into the pavilion.

Trumpeters on the roof of the palace sounded the familiar notes of the princes of Judah. Then Absalom appeared dressed in royal robes. The setting sun glinted on his jeweled cloak and the crown of his father sat firmly on his head of thick, long hair which fell over his shoulders in abundance. He looked just as the people wanted their king to look—young, proud, and arrogant. He carried his head with nobility, and they noticed that he was surrounded by other young men who had about them the same careless hauteur.

"Absalom, our king! Absalom, the ruler of Urusalim!" The people broke into uncontrolled excitement and would not be silenced until the trumpeters blew another series of blasts. Absalom waved in triumph to the people who now stood crushed together, tense with anticipation.

They saw Absalom's friends anoint his hair, adjust his cloak, and then set the crown at a more casual angle. There was more laughter and boisterous shouting. Again Absalom leaned over the parapet and waved to the people; winking he made an obscene gesture, and the people roared with laughter. Then he turned to the pavilion, raised the flap and entered, leaving the crowds outside riotous with anticipation.

The dancers danced and the drums beat while the people shouted advice just as they would have done at one of their local weddings. On the roof the dancers tired before the onlookers finally heard a shout, and Absalom again appeared at the door of the pavilion. His crown was not on his head, his jeweled robe had been thrown off, but other than that he looked fresh and relaxed. He walked to the edge of the parapet and waved at the chanting, cheering crowd, and then turned to Ahithophel who was waiting to lead him back down to his royal bedchamber.

"My lord," Ahithophel hissed as soon as they were out of range of the other attendants who followed behind, "how did you manage such a feat? I mean ten women, well. . . !"

Absalom looked surprised and then broke out into laughter. "You thought I. . . ." He laughed again until he saw Ahithophel was red with embarrassment.

"My friend, I simply had the maids undress and ordered them to dance before me until I picked the one that suited me the best. The serving maid will bring her to my room when all this show is finished."

"What took so long?"

"My wise friend, I can see that you are knowledgeable in matters of state but know little of love. I take my pleasures in the right atmosphere, with soft lights, music and tender words. I have assigned each one of them a night."

"Then you have not yet . . ."

"I'm not a dog, Ahithophel. I take my pleasures like a man, and though I go along with your idea of disgracing my father, still this is my affair, and I will manage as I please. Those people had their excitement, and I'll have mine in my own way." Absalom turned into his chamber, leaving Ahithophel staring somberly after him.

Ahithophel was somehow deflated. He had planned so carefully for his revenge to take place in the same cursed pavilion where David had defiled his granddaughter. It was a shock to find it had not happened as he expected. "The people do not know the difference," he reasoned, and yet try as he might, he could find no joy in it.

His torch wavered and he stopped to steady the flame. "That young fool thinks he will spend the next ten nights in Urusalim dallying with his father's concubines, but there is no time. He must attack his father before David has a chance to cross the Jordan."

Ahithophel spent a sleepless night tossing and turning on his narrow pallet. He estimated the number of men Absalom would need, the supplies to be taken, and the weapons best suited for such an attack. The sense of urgency overwhelmed him. While the cocks were still crowing in the valley and the morning mists had not yet been driven back by the rising sun, Ahithophel made his way to the palace. The common room was still heavy with incense; the torches had burned low and were sputtering. He shook one of the men who lay sleeping on the floor and asked after the young king.

"There was a party in the pavilion," the young man said sleepily. "And then Absalom called for one of the concubines. It will be late morning before he holds court." He rolled over and closed his eyes.

With one swift motion Ahithophel pulled the cloak from around him. "This is no time to sleep. You have won nothing yet. Get up and go to your master and tell him Ahithophel is here." The young man jumped up in alarm and ran to deliver the message.

Ahithophel then noticed that only two guards had been left on duty and the common room was filled with the drunken young men of Absalom's army, all sleeping soundly. He was appalled that

Absalom would be so lax. This abandonment to pleasure and celebration angered him.

Within minutes the young man was back with the message that Absalom would see his chief counselor. Ahithophel mounted the stairs to the roof, amazed that in such a short time the whole atmosphere of David's palace had changed. A young, beardless guard drew aside the curtain and Ahithophel stepped into the king's pavilion. It was dark inside and heavy with the odor of spikenard and rosewater.

"Is not this very early for my chief counselor to be out?" The voice came from the dais where Absalom was sitting crosslegged, his arm resting on one of the lion's heads and a brass goblet of wine balanced in his hand.

"My lord," Ahithophel said, trying to maintain his composure, "we must move quickly. If David's men cross the Jordan we may not be able to overtake them at all."

"Come, sit down, my friend. We'll have some grapes and figs and . . . not there but over here." Ahithophel was about to sit down when Absalom reached out to stop him. "Amital is still sleeping."

To Ahithophel's horror he saw that in the darkened room he had been about to sit down on a naked young concubine who was still sleeping among the cushions of the dais. She was curled up like a kitten with one arm flung out to the side, her head back on the cushion. Her long, luxurious hair fell down over her young breasts. Instinctively, Ahithophel's hand covered his eyes.

"Is not this what you had imagined?" Absalom's tone showed his amusement.

"It was just the shock."

"You must be exhilarated with the revenge you've had on my father."

"It is not as I had imagined."

"What did you expect? Perhaps a drunken orgy with all ten concubines?"

"No, no. . . ." Ahithophel was uncomfortable and became even more uncomfortable when the young concubine awoke, stretched and smiled at Absalom.

"My lord," he said, "dismiss the girl. We must discuss important matters."

"She makes you nervous, does she?" Absalom slipped his arm around the young girl, and his eyes glinted with amusement at Ahithophel's discomfiture.

"It is urgent that you overtake your father before he has a chance to cross the Jordan."

"I am not going to the Jordan." Absalom stretched languidly.

"Not going to the Jordan?"

"No, I have had new advice, and I am inclined to take it."

Ahithophel was on his feet and angry. "Who would give you such wrong advice?" He followed Absalom through the curtained door onto the roof where the sun was just coming up over the mountain of Olivet.

"Hushai. He's just returned from following my father's forces. He reports they are weaponless, barefoot, and without food. He does not expect that we will have to fight at all; but if we do, he advises us to wait until we're better organized."

Absalom leaned out over the parapet and breathed in the fresh morning air with obvious relish. "His advice suits my pleasure. I have nine more concubines to enjoy, and if they are all as charming as Amital, it will be quite a celebration."

Ahithophel was stunned. "You must realize that

Hushai is working for your father. He's always been his friend."

"Whether his advice is false or not, it suits me, and I'll take it." With a casual nod Absalom left Ahithophel standing by the parapet and returned to the curtained pavilion and to Amital.

Ahithophel walked down the stairs in a fury of frustration. Instead of relishing the revenge he'd planned, he found himself totally disgusted with Absalom's irresponsibility.

That evening when the men gathered for their daily meal, Ahithophel was further incensed to find that Hushai had been given what had been his seat of honor. Hushai repeated his advice to the assembled men, and Absalom nodded his approval, ordering his men to put up their swords and hang their shields in place around the wall. "There's no need for war," he shouted to them joyfully. "Instead we'll feast and celebrate our victory."

It was useless to argue further. Ahithophel left the brightly lit room and made his way across the courtyard to the empty guardhouse which was cold and only dimly lit. Depression and despair crowded in on him. The revenge against David was not the triumph he had planned; it was cheap and disgusting. Absalom's actions would hurt David but not much worse than what the king would have suffered in seeing his son dally in Urusalim with these same women.

Faint and faraway he could still hear bursts of laughter from the palace. He drew his cloak around him and shivered in the dampness. He was no longer a part of Absalom's inner group of friends. He was no longer a part of anything. Life was total futility. With sudden resolve he walked from the guardhouse to the stable, untied his mule, and led it outside. After a final look at the palace, he mounted the animal and headed toward the city gate.

It was dark when Ahithophel arrived in the courtyard of his old house in Giloh. The night was moonless, and there was a strange stillness in the air that made the slightest sound seem loud and ominous. The scraping of the gate, his sandals shuffling across the smooth stones of the court and even his labored breathing resounded in his ears as he felt for the door of the cook room.

The servants had gone home for the night, leaving a warm bed of live coals carefully banked to last until morning. Ahithophel ran his hand over the wall until he felt the niche and then the old lamp, half filled with oil. He needed tongs. He groped along the mud-packed counter.

As his eyes became accustomed to the darkness, he saw the tongs lying beside the oven. Quickly he chose a coal and held it to the wick. A small flame flickered and grew in the shelter of his cupped hand.

Now he must write. He must explain to those he loved in Lodebar. With his free hand he fingered the parchment in his belt and then his writing pouch.

Holding the lamp high so that it cast patches of light before him on the irregular stones of the court, he made his way to the far wall where his yoke and plow had stood and where the pigeons' nests had always hung. He settled himself in the corner away from the wind, stretched out the parchment, and prepared to write.

He could not explain to them his failure and despair, but he must write something to his family. He had come home to die. It did not matter by what means he chose to end his life. Nothing mattered now. Even his family was remote, but he owed them an explanation.

He dipped his pen into the ink and watched the dark globules drip from its point while he thought about the failures of his life. First his son, his only son, the hub of all his plans, had been cut down in his prime. Next Bathsheba. He dropped his pen and wiped the beads of sweat breaking out on his forehead. His granddaughter had been chosen by the king, only to be branded an adulteress before the whole world, and his great-grandson lay dead within a week. Then Reba had died. David had disillusioned him. Absalom had betrayed him.

Defiantly he wound the end of the headpiece around his head, and with a grimace he picked up the pen. For a moment he held the quill above the parchment. How close he'd been to his revenge against David. His mouth tightened, and his eyes grew dull. Somehow David had missed the final, bitter dregs. He had escaped the final blow, and Ahithophel could not endure to live and see him recover and win.

Hastily he wrote the message for those he loved in Lodebar, then rolled the skin carefully, melting the wax and watching its red drops gather on the edge to seal it.

Calmly he rose and walked to the well-curb and felt for the old, hemp rope that had been used to draw water since he was a boy. He flung it over his arm, tucked the scroll in his belt and mounted the stairs to the roof.

Deliberately and surely, so it would not fail him at last, he tied the rope to one of the new rafters and then fashioned a noose around his neck. He stood a moment, letting his whole soul harden with bitterness toward what he felt was God's unfairness and life's utter futility. Then he plunged forward into darkness.

8

THE PEOPLE OF Lodebar were shocked to hear that Absalom had proclaimed himself king and that David had fled from Urusalim with a small band of followers. Machir made a quick decision, then gathered up sleeping mats, cooking pots, serving bowls, wheat, barley, flour, parched grain, honey, butter, and cheese. He and a friend rode, without stopping, to join David's band of tired and discouraged forces just as they were crossing the Jordan.

So it was that Machir was not at home when Ahithophel's message arrived in Lodebar. A camel caravan delivered it to the elders at the village gate who, in turn, brought it to the house of Machir. Immediately Bathsheba recognized the seal. With trembling hands she broke the stubborn wax and read the small precisely written words quickly. Then she read them again with growing distress.

Ahithophel to my dear family in Lodebar: Greetings. From the first it has been evident to me that I have not been favored by either the God of my people or the earth gods of my friends. Now I am a broken man. Absalom has turned from my advice and is listening to those who will lead him to defeat. This world is not the place for wisdom and justice. Give up your foolish hope that Solomon will ever sit on

David's throne. The gods are all against us. The world is a place of foolishness and folly. Farewell.

Bathsheba was filled with a terrible apprehension. What did Ahithophel's letter mean? There was no indication of his coming home to them, and his words of farewell were confusing. Quickly she called for Phineas to go and find the man who brought the parchment.

Within minutes Phineas had returned with the young traveler from Giloh. "The old man's dead," he said abruptly. "The servants found his body hanging by a rope from one of the house beams and this parchment at his feet."

The young man turned and hurried out the gate, while Bathsheba, torn with grief, felt her way up the stairs to the roof. There she sank down on the bench by the loom and with trembling hands again unrolled the parchment. With her finger she traced the small, square characters that had made Ahithophel's handwriting so distinctive and wept, remembering her grandfather as she had last seen him. His jaw had been set firmly, his mouth tense with hurt, and his eyes which had looked out from under heavy brows were dark with pain. How she had hurt him! Bathsheba groaned as she pictured him alone in his house in Giloh and the terrible suffering he must have endured.

When the news came that Absalom's men were making a determined effort to track down and kill David, Bathsheba's torment grew unbearable. Dark premonitions of defeat and doom weighed down upon her. She did not cry but sat tense and waiting, expecting at any moment to hear the messenger pounding on the gate to bring her word of David's death.

413

Over and over again she relived what had happened to her since she had left Lodebar to marry Uriah. She pictured again his dark, depressing house, the cruelty of ImAshtah and how resentful she had become. She remembered how righteous she had felt in defying ImAshtah to carry out her ceremonial cleansing on the roof, even making sure to use the acceptable rainwater for the ritual. She recalled distinctly how pure and clean she had felt on that night. It was hard to imagine that on that same night she had so willingly given herself to David with little thought of the law or of the consequences.

Everything looked so different now. She was no longer the innocent victim being crushed but had somehow joined those evil forces that crushed others. There had followed Uriah's cruel death, ImAshtah's suicide, and her own baby's death. Then had come Amnon's sin and murder, Absalom's revolt, and now her grandfather's bitter suicide. And a blight still hung over her little son, Solomon. All of this had stemmed from that first wrong deed.

As long as she had been sheltered in David's love, she had seen none of this. Now she knew that even the treasure of their love was almost extinguished by the guilt she carried. Nothing but evil had come upon the house of David since she entered it. Now the final blow was about to fall, and there was nothing she could do to prevent it. If God dealt out His justice as a judge or king, it would be a life for a life. Thus David must die and Absalom take the crown.

She sank down onto the hard mud floor of the roof and covered her face with her mantle, sobbing and praying, her words coming in broken gasps: "O God, God of Abraham, Isaac, and Jacob: I am the one who has done evil in Your sight. Take from me my life but spare the king."

"Bathsheba," the voice was gentle and familiar. Judah had climbed the stairs and had heard her prayer. She looked up and saw that he was standing beside her with a look of infinite compassion. "Do not lose hope. The king will live. Have faith in God."

"Judah, you don't understand. Before God, the king and I are both guilty of such evil that there's only punishment in store for us. The good days are all gone, our love is gone, our hope is gone."

Judah sat down on the rough bench beside her and took her hand in his. "Expect the worst, and it will happen. This is one of life's unwritten laws. You must have faith in God—in His promises, in His goodness."

"Oh, Judah, if we deserved God's goodness then I could believe in it. I could have faith that God would bring David back to me and that Nathan's prophecy would come true. But now I feel we can ask no blessing from His hand."

"Guilt kills many things, among them love and faith and hope. You cannot rid yourself of guilt until you first accept it, admit it, and then apply the remedy."

"The remedy? What is the remedy?"

"Bathsheba, think. You have gone often to the mikvah and washed in the clear running water to cleanse yourself of all defilement. It is one of God's ways to free you from guilt."

Bathsheba shook her head sadly. "There is no mikvah in all the world large enough to wash away my guilt."

"It is not the washing of the mikvah; it is God who makes us clean. It is a mystery. It is our part to obey and His to perform the cleansing." There was silence between them, and then Judah rose and left as quietly as he had come.

Bathsheba stood up, dusted off her robe, and dried her eyes. The sun was low on the horizon, but if she hurrried she could get to the mikvah before old Tiva locked it for the night.

The door to the mikvah stood open, but Tiva was nowhere in sight. The women who sometimes came at this hour to bathe were gone. The dark pool was deserted. Bathsheba shivered as she thought of all the women who had been stoned outside the city wall. For them there'd been no cleansing possible.

Alone in the cool darkness she felt as though she were in the very antechamber of God's presence. She bowed down and did obeisance with her forehead on the cool tiles.

Oh, God, I am no longer worthy to enter Your presence. I am a woman who is scorned and shunned by those who love Your law. I have brought disgrace to my family and death to Uriah. Everything I touch is defiled. Even my love for David and his love for me have become blighted and tarnished. Purge me with hyssop. Wash me so I will be clean.

She rose and slowly removed her clothes, folding them as she had done so many times before. Now as she felt the cool water rise up over her waist and then her shoulders and finally cover her completely, there was a moment when she paused to release the old dark memories of guilt, failure, and resentment. Then to her surprise, the joy came! Unexplainable, radiant joy!

She rose from the water feeling accepted, loved,

forgiven. She felt cleansed and whole. As she recited the old familiar blessings, she knew there was no barrier now, the guilt was gone, the light of God's countenance shone upon her as it had not done since she was a child.

She found her clothes and put them on, then paused, afraid to leave the mikvah. What if the joy would go and all the guilt and fear return to haunt her? She looked down at her hands and saw how white and clean they were in the dim light. *They will become soiled again,* she thought, *but I know how to wash them clean.* Quietly she closed the door and walked down the lane to her house, remembering the words of the blessing.

As Bathsheba approached her house, the sun had gone down and a mauve twilight had settled on Lodebar. Outside the gate she reached for the latch and paused. A sixth sense warned her that something was wrong.

She listened. Nothing. The gate was ajar, which was strange. It was usually locked, especially at dusk.

Slowly she pushed the gate open and stepped inside. Then she froze. At the other end of the courtyard were three figures. One she did not know, a heavy-set, swarthy man. He had his left arm wrapped around Solomon. The right hand held a knife.

Opposite them was Judah, unarmed, but moving slowly toward the intruder and Solomon.

"Stop where you are or the boy dies."

Judah stopped.

The swarthy man began backing toward the gate, still holding Solomon.

Beside the gate lay the heavy metal bar used to secure the latch. Soundlessly Bathsheba picked it up. She waited, then stepped forward and with all her strength aimed her weapon at the intruder's head.

The metal bar glanced off the right side of the man's head, hitting his shoulder. He cursed, as the knife clattered onto the stones of the courtyard.

With a cry of pain, he turned around, letting Solomon go, and lunged at Bathsheba. The impact knocked her to the ground.

Instantly, Judah bounded forward, grabbed the knife, ordered Solomon to flee, and faced the intruder.

The two men stared at each other warily, crouching and circling, seeking an opening. With a growl the swarthy man dived at Judah and grabbed the arm holding the knife. They both fell to the ground, grappling for control of the weapon.

The strength of the younger man prevailed as he slowly wrested the knife from Judah and raised his hand to plunge it into Judah's heart.

As he held the knife upraised, Solomon sprang from the shadows and threw his small body against the intruder. Once again the knife dropped to the ground as the assailant was knocked off balance.

Judah quickly snatched up the knife, pushed Solomon aside, and drove it into the attacker's chest. The man groaned, coughed, tried to regain his feet, then crumpled to the ground, limp and lifeless.

Solomon scrambled up and rushed to his mother, sobbing, and Bathsheba, too shaken to move, held him tight.

Judah rose slowly and stood over the intruder, the blood-stained knife still in his hand, a dazed look on his face. "He's dead. We'll probably never know who sent him. But I can guess."

"Absalom?" questioned Bathsheba.

"Or one of his followers." Judah looked with distaste at the knife in his hand.

Bathsheba turned away from the ugly scene. She felt nauseated and shaken. Lodebar had always seemed so safe, but now she saw that for a king's son there was no safe place.

"In spite of all of my careful planning Solomon was almost killed right here in Lodebar," she whispered to herself. How like Ahithophel she had become as she sought to control those she loved. And how futile all her efforts had proved to be! Fear had loomed larger than her faith and larger than her love for David.

It was my fear that came between us, she thought, *not Absalom.*

Early the next morning Machir returned to Lodebar. He had been told of the attack on Solomon's life, and he expected to find Bathsheba tearful and distraught. Instead he was surprised to find her busy about the house, strangely at peace.

"David is safe," Machir said simply as Bathsheba ran joyfully to welcome him home, flinging her arms around his neck.

"Bathsheba," he said, taking both of her arms from around his neck and holding her hands in both of his securely, "there is something you must know. Though David is safe he is almost prostrate with grief."

"I must go to him." Bathsheba said simply, her eyes large and anxious, full of love.

"It is not just Absalom. David's whole world has come crashing down around him. Men he thought of as his friends have turned on him as Ahithophel did. His family is divided and scattered, and now the very worst has happened. Not only was Absalom killed, but Joab was the one who did it."

419

"Joab. . . ."

"Absalom's long hair and crown caught in the branches of a tree as he was fleeing from David's men. As he hung helpless begging for his life, Joab rode up and stabbed him."

"Oh, Machir, how awful for David! Where is he now?"

"He is there in the room above the gate at Mahanaim. He just sits there with his head in his hands and moans, 'Absalom, my son, my son. Would to God I had died in your place.' He means it too. He no longer wants to live. We are hoping that when he sees that you have come back to him. . . ."

"Machir, I should never have gone away and left him."

"No," Machir assured her, "you did the right thing. He couldn't see it at the time but now he will. Especially since everything has turned out as you told him it would."

"I will go just as I am." Bathsheba started for the door. "Tell Phineas to bring my mule and some provisions, and I will get Solomon."

9

WHEN THEY ARRIVED before the gates of Mahanaim, Bathsheba was startled to remember that night long ago when as a little girl she had entered this same gate with her family, seeking refuge. Now it was necessary for Machir to get down from his donkey to make a path through the men who were crowded around the gate. Bathsheba could see that most of them were dusty, tired, and blood-stained. Some were dressed in armor, but others were just young men who had left their sheep or plow in order to fight.

They looked curiously at her and then at the young boy sitting so regally on his own donkey in front of her. She could see them move to whisper to each other, and faint and indistinctly she heard her name. "Bathsheba!"

She left Solomon in the guardroom and then followed Machir up the dark and winding stairs to the room above the gate where David was sitting with his tribesmen. Machir signaled to the men, and one by one they rose and departed, leaving Bathsheba alone with David.

She entered the darkened room, noticing the closed shutters, the clutter of shields, spears, and rumpled pallets, signs that it had been the headquarters for David and his men. As her eyes grew accustomed to the dim light, she saw him, sitting dejected and alone, his head in his hands, his robes torn. Before him on the floor were several pieces of armor and a golden crown.

As she came slowly toward him, she could see his lips moving almost soundlessly: "Absalom, oh, my God, not Absalom." She knelt before him and gently took his hand and pressed it to her cheek which was already damp with tears.

David raised his head and looked at her as though he could not comprehend what he was seeing. She noticed that his face was gaunt with pain and streaked with tears; his eyes were red and swollen.

"My lord," her voice was choked, and she could say no more.

He turned from her and motioned to the armor and the crown. "This was his armor, and there's the cursed crown that caused his death. They want to put it on my head, but I'll not have it."

For one brief moment she felt resentment that Absalom, even in his death, should come between them in this way. With the attempt on Solomon's life and her suspicions of Absalom's treachery, she wanted to cry out again against this love that David held for Absalom. But the new spirit inside her dissolved the resentment. She stretched out her hand and touched the golden armor, then the greaves, breastplate, and shield. "My lord, tell me of Absalom. I want to hear it all, and then perhaps I'll come to love him as you do."

Slowly David turned to her, and for the first time she saw a faint flicker of the love she'd known before the trouble had begun. "They didn't bring my son here so I could see his face before they buried him."

This had hurt him in some deep, profound way. "I want to hear it all," she said, "all that has happened to you and to Absalom."

Hesitantly at first and then almost compulsively, he began to talk of Absalom, sharing with her each memory of the happy, laughing boy, his brilliance and his charm, leaving out any hint of criticism or of blame. Sometimes he paused and looked at her as though waiting for her to add some word of disagreement. Then seeing nothing but open acceptance in her eyes, he continued. Finally, like one returning from some dark journey, he was spent and relaxed enough to fall asleep, cradled in her arms.

No one knocked or came near the room in which they sat, and Bathsheba had time to ponder the strange course of her love. It seemed to her that she had always loved David, at first foolishly and blindly, dazzled by his charm and winning manner. Then through dark days when everything went wrong they had clung to each other like shipwrecked mariners. And now sitting here in this strange room filled with armor and the stale smell of battle, the love she felt for him was warm and protective. They had lived through so much. They had learned so much. They had paid so dearly for their love that they must not let it slip away.

A cock in some nearby courtyard crowed and David stirred, then opened his eyes and looked at her as though he were seeing her for the first time. "You must be hungry," she said tucking in a stray wisp of hair as she rose and looked around the room for the cooking utensils and flour she had brought with her from Lodebar.

David insisted he was not hungry, but when she brought a wooden bowl and came to sit by him he did not object. And when she blew on the coals of the brazier until they flared up and heated the clay griddle so that the smell of the baking cakes filled the room, David admitted he was quite hungry. The cakes spread out in wide circles, and when she gathered them up and placed them on the woven mat before David, he reached for them eagerly.

They spoke of trivial things until he'd finished eating. Then their eyes met and held and met again questioningly. Bathsheba saw his eyes slowly grow warm and tender as they moved over her face and back to her eyes. She reached out to him and felt his arms go around her. "Bathsheba, my love, my only love," he said brokenly. He pulled her to him and held her as though he would never let her go.

It was three days later when David and all his household said farewell to those who had helped him during the dark days of exile. Then they started back on the long road to Urusalim. Bathsheba rode with her servants, rejoicing to see the young Solomon riding for the first time beside his father.

423

She would have been more astonished if she could have heard the conversation carried on between father and son. "Are you a very great king?" the young boy asked his father, looking with obvious admiration at the strong, handsome features of the older man beside him.

The king looked down at his son with just a touch of a smile. "No, my son. I am not a great king, and my kingdom is actually very small. When I die and lie with my fathers in the tomb of Bethlehem, I shall soon be forgotten."

He paused in thought and then continued. "You, my son, will not be forgotten, for you will be known through all these lands as the one who built a temple to our God—a temple of such beauty that there will be none like it in all the earth. And when men shall ask you how you were able to gather all that was needed for such a temple, you will tell them this: 'My father gathered the materials so that this temple might be built to the glory of God. He was an imperfect man, but one who loved his God with all his heart.' "

The Genealogy of Jesus Christ

According to the Gospel of Matthew (1:1-16)

Abraham was the father of Isaac,
Isaac was the father of Jacob,
Jacob the father of Judah and his brothers.
Judah the father of Perez and Zerah, whose mother
    was Tamar;
Perez the father of Hezron,
Hezron the father of Aram,
Aram the father of Aminadab,
Aminadab the father of Nashon,
Nashon the father of Salmon,
Salmon the father of Boaz, whose mother was
    Rahab;
Boaz the father of Obed, whose mother was Ruth;
Obed the father of Jesse,
Jesse the father of King David,
KING DAVID THE FATHER OF SOLOMON,
    WHOSE MOTHER HAD BEEN THE WIFE OF
    URIAH;
Solomon the father of Rehoboam,

Rehoboam the father of Abijah,
Abijah the father of Asa,
Asa the father of Jehoshaphat,
Jehoshaphat the father of Joram,
Joram the father of Uzziah,
Uzziah the father of Jotham,
Jotham, the father of Ahaz,
Ahaz the father of Hezekiah,
Hezekiah the father of Manasseh,
Manasseh the father of Amon,
Amon the father of Josiah,
Josiah became the father of Jechoniah and his
    brothers about the time of the deportation to
    Babylon. After the exile to Babylon
Jechoniah became the father of Shealtiel,
Shealtiel the father of Zerubbabel,
Zerubbabel the father of Abiud,
Abiud the father of Eliakim,
Eliakim the father of Azor,
Azor the father of Sadoc,
Sadoc the father of Achim,
Achim the father of Eliud,
Eliud the father of Eleazar,
Eleazar the father of Matthan,
Matthan the father of Jacob,
Jacob the father of Joseph, the husband of Mary of
    whom was born Jesus who is called the Christ.

Inspirational Best Sellers
from Tyndale House

SECOND CHANCE by Darla Milne. The chilling but true experiences of Nicky Cruz's gang leader Israel Narvaez. 07-5843 $2.95.

THE CHASE by Richard Walsh. How could a man be so tremendously successful in business and such a failure in life? Richard Walsh was on an endless run until a mountain accident broke his neck. What follows turns a tragedy into triumph in this inspiring story of courage and renewal. 07-0221 $2.95.

ELIJAH by William H. Stephens. He was a rough-hewn farmer who strolled onto the stage of history to deliver warnings to Ahab the king and to defy Jezebel the queen. A powerful biblical novel you will never forget. 07- 4023 $3.50.

SEARCH FOR THE TWELVE APOSTLES by William Steuart McBirnie. What really happened to the original disciples of Jesus? The author, a Bible scholar and television personality, has uncovered the history of the apostles and their activities after Christ's death. A dramatic tale of men of courage and dedication. 07-5839 $3.50.

THE TOTAL MAN by Dan Benson. A practical guide on how to gain confidence and fulfillment. Covering areas such as budgeting of time, money matters, and marital relationships. 07-7289 $3.50.

HOW TO HAVE ALL THE TIME YOU NEED EVERY DAY by Pat King. Drawing from her own and other women's experiences as well as from the Bible and the research of time experts, Pat has written a warm and personal book for every Christian woman. 07-1529 $2.95.

IT'S INCREDIBLE by Ann Kiemel. "It's incredible" is what some people say when a slim young woman says, "Hi. I'm Ann," and starts talking about love and good and beauty. As Ann tells about a Jesus who can make all the difference in their lives, some call that incredible, and turn away. But others begin to see miracles happening in their lives. They become miracles themselves, agreeing with Ann that it's incredible. 07-1818 $2.50.

SLIM LIVING DAY BY DAY by JoAnne Ploeger. The official book of the YMCA's Slim Living Program. It contains the same wit, wisdom, and inspiration which has made the Slim Living Program work in hundreds of cities and thousands of lives. 07-5913 $2.50.

JOHN, SON OF THUNDER by Ellen Gunderson Traylor. Travel with John down the desert paths, through the courts of the Holy City, and to the foot of the cross. Journey with him from his luxury as a privileged son of Israel to the bitter hardship of his exile on Patmos. This is a saga of adventure, romance, and discovery—of a man bigger than life—the disciple "whom Jesus loved." 07-1903 $3.95.

RAISING CHILDREN, Linda Raney Wright. In this book twelve prominent women share their successes and failures in raising children. They have no pat answers—just a willingness to share their unique observations. And because their families are famous, their lives may not even be typical. But the insights they have gained while raising their children may be important help for every home! 07-5136 $2.50.

Forthcoming Best Sellers from Living Books

TOO MEAN TO DIE by Nick Pirovolos with William Proctor. In this action-packed story, Nick the Greek tells how he grew from a scrappy immigrant boy to a fearless underworld criminal. Finally caught, he was imprisoned. But something remarkable happened and he was set free—truly set free! 07-7283 $3.50. Available February 1982.

FOR WOMEN ONLY. This best seller gives a balanced, entertaining, diversified treatment of all aspects of womanhood. Edited by Evelyn and J. Allan Petersen, Founder of Family Concern. 07-0897 $3.50. Available March 1982.

FOR MEN ONLY. Edited by J. Allan Petersen, this book gives solid advice on how men can cope with the tremendous pressures they face every day as fathers, husbands, workers. 07-0892 $3.50. Available March 1982.

ROCK. What is rock music really doing to you? Bob Larson presents a well-researched and penetrating look at today's rock music and rock performers. What are lyrics really saying? Who are the top performers and what are their life-styles? 07-5686 $2.95. Available April 1982.

THE ALCOHOL TRAP by Fred Foster. A successful film executive was about to lose everything—his family's vacation home, his house in New Jersey, his reputation in the film industry, his wife. This is an emotion-packed story of hope and encouragement, offering valuable insights into the troubled world of high pressure living and alcoholism. 07-0078 $2.95. Available April 1982.

LET ME BE A WOMAN. Best selling author Elisabeth Elliot (author of *THROUGH GATES OF SPLENDOR*) presents her profound and unique perspective on womanhood. This is a significant book on a continuing controversial subject. 07-2162 $2.95. Available May 1982.

WE'RE IN THE ARMY NOW by Imeldia Morris Eller. Five children become their older brother's "army" as they work together to keep their family intact during a time of crisis for their mother. 07-7862 $2.95. Available May 1982.

THE WILD CHILD by Mari Hanes. A heartrending story of a young boy who was abandoned and struggled alone for survival. You will be moved as you read how one woman's love tamed this boy who was more animal than human. 07-0223 $2.95. Available June 1982.

THE SURGEON'S FAMILY by David Hernandez with Carole Gift Page. This is an incredible three-generation story of a family that has faced danger and death—and has survived. Walking dead-end streets of violence and poverty, often seemingly without hope, the family of David Hernandez has struggled to find a new kind of life. 07-6684 $2.95. Available February 1982.

The books listed are available at your bookstore. If unavailable, send check with order to cover retail price plus 10% for postage and handling to:

Tyndale House Publishers, Inc.
Box 80
Wheaton, Illinois 60187

Prices and availability subject to change without notice. Allow 4-6 weeks for delivery.